D0301686

WITHDRAWN

ESSAYS ON THE SOCIOLOGY OF CULTURE

Although Mannheim's contributions to the sociology of knowledge are well known and widely discussed, his analysis of the problems of cultural sociology has been neglected by sociologists. This is a pity, because the sociology of culture has become one of the most popular and exciting areas of sociological debate in recent years and Mannheim's work has much to contribute.

In this book Mannheim provides an overview of the nature and content of the cultural sciences within the context of his historical approach to questions of knowledge. The essays are organized around two important questions: what is the relationship between the organization of intellectuals and the ideas which they produce, and, given the development of a democratic ethos in society, what form would the democratization of culture assume? These two questions continue to be central to the humanities and social sciences, and therefore Mannheim's contribution remains a fascinating input to contemporary debate. In considering the role of the intelligentsia in the production of culture, Mannheim provides us with a brilliant sketch of their historical development from medieval times, while his work on culture and democracy presents many stimulating perspectives on the problem of culture and citizenship. Mannheim's analysis of the intellectual and culture anticipated a number of current debates about the decline of the intellectual, the commodification of culture, the problem of cultural citizenship, the fragmentation of culture and the postmodern challenge.

This is one of Mannheim's most important books and the new edition constitutes a major contribution to the sociology of culture.

Bryan S. Turner is Professor in Sociology at the University of Essex.

ROUTLEDGE SOCIOLOGY CLASSICS

Editor: Bryan S. Turner

IDEOLOGY AND UTOPIA
Karl Mannheim

THE SOCIAL SYSTEM
Talcott Parsons

FROM MAX WEBER:
ESSAYS IN SOCIOLOGY
H.H. Gerth and C. Wright Mills

ESSAYS ON THE SOCIOLOGY OF CULTURE

by

KARL MANNHEIM

WITH A NEW PREFACE
BY BRYAN S. TURNER

London and New York

First published in 1956
by Routledge & Kegan Paul Limited

This edition published in 1992
by Routledge
11 New Fetter Lane, London EC4P 4EE

Simultaneously published in the USA and Canada
by Routledge
a division of Routledge, Chapman and Hall Inc.
29 West 35th Street, New York, NY 10001

Printed and Bound in Great Britain by
Hartnolls Limited, Bodmin, Cornwall.

British Library Cataloguing in Publication Data
Mannheim, Karl, 1893–1947
Essays on the sociology of culture.
I. Title
306

Library of Congress Cataloging in Publication Data
Available on request

ISBN 0 415 07553 X

CONTENTS

CONTENTS

PART THREE

THE DEMOCRATIZATION OF CULTURE

PREFACE TO THE NEW EDITION

BRYAN S. TURNER

INTRODUCTION

KARL Mannheim (1893–1947) is famous for his contribution to the development of the sociology of knowledge (Turner 1991), but his contribution to the sociology of culture is unfortunately less well known or appreciated. These two aspects of Mannheim's sociology are clearly closely related. Consequently, these essays on culture can be suitably read alongside Mannheim's influential *Ideology and Utopia* (1991). The sociological study of culture can be considered as an extension of the sociology of knowledge, because it develops a sociological perspective on the symbolic field. Although Mannheim's essays on the sociology of culture were begun originally in Germany before his exile in 1933, they have retained their intellectual freshness and relevance to our times.

There are two reasons why it is still very profitable to study these essays. Firstly, Mannheim developed a method of studying systems of ideas which has continued to be revolutionary in challenging our assumptions about the relationship between knowledge and society. This revolutionary method was in fact the sociology of knowledge which, among other things, is concerned with the social determination of ideas. His approach raised, and continues to raise, fundamental problems about the truth and falsity of ideas which are, for example, produced by the social competition between groups (Merton 1945; Abercrombie 1980; Meja and Stehr 1990).

Secondly, Mannheim's views remain compelling because he explored issues which have continued to dominate contemporary debates. Two such issues are central to *Essays on the Sociology of Culture.* They can be expressed in the form of two questions: What is the relationship between the social organization of intellectuals and the ideas which they produce? Given the changing nature of equality in contemporary societies, can we expect a certain democratization of culture? In this new preface to Mannheim's work on culture, I shall address myself to these two profoundly significant questions. However, before considering the problems of the intelligentsia and democratization, we need to concern ourselves briefly with the concept of 'culture'.

SOCIOLOGY OF CULTURE

Although the concept of culture is central to both sociology and anthropology, there is little agreement about its meaning or significance. Although there have recently been a number of major contributions to the sociology of culture (Archer 1988; Wuthnow 1987), Raymond Williams' observation that 'culture is one of the two or three most complicated words in the English language' (Williams 1976:76) is still obviously accurate. As a broad definition, we can say that culture refers to the symbolic and learned components of human behaviour such as language, religion, custom and convention. As contrasted with instinct, culture is often thought to mark out the significant division between the human and the animal world. In sociology, much of the difficulty with culture is whether it is necessary to have a sociology of culture or cultural sociology; that is, does sociology attempt to study a special phenomenon called 'culture', or should we attempt to develop a special perspective on social relations which would be encapsulated by the notion of 'cultural sociology'?

While there are these general difficulties, there are quite specific problems in terms of how we are to approach Mannheim's 'sociology of culture' in order to understand it properly within its German sociology context. Mannheim's understanding of the issues is developed in Part One, where he attempts to outline a sociology of mind in response to the legacies of idealism and materialism in German philosophy. He defines the sociology of mind as 'the study of mental functions in the context of action' (Mannheim 1956:20). The sociology of the mind will provide 'the wider frame of reference for our earlier inquiries into the sociology of knowledge' (Mannheim 1956:24). There are a number of problems and difficulties with Mannheim's presentation of the sociology of mind.

To begin with a problem of translation, the German term *Geist*, which has been translated here as both 'mind' and 'culture', is in fact problematic because of its very richness. As the translator's footnote on page 171 acknowledges, *Geist* in Mannheim's essay *Demokratisierung des Geistes* has been translated as 'culture' rather than 'mind', because Mannheim was concerned to understand social and cultural processes rather than processes in thought. In the English translation of the *Essays*, 'mind' and 'culture' are therefore employed interchangeably (Mannheim 1956:81). The English reader of Mannheim should not be misled by thinking that Part One on the sociology of the mind is either a psychological treatise or a contribution to analytical philosophy. Mannheim explores the legacy of Hegel's phenomenology and philosophy of mind in order to develop his own distinctive approach to culture and knowledge from a sociological point of view.

Geist is thus a particularly important concept in the development of German philosophy and social science. In discussing the concept, Mannheim typically analyses *Geist* from the point of view of the sociology of knowledge. The concept was part of a religious tradition, and it was Martin Luther who contributed to its transmission into German idealism. The educated German middle classes (*Bildungsbürgertum*) embraced the concept in 'their accommodation to the bureaucratic state and spiritualized the idea of freedom to mean intellectual indeterminism' (Mannheim 1956:31). For Mannheim, the consequence was to set up a false polarity between ideas and matter, but it also placed a special emphasis on the idea of individual autonomy. In short, German idealism blocked the emergence of the sociology of knowledge which has attacked the basic assumptions of 'the immanence theory' (Mannheim 1956:32). The argument of Part One is thus an attempt to clear the ground of misconceptions in order for the sociology of knowledge and the sociology of culture to emerge as legitimate lines of enquiry without the burden of the false starts in immanence theory. Mannheim's intention was, for example, to avoid the reification and separation of the individual and society. He argues that 'it is misleading to speak of the social determination of the individual—as though the person and his society confronted one another as discrete entities' (Mannheim 1956:46). The problem of the relationship between the 'individual' and 'society' has continued to dominate the sociological imagination without any clear resolution (Elias 1991), but Mannheim's approach remains influential because he attempted to avoid reification (treating individual and society as dichotomous, static, concrete phenomena) and he approached the issue from a resolutely historical perspective.

Mannheim's intention is relatively clear, but there are still problems about translation. In referring to the human mind, *Geist* is normally contrasted with *Körper*, the body, as in 'body and mind'; it can also be used in the sense of 'spirit', as in the spirit of the times (*der Geist der Zeit*), or *Phänomenologie des Geistes* (phenomenology of the spirit). In the famous study by Ludwig Klages, we see this contrast in the idea of 'the mind as the antagonist of the soul' (*Der Geist als Widersacher der Seele*) (Klages 1981). The intellectual or conscious life of people was seen to negate their spiritual or emotional life. It is also contrasted with *der Seele* or 'soul'. In German philosophy, it was common to structure thought around these three realities—mind, soul and body. By interpreting *Geist* as 'culture', we are implicitly accepting these divisions between culture, spirituality and nature.

These intellectual divisions which were inherited from theology and philosophy eventually came to shape the way in which sociology was thought of as a discipline existing within the *Geisteswissenchaften* or, broadly speaking, 'the cultural and humanistic sciences' (Weber 1949:145). Weber saw sociology as 'a science concerning itself with the interpretive understanding of social action' (Weber 1978:4). The cultural sciences were to have their own special methods of inquiry which are appropriate to the study of the meaning of social action. This formulation of the contrast between *Geisteswissenschaften* and *Naturwissenschaften*, between what we commonly refer to as the social sciences and the natural sciences, has remained problematic: are they opposed or merely different? Is causal explanation with which we are familiar in the experimental methodology of the natural sciences inappropriate in social science? Is social science interpretation a form of explanation? These issues were central to the *Wissenschaftslehre* of Weber (Weber 1949;1975;1977), who claimed that socio-cultural analysis of human conduct was, by comparison with causal analysis in the natural sciences, 'qualitatively quite different' (Weber 1975:125). If we accept natural science as the only legitimate model of scientific activity, then we ultimately reduce values and meaning to observable behaviour. For many German sociologists and philosophers, this intellectual 'surrender' was merely a further step in the colonization and subordination of the life of the mind to the impulses of matter. Much of German phenomenology was bitterly opposed to this travesty, as they regarded it (Scheler 1980).

It is important to understand that Weber's theory of social science methodology was very influential in the development of Mannheim's sociology of culture. In formulating a sociology of mind (culture), Mannheim was trying to avoid what he regarded as the pitfalls of reductionism; he wanted to avoid the use of mechanistic metaphors of causal explanation (such as levers, switches, motors or tracks) when dealing sociologically with the symbolic life of social groups. These essays on culture were regarded by Mannheim, following an expression of Montaigne, as merely 'attempts' (Mannheim 1956:24) at a final solution of the very difficult and complex philosophical difficulties facing the sociology of the mind. Hence sociological theory is at an exploratory and tentative stage of development. The essay form was thus best suited to an attempt at a sociology of mind.

Mannheim did not believe that it was necessary or desirable to exclude causal and functional analysis in sociology by concentrating only on meaningful interpretation of events; despite their very obvious differences it is unnecessary to polarize natural science and social science. For Mannheim, 'We identify such things as clans, nations, castes or pressure groups not causally, but through their structural setting' (Mannheim 1956:77). Sociology requires causal, functional and interpretative approaches. In accepting Mannheim's approach, however, the English-speaking reader needs to keep in mind the fact that the concept of science in German (*Wissenschaft*) has a much broader range of meaning than in English, where in everyday parlance 'science' means the methods of the natural sciences, especially controlled experimentation. The gap between the German and English understanding of 'science' is perhaps best illustrated by Weber's essays on interpretation in the methodology of social science in *The Methodology of the Social Sciences* (Weber 1949) and J.S. Mill's argument (Mill 1952) in *A System of Logic* in 1843, where he asserted that the methods of physical science are the only proper scientific methods (Oakes 1975:22). Because *Wissenschaft* is derived from *Wissen* or 'knowledge', the German debate about the methodology of the social sciences (the famous *Methodenstreit*) has not been so hampered by a specifically narrow understanding of 'science' (Apel 1984).

There is one further issue which we must take into account if we are to understand the context of Mannheim's sociology of culture, namely the contrast in German social science analysis between 'civilization' and 'culture'. While in English it would not be considered inappropriate to use these terms as equivalent descriptions, in both French and German they had a distinctive and often opposed meaning. In France, the verb 'to civilize' had been overshadowed by the noun 'civilization' as the civilized West came to take its global superiority over uncivilized societies for granted in the eighteenth and nineteenth centuries. Civilization was associated with progress. By contrast, in Germany, *Zivilisation* was regarded as useful, but superficial. Genuine values coincided with *Kultur*, not *Zivilisation.* It was only through inner development and refinement that a person (in fact an intellectual) could obtain genuine culture (Elias 1978). Education and culture (*Bildung* and *Kultur*) are crucial for drawing a line between the educated/cultured classes or nations, and those lives which are dominated by utility, or civilization. This debate was an important context for Mannheim's development, since at Heidelberg, where Mannheim worked from 1920 to 1929, Alfred Weber, the brother of Max Weber, developed a sociology of the 'civilizing process' around the contrast between culture and civilization. Mannheim argues that a sociology of culture must go beyond an ethnography of customs, which he associated with the existing historical studies of *Sittengeschichte* (Mannheim 1956:52). As sociologists, we must understand civilization as a long process of constant struggle between social groups to assert their interpretations over cultural forces. Thus Mannheim was concerned to understand the process of civilization as the growth of new patterns of self-regulation—'contemporary society has evolved a great variety of controls which take the place of coercive power as the main guarantee of super- and subordination' (Mannheim 1956:98). This process of self-regulation was part of the growth of the 'self-discovery of groups' in the context of the democratization of culture and the autonomy of intellectuals.

MANNHEIM AND THE INTELLIGENTSIA

At various points in his academic career, Mannheim made an attempt to develop a sociology of the intellectuals. In *Ideology and Utopia*, he discussed the idea of the 'free-floating intellectuals' (Mannheim 1991:137) who might be able to achieve an independent, autonomous view of society as a whole. In *Conservatism*, Mannheim (1986) considered how various forms of conservatism were related to different patterns of intellectual life and to different social circumstances. In *Essays on the Sociology of Culture*, Part Two is devoted to an elaborate analysis of the historical development of the intelligentsia. Again there are problems in English where an educated reader might shrink from the idea of an 'intelligentsia' as a meaningful concept. The concept refers originally to an organized social group of educated people, typically in a revolutionary context. The debate originated in the contexts of the French and Russian Revolutions. The empiricism of English culture, the absence of a revolutionary (socialist) tradition, and the dominance of Oxford and Cambridge as training grounds for gentlemen and theologians, have blocked the acceptance in English of the idea of an intelligentsia.

Why is there this preoccupation with the life of intellectuals in the sociology of Mannheim? There is a cynical answer. A self-interest in the life of the intellectual might be expected from that social group which is narcissistically concerned with its own historical evolution and autonomy, namely academic intellectuals (Bauman, 1987:8). There are two more respectable answers.

The first is that, because the sociology of knowledge is concerned with understanding the structure and history of *systems* of belief and knowledge rather than the particular forms of knowledge held by individuals, it will be concerned with understanding the social organization of that group in society (the intelligentsia) whose special social function is collectively to produce, analyse and explain systems of belief. They are crucial to our understanding of the production of knowledge. Secondly, because the problem of relativism is endemic to the sociology of knowledge, it is important to understand the social location of intellectuals.

The problem of relativism, relationalism and reductionism in Mannheim's thought has been widely discussed and debated (Abercrombie 1980; Abercrombie and Longhurst 1983; Kettler *et al* 1984; Meja and Stehr 1990). I cannot analyse these problems here in any detail. However, relativism tends to be self-defeating: if all thought is relative to certain existential conditions (such as social class), then this statement about relativism also suffers from relativism. Hence, Mannheim attempted to articulate various solutions to the problem, including the weaker notion of a relationship between society and thought. Part of the problem is a confusion between the social determination of ideas, their truth and falsity, and the rational or irrational ways in which ideas might be held. The emergence of a scientifically valid view of the planetary system was a socially determined process, but whether or not it is true that the earth moves around the sun has to be established by scientific processes, which are also obviously determined. There is no *necessary* relationship between determinism and falsity. Once we accept the idea that there are no systems of thought which are not socially determined, then some aspects of Mannheim's problem simply disappear. Mannheim appears to have assumed that a belief system which is socially determined cannot be valid; he was therefore concerned to understand how some groups of intellectuals might be free-floating: that is, not entirely determined by social interests and social forces. This quest to discover a 'socially unattached intelligentsia' (*freischwebende Intelligenz*, in Alfred Weber's words) is a rather misguided search, on the grounds that all systems of belief and knowledge are socially determined. Of course, we must keep in mind the social context in which Mannheim's views about the relationship between knowledge, intellectuals and politics emerged, namely in the context of the rise of fascism. The activities of Nazi students in the University of Heidelberg are particularly important historically. In retrospect, it now appears that many major thinkers such as Martin Heidegger were seriously compromised by fascism (Wollin 1991). Mannheim and his assistant Norbert Elias (Mennell 1989:16) were forced to flee Germany, both eventually seeking exile in Britain. We can therefore see that the political role and social autonomy of intellectuals was, for Mannheim, both an intellectual and a personal issue.

Mannheim treats the rise of the intelligentsia as a historical issue, as part of the growing self-awareness or self-discovery of social groups. Whereas in mediaeval times the individual could live relatively naïvely in the context of well-worn traditions, in the contemporary world, where social change is extremely rapid and all-pervasive, customs and traditions are constantly superseded. Mannheim wanted to understand both the historical evolution of this consciousness of change, and how this consciousness was itself shaped by the competition between groups; that is, how the 'history of the human mind expresses the consecutive tensions and reconciliations of groups' (Mannhein 1956:94). In particular, he was interested in the coming-to-consciousness of the proletariat in terms of class-consciousness. He briefly referred to the emergence of a feminist consciousness as women entered the labour force under competitive market circumstances, but his main preoccupation was of course with the rise of consciousness among the intellectuals.

There are certain peculiar features of the intellectuals as a social group which Mannheim thinks are particularly significant. Firstly, their non-manual labour typically requires some system of patronage, whereby intellectuals can avoid entering into the labour force in order to withdraw into a contemplative role. In Western societies, the two major patrons of the intellectuals historically have been the Church and the State, but this very dependence on patronage does, of course, threaten that autonomy which is an essential feature of their intellectual independence. This paradox has continued to exercise the attention of sociologists (Bauman 1987; Gouldner 1982; Jacoby 1987). Secondly, the intellectuals are an interstitial stratum existing between social classes and parties. Thirdly, because these interstitial intellectuals are also recruited from a broad range of social groups and classes, they are potentially able to see social reality in neutral terms or from many perspectives. They are in this specific sense a 'relatively uncommitted intelligentsia' (*relativ freischwebende Intelligenz*) (Mannheim 1956:106).

Having provided a general outline of the problem of the sociology of the intellectuals, Mannheim then developed a more detailed historical view of the rise of the intellectuals in Europe in terms of a division of labour between manual and non-manual activities, between trades and professions, the growth of the concept of the cultured gentleman, and the growth of certification. This history is concerned to trace the shifting contexts of intellectual life—the Court, the Church, the State and, in modern societies, the University—and the changing organization of intellectual activity. Mannheim identifies an issue which is crucial to our understanding of the contemporary intellectual. This is the erosion of the authority of the intelligentsia as a closed and privileged status group and their transformation into a social group which has, in some industrial societies, forced the intellectual into the market-place of credentialization in search of employment in universities or government agencies or the media. Mannheim argues that 'the group of the learned has lost its caste organization and its prerogative to formulate authoritative answers to the questions of the time' (Mannheim 1956:117). With secularization, intellectuals no longer have the normative authority to pronounce definitively on events. For some writers, the dominance of large, commercially funded, public universities has meant that intellectuals can find employment as academics, but at the cost of their intellectual independence (Jacoby 1987).

The role of the modern intellectual presents a number of paradoxes. The loss of religious patronage has been partly replaced in the post-war period with the patronage of the modern university, the growth of which was, in part at least, an effect of the democratization of higher education, especially in societies such as the United States (Parsons and Platt 1973). Critics of these developments have suggested that the intellectuals have now lost their 'free-floating' character because, as hired labour, they are forced to serve interests over which they have little control. Furthermore, the modern university is merely an educational factory producing low-grade certification of a middle-class sector of the labour force. This rationalization of higher education undermines genuine academic vocations in a context where the intellectual is simply alienated labour. The political role of the intellectual-as-academic has become increasingly problematic and uncertain, but the relationship of intellectuals to modern culture is equally difficult. Is the intellectual somebody who merely reproduces the 'cultural capital' of the dominant social groups, and is the role of the university to preserve the hierarchy of aesthetic standards? Is the structure of the intellectual field produced by the competition for academic dominance between social groups (Bourdieu 1988)? The question of the possibility of a democratization of culture as a development which is necessarily related to the democratization of politics through the institution of modern citizenship is thus necessarily connected with issues in the social organization of intellectual life.

CULTURE AND DEMOCRATIZATION

In this section I want to explore a rather traditional question; namely, is it possible to anticipate some democratiziation of modern culture as a consequence of the enhancement of citizenship rights? Although this issue was much debated—as I want to show subsequently by writers not only such as Mannheim, but by Theodor Adorno and Talcott Parsons in classical sociology—in our period this conventional question has acquired a new dimension, namely the consequences of a (partial) postmodernization of culture. I shall not in this preface attempt to explore all of the complexities of the idea of postmodernization (Turner 1990). By the postmodernization of culture in this discussion, I shall simply mean an increasing fragmentation and differentiation of culture as a consequence of the pluralization of life-styles; the employment of irony, pastiche and montage as cultural styles; the erosion of traditional 'grand narratives' of legitimation; the celebration of the principles of difference and heterogeneity as normative guidelines in politics and morality; the globalization of postmodern culture with the emergence of global networks of communication through satellites; and the erosion of industrial society and its replacement by post-industrialism.

The cultural consequences of these changes are very profound. They bring into question the traditional division between high and low culture, because postmodernization mixes and conflates these two aspects of a national culture. As a result, the traditional authority of intellectuals and universities (as carriers and producers of high culture) is challenged (Baumann 1987). Secondly, mass culture, which emerged after the Second World War with the mass availability of radio, television and motor cars, and with the creation of the means of mass consumption, has also been eroded by a growing diversification of patterns of consumption and life-style (Featherstone 1991).

While these claims are clearly contentious, I believe they can be defended with both sociological argument and evidence, but in this presentation I shall have to take much of this debate for granted. However, I want to point out a number of important qualifications to this claim. Firstly, just as in the neo-Marxist language of development theory, sociologists noted the continuity of traditionalism and underdevelopment alongside development, so we may expect traditional and modernist culture to continue alongside postmodernism. These elements or dimensions will persist in an uneven balance. Furthermore, as a response to both postmodernization and globalization, we can anticipate a corresponding (and literally reactionary) fundamentalization of culture and society by social groups who want to oppose postmodern consumerism, irony and relativism. The second aspect of my argument is equally controversial. The great majority of theorists have taken the somewhat pessimistic position that a democratization of culture is not feasible, and furthermore that the commercialization of culture is in fact an inauthentication of culture. By contrast, I want to present an optimistic interpretation. Postmodernization is a process which may offer us both the dehierarchization of cultural systems (and hence a democratization of culture), while also permitting and indeed celebrating the differentiation of culture which is an inevitable outcome of the differentiation of social structure and life-style in postindustrial civilizations. As I have said elsewhere, we can summarize the ethic of postmodernism under the slogan 'Here's to heterogeneity!' (Turner 1990:12).

CITIZENSHIP

I want to link Mannheim's idea of cultural democratization with the sociology of citizenship which was developed by the English sociologist T.H. Marshall (1950). What are the implications of this for citizenship as the crucial element in the democratization of modern societies? Firstly, I do not believe that the nation-state is any longer the most appropriate or viable political context within which citizenship rights are 'housed'. If we think about the meaning and history of citizenship, then there have been, in Europe, a number of important evolutionary steps towards modern citizenship: the public space of the Greek polis as a debating chamber for rational citizens; the development of Christendom as a religio-political entity within which political membership came to depend on the sharing of a common faith; the rise of the autonomous European cities of the late mediaeval period; and the development of nationalism and the nation-state as the carrier of rights (Turner 1986a).

At present, there are socio-political and cultural changes which are challenging the idea that the state is the instrument through which citizenship is expressed. For example, in Europe the growth of community-wide institutions such as the European parliament and the European court of justice means that the sovereignty of the state is increasingly limited. There is a growing cultural awareness of a 'European identity' which transforms nationalistic conceptions of political citizenship. More fundamentally, the processes of globalization undermine—especially in the most privileged social classes in society—the emotive and institutional commitment to citizenship within the nation-state. At the same time that the state is eroded in terms of its political sovereignty and cultural hegemony by globalization, localism as a response to such changes 'squeezes' the state from below. The state has to respond simultaneously to these global pressures which challenge its monopoly over emotive commitments, and to local, regional and ethnic challenges to its authority. In a more profound fashion, the traditional language of nation-state citizenship is confronted by the alternative discourse of human rights and humanity as the normatively superior paradigm of political loyalty. This idea is certainly not new. Emile Durkheim in

Professional Ethics and Civic Morals (1957) argued that the moral system of the state would give way eventually to a cosmopolitan ethic of humanity.

By examining the postmodernization of culture and globalization of politics, I have been preparing the way for an argument which claims that much of the traditional literature on democracy and citizenship is now antiquated. Let us take the theory of Marshall (1950), who defined citizenship in terms of three levels of entitlement (legal, political and social) which were institutionalized in the law courts, parliament and welfare state. In Marshall's theory, citizenship counteracts the effects of the capitalist market by providing individuals with minimum guarantees to a civilized life. In a capitalist society, citizenship and class stand in a relationship of tension or contradiction. A number of critics have noted that Marshall did not extend his idea of citizenship to include economic citizenship; that is, economic democracy. I want to take a parallel position by suggesting that Marshall failed to consider the nature of cultural citizenship in modern societies. It is in this context of the absence of a notion of cultural citizenship that we can more adequately appreciate the importance of Mannheim's attempt to outline a theory of cultural democratization.

By 'citizenship', I mean that set of practices which constitute individuals as competent members of a community. I adopt this definition in order, as a sociologist, to avoid putting too much emphasis on juridical or political definitions of citizenship. It would be more conventional for example to define citizenship as a status within a polity which determines the nature of rights and obligations. I prefer a sociological definition which identifies (1) a bundle or ensemble of practices which are social, legal, political and cultural, (2) which constitutes rather than merely defines the citizenship, (3) which, over time, becomes institutionalized as normative social arrangements, and (4) which as a consequence determines membership of a community. I am thus trying to avoid the idea that citizenship is a narrow juridical status which defines the conditions of participation in a state. Within this perspective then, cultural citizenship is composed of those social practices which enable a citizen to participate fully and competently in the national culture. Educational institutions, especially universities, are thus crucial to cultural citizenship, because they are an essential aspect of the socialization of the child into this national system of values.

There are some obvious problems with the way in which I have attempted to reiterate Mannheim's notion of the 'democratization of culture'. In those societies which have a large aboriginal population, such as Australia, the expansion of national-cultural citizenship may in fact be a form of cultural colonialism; cultural citizenship involves the destruction or co-optation of indigenous or aboriginal cultures. In this case, there may be a contradiction between citizen rights and human rights. A similar argument may well apply to societies which are divided by class so that cultural citizenship involves the exclusion or marginalization of subordinate class cultures by the cultural élite which surrounds the state. Both objections in fact amount to throwing doubt on the idea of a 'national' culture because very few modern societies have a uniform, national culture. Multiculturalism is the fate of us all. Finally, there is the view that formal participation in the national culture may simply disguise major *de facto* forms of exclusion. In Britain, to take a possibly trivial example, regional and class differences in speech and vocabulary continue to function in everyday life as major markers of cultural inferiority and superiority, despite the efforts of the BBC to legitimize certain regional accents as acceptable forms of speech.

Talcott Parsons played an important role in developing this notion of cultural citizenship in his discussion of his 'educational revolution' of the twentieth century. Parsons, who was in any case influenced by Marshall in his study of the absence of citizenship for the black American, adopted the notion of citizenship as part of his general view of the process of modernization (Holton and Turner 1986; Robertson and Turner 1991). We can regard citizenship within a Parsonian paradigm as the institutionalization of the *Gesellschaft* side of the pattern variables. Citizenship is a secular principle of membership of society which emerges with social differentiation and the institutionalization of achievement-ascription as dominant values of modern capitalism. For Parsons, therefore, especially in *Societies: Evolutionary and Comparative Perspectives* (Parsons 1966) and *The System of Modern Societies*

(Parsons 1971), the rise of a mass, comprehensive and national system of education, and especially the university, was a critical step in the evolution of modern societies. Indeed, Parsons wanted to talk about an 'educational revolution' which in his view was as significant historically as the industrial and French revolutions. A comprehensive education system was the necessary prerequisite for the education of citizens as active participants in society, and on those grounds Parsons compared the historical experience of the USA favourably against Europe, where educational opportunity had remained narrow as a consequence of its class basis.

CULTURAL DEMOCRATIZATION

However, one of the strongest arguments in favour of the idea of cultural democratization is to be found in Part Three of Mannheim's *Essays.* Mannheim rather baldly starts his argument with the statement that 'a democratizing trend is our predestined fate, not only in politics, but also in intellectual and cultural life as a whole. Whether we like it or not, the trend is irreversible' (Mannheim 1956:171). Although Mannheim recognized the dangers of cultural democratization in terms of Nietzsche's critique of the levelling consequences of the political dominance of the 'herd' ('democracy levels everything, it ushers in the dominance of mediocrity and the mass'), he argues that this position is ultimately a superficial view of the sociological relationship between aristocratic and democratic cultures (Mannheim 1956:175).

Mannheim felt that the underlying principles of democracy (the ontological equality of human beings, the idea of individual autonomy and the principle of open recruitment to élite positions in society) had fundamentally shaped the nature of culture in the modern world. He claimed that cultural democratization had the following socio-cultural consequences: (1) it was associated with 'pedagogical optimism' in which the educational system assumes that all children are able to achieve the highest levels of cultural excellence; (2) it is sceptical of the monopolistic character of 'expert knowledge'; and (3) cultural democratization brings about what Mannheim called the 'de-distantiation' of culture: that is, the erosion of the distinction between high and low culture (Mannheim 1956:208).

These democratic ideals which assume the ontological plasticity of human beings conflict sharply with the aristocratic ideal of charismatic cultural authority whereby the cultured person is transformed by illumination or conversion rather than education. The aristocratic ideal requires distantiation and wants to create an 'élite culture'. It is assumed that their knowledge, cultural techniques, patterns of speech and leisure activities will be 'unshareable by the many' (Mannheim 1956:211). This élite is a genuine leisure class which cultivates 'finickiness and delicacy' to distinguish itself from the masses.

In terms of the historical evolution of the democratic ideal, Mannheim claimed that a strong democratic trend is discernible from 1370 in late mediaeval art which developed 'intimate realism', where everyday life activities were represented in a naturalistic style. The highly stylized and unrealistic attitude of early mediaevalism was no longer attractive to new urban groups. Later the Reformation challenged the hierarchical assumptions of Catholicism and produced another stage in the historical development of democratic cultural norms. Baroque culture in the age of absolutism was treated by Mannheim as a reversal of this trend; baroque culture was characterized by ecstasy 'in the form of an intensification of fervour beyond all measure, in a kind of overheated and sublimated eroticism' (Mannheim 1956:224). Baroque effervescence contrasts strongly with modern popular cultural forms. Interestingly, Mannheim treated photography as the most characteristic expression of modern democratization. Its principle is supremely that of de-distantiation. Photography 'marks the greatest closeness to all things without distinction. The snapshot is a form of pictorial representation that is most congenial to the modern mind with its interest in the unretouched and uncensored "moment"' (Mannheim 1956:226).

The democratic cultural ethic also has its impact on religion where the traditional conceptualization of an all-powerful patriarchal God is the epitome of distantiation. The democratic trend brings about an equalization of the relationship between men and gods. Thus Mannheim argued that

The metaphysical aura which surrounds the things of the world in pantheism is dispersed in modern naturalism, positivism and pragmatism. As a result of this radical this-worldliness, the mind of man becomes perfectly congruent with 'reality' ... We have to do here with a radically analytical and nominalistic outlook that leaves no room for the 'distantiation' and idealization of everything.

(Mannheim 1956:229)

A CRITIQUE OF CULTURAL DEMOCRATIZATION

I have briefly identified in Marshall, Parsons and Mannheim a view of modernization which involves the idea, or is compatible with the idea, that cultural citizenship will require a democratization of culture, or, in Mannheim's words, will involve the replacement of an aristocratic ethos by a democratic one. The two main arguments against the possibility of cultural democratization which I want to consider are firstly, the studies of modern society which show that cultural divisions between classes are illimitable and irreducible, and secondly, those traditions of social analysis which suggest that any democratization of culture in capitalism will in fact produce the inauthentication of culture by a process of trivialization. Thus, from a sociological perspective, these claims about democratization of culture in modern capitalism do not appear immediately persuasive. To take two widely contrasted positions, Veblen's notion of 'the leisure class' (Veblen 1899) suggests that some form of the high culture/low culture division is likely to persist in a capitalist society where the lower class is characteristically referred to as a 'working class' or 'labouring class'. An upper class is likely to assume a leisure life-style as a mark of distinction from subordinate labouring classes; hence the typical division in the occupational hierarchy between the manual and non-manual sectors. It is through leisure that these social classes can gain an easy familiarity with a cultured way of life.

The second example would be that the sociology of education has shown that the competitive educational systems which were characteristic of the post-war period, far from bringing about a major equalization of social outcomes, tended merely to reproduce the existing class structure. Formal equality of opportunity in the educational field was an important feature of the extension of citizenship rights to the whole population. However, the continuity of cultural deprivation and cultural differences between social classes meant that actual social mobility through educational attainment was well below the level anticipated by post-war educational reforms. The result has been that the educational system has reproduced the culture of the dominant class (Bourdieu and Passeron 1990).

Pierre Bourdieu has further elaborated this idea in his study of social distinction (Bourdieu 1984), which we can interpret as a sociological critique of Kant's theory of aesthetics. Whereas Kant wanted to argue that the aesthetic judgement is individual, neutral, objective and disinterested, Bourdieu wants to demonstrate empirically that taste is social, structured and committed. Our taste for goods, both symbolic and material, is simultaneously a classification which classifies the classifier; as such, it cannot be neutral and disinterested because it is a consequence of class position. Life-style, cultural taste, and consumer preferences are related to particular divisions within the occupational structure of society, and especially in terms of educational attainment. With the decline of a rigid status order in society, there is constant competition between classes and class factions to secure dominance over the definition of cultural taste (Featherstone 1991). These patterns of cultural distinction are so profound and pervasive that they also dictate how the body should be correctly developed and presented, because the body is also part of the symbolic capital of a class. Because the flow of symbolic goods is so extensive in the modern market-place, there develops the possibility of endless interpretation and reinterpretation of new cultural products. To provide this service, a class of new cultural intermediaries emerges (especially in the media, advertising and fashion) to inform society on matters of distinction. These intermediaries transmit the distinctive life-style of the intellectuals and the leisure class to a wider social audience. These processes within the world of consumer goods therefore force upper, educated social classes to invest in new knowledge and new cultural goods. These dominant groups will turn to 'positional goods' (Leiss 1983) which are prestigious because of an artificial scarcity of supply in order to reassert their distinctive cultural distinction.

What is the implication of these studies of class and culture for the Mannheimian argument that we have entered a period in which the democratization of culture is inevitable? It implies obviously that any process of cultural equalization or levelling will be met by a counter-process of distantiation and hierarchization. Within a competitive market of symbolic goods, some pattern of social distinction will be imposed upon the market by cultural intermediaries. Although governments may attempt to reform the educational system to provide equality of educational opportunity, there will always be inequality in social outcomes, because different social classes and social groups already possess different types and amounts of cultural capital which they inevitably transfer to their children. Furthermore, because, for Bourdieu, intellectuals play a very important role in defining standards of appropriate cultural production and consumption, intellectuals as a stratum of cultural intermediaries have a distinctive, if often contradictory, interest in maintaining a hierarchy of taste.

In this sense, Bourdieu's work has very pessimistic implications for cultural democratization, because it would rule out any possibility of the majority of the population participating freely and fully in the 'national' culture. According to Bourdieu's work, any national culture will always be overlaid and structured by a class system which requires cultural distantiation. There may be two criticisms of, or alternatives to, Bourdieu's analysis which we should consider. The first is taken from Zygmunt Bauman's book *Legislators and Interpreters* (1987) in which Bauman argues that one important feature of modern society is that the state no longer exercises direct hegemony and regulation over culture. A fissure has opened up between the polity and the national culture, with the result that the intellectuals no longer have effective authority over cultural symbols. They have lost a considerable amount of social and political power as a result. This separation of politics and culture, and the conversion of intellectuals from legislators into interpreters, is associated with the postmodernization of cultures, namely their fragmentation and pluralization. Perhaps, therefore, the cultural field is more fluid and uncertain than Bourdieu suggests, and as a consequence it may be much more difficult than he imagines for cultural élites to impose their authority over cultural capital.

A second modification of Bourdieu's argument which may be important is that his view of the working class and working-class culture is extremely passive. In my typology, his view of cultural citizenship for the working class is private and passive. They are merely the recipients of the cultural products of the market. In *Common Culture*, Paul Willis *et al* (1990) present us with an alternative view of the working class as active users and creators of culture which is resistant to total cultural incorporation. Following the work of Michel de Certeau (1984), Willis shows how consumers or users of cultural objects constantly change and modify cultural products to their own local needs and requirements. In short, people are not merely passive recipients of cultural products, and 'reception theory' has suggested that consumers have varied and complex methods of cultural appropriation (Morley 1986; Abercrombie 1990). This argument may be an important corrective to the 'top-down' view of cultural capital which appears to dominate Bourdieu's view of the cultural market-place in capitalism.

I shall now turn to the rather different issue of the inauthentication of culture by commodification and the growth of mass cultures in the western liberal democracies. Mannheim's essays were in fact originally composed in the early 1930s shortly before the rise of National Socialism forced Mannheim to seek asylum in England. Mannheim's optimistic view of the potential for cultural democratization thus contrasts sharply with the view of the 'culture industry' which was advanced by Theodor Adorno, who has provided one of the most sustained and original critiques of consumer culture. We must remember of course that Adorno's aesthetic theory was set within the specific context of the employment of film by the national socialists to manipulate public opinion, and that his attack on the culture industry took place within a wider set of objections to the problems of instrumental rationality and rationalization (Adorno 1991). Adorno rejected the false universalism of mass art and entertainment, which he regarded as merely a respite from labour. Mass culture imposes a uniformity of culture on society; cultural production follows the same logic as all forms of capitalist production; real pleasure is converted into an illusory promise.

Although Adorno's aim was to break down the division

between high and low art in conservative aesthetics, and to provide a critique of the falsification of culture by commodification, Adorno's own position has been criticized as an élitist defence of high art, given, for example, Adorno's rejection of jazz music as part of the culture industry. Adorno's form of critical theory has also been attacked as a nostalgic defence of high modernity against the emergence of popular culture (Stauth and Turner 1988). Critical theory's attack on mass culture often in practice appears to be a condemnation of the Americanization of western popular culture. Other critics have argued that Adorno and critical theory failed to identify the oppositional and critical elements of popular culture—a theme developed in the work of the Birmingham Centre for Contemporary Cultural Studies, for whom popular culture is pre-eminently low and oppositional (Brantlinger 1990). Another argument against Adorno is that we no longer live in a world of standardized mass fashion. Instead, the world of popular taste is highly fragmented and diverse, catering to specific and distinctive audiences. Although a number of writers have recently come to Adorno's defence—for example Frederic Jameson in *Signatures of the Visible* (1990)—it is interesting that Walter Benjamin's 'Art in an age of mechanical reproduction', which was one target of Adorno's critique, has had more influence on our understanding of mass and popular culture than Adorno's aesthetics.

CONCLUSION

I have identified a number of important critiques of the idea of a democratization of culture in modern societies; yet it appears to be necessary to defend Mannheim, because the alternative (namely, acceptance of a pessimistic view of inevitable hierarchization) would leave us with no normative programme for educational and cultural reform. Pessimism is not a particularly useful framework for social change. By contrast, Mannheim never entirely abandoned the idea of utopian mentalities as a requirement for social reorganization. Mannheim's views on cultural democratization, which were originally developed in Germany in the late 1920s and early 1930s, may as a consequence be seen as foundations for his subsequent writing in England on the problems of rational reconstruction of a democratic society in the aftermath of war, and the importance of planning for progressive social change (Mannheim 1950). It is partly for that reason that I believe it is appropriate to compare and contrast Mannheim (1893–1947) and Marshall (1873–1982) on the nature of citizenship in modern societies. Marshall, whose ideas on citizenship became important in the development of social policy in Britain, was Professor of Sociology and Head of the Social Science Department at the London School of Economics from 1946. Both sociologists had a commitment to the principles of citizenship as a basis for attempting to transform inequalities in a democratic context. The difference between them is, not only the greater scope of Mannheim's sociology, but Mannheim's commitment to a principle of utopian imagination as a counterweight to pessimism.

Sociologists tend to write about inequality, not equality (Turner 1986b:15), and therefore a sociologist like Mannheim who has an interest in the democratization of culture is likely to find himself working against the grain. Elias' ideas about civilization in an epoch which appears predominantly uncivilized (in terms of total war) received an equally negative reception in mainstream sociology. On the specific issue of cultural democratization, one important conclusion must be that the processes of hierarchization and democratization occur simultaneously in the cultural sphere as social groups compete with each other for social dominance, but an emphasis on cultural inequality in mainstream sociology has often neglected important aspects of cultural democratization. Thus the democratizating implications of the motor car, tourism, the cinema and television, are often ignored in favour of pessimistic analyses of the culture industry, the inauthentication of cultural meaning and the endless simulations in media representation (Baudrillard 1990). Unfortunately, this critique of the cultural industry often leads implicitly to both an élitist defence of high culture against democratization and a nostalgia for lost communalism and wholeness. Thus Mannheim's contrast between the aristocratic and the democratic ethic in cultural life provides an important sociological insight into many of the educational and political dilemmas of our age, which is an antidote to nostalgia and élitism.

GENERAL REFERENCES

Abercrombie, N. *Class Structure and Knowledge.* Oxford: Basil Blackwell, 1980.

Abercrombie, N. 'Popular culture and ideological effects', in N. Abercrombie, S. Hill and B.S. Turner (eds), *Dominant Ideologies.* London: Unwin Hyman, pp. 199–228, 1990.

Abercrombie, N. and Longhurst, B. 'Interpreting Mannheim', *Theory Culture & Society* 2(1): 5–15, 1983.

Adorno, T. *The Culture Industry. Selected Essays on Mass Culture.* London: Routledge, 1991.

Apel, K.-O. *Understanding and Explanation, a Transcendental-Pragmatic Perspective.* Cambridge, MA: MIT Press, 1984.

Archer, M. *Culture and Agency. The Place of Culture in Social Theory.* Cambridge: Cambridge University Press, 1988.

Baudrillard, J. *Revenge of the Crystal. Selected Writings on the Modern Object and its Destiny, 1968–1983.* London: Pluto Press, 1990.

Bauman, Z. *Legislators and Interpreters. On Modernity, Post-modernity and Intellectuals.* Oxford: Polity Press, 1987.

Bourdieu, P. *Distinction. A Social Critique of the Judgement of Taste.* London: Routledge & Kegan Paul, 1984.

Bourdieu, P. *Homo Academicus.* Stanford, CA: Stanford University Press, 1988.

Bourdieu, P. and Passeron, J.C. *Reproduction in Education, Society and Culture.* London: Sage, 1990.

Brantlinger, P. *Crusoe's Footprints, Cultural Studies in Britain and America.* New York and London: Routledge, 1990.

Certeau, M. de. *The Practice of Everyday Life.* Berkeley, CA: University of California Press, 1984.

Durkheim, E. *Professional Ethics and Civic Morals.* London: Routledge & Kegan Paul, 1957.

Elias, N. *The Civilizing Process.* Oxford: Basil Blackwell, 1978.

Elias, N. *The Society of Individuals.* Oxford: Basil Blackwell, 1991.

Featherstone, M. *Consumer Culture and Postmodernism.* London: Sage, 1991.

Gouldner, A.W. *The Future of Intellectuals and the Rise of the New Class.* New York: Oxford University Press, 1982.

Holton, R.J. and Turner, B.S. *Talcott Parsons on Economy and Society.* London: Routledge & Kegan Paul, 1986.

Jacoby, R. *The Last Intellectuals, American Culture in the Age of Academe.* New York: Farrar, Strauss and Giroux, 1987.

Jameson, F. *Signatures of the Visible.* London: Routledge, 1990.

Kettler, D., Meja, V. and Stehr, N. *Karl Mannheim.* Chichester: Ellis Horwood, and London and New York: Tavistock Publications, 1984.

Klages, L. *Der Geist als Widersacher der Seele.* Bonn: Bouvier, 1981.

Leiss, W. 'The icons of the marketplace', *Theory Culture & Society.* 1(3): 10–21, 1983.

Mannheim, K. *Freedom, Power and Democratic Planning.* London: Routledge & Kegan Paul, 1950.

Mannheim, K. *Essays on the Sociology of Culture.* London: Routledge & Kegan Paul, 1956.

Mannheim, K. *Conservatism, a Contribution to the Sociology of Knowledge.* London: Routledge & Kegan Paul, 1986.

Mannheim, K. *Ideology and Utopia.* London: Routledge, 1991.

Marshall, T.H. *Citizenship and Social Class and Other Essays.* Cambridge: Cambridge University Press, 1950.

Mennell, S. *Norbert Elias, Civilization and the Human Self Image.* Oxford: Basil Blackwell, 1989.

Meja, V. and Stehr, N. (eds) *Knowledge and Politics, the Sociology of Knowledge Dispute.* London: Routledge, 1990.

Morley, D. *Family Television: Cultural Power and Domestic Leisure.* London: Comedia, 1986.

Merton, R.K. 'Sociology of knowledge', in G. Gurvitch and W.E. Moore (eds), *Twentieth Century Sociology.* New York: The Philosophical Library, pp. 366–405, 1945.

Mill, J.S. *A System of Logic.* London: Longman and Green, 1952.

Oakes, G. 'Introductory essay' to Max Weber, *Roscher and Knies. The Logical Problems of Historical Economics.* New York: The Free Press, pp. 1–49, 1975.

Parsons, T. *Societies: Evolutionary and Comparative Perspectives.* Englewood Cliffs: Prentice-Hall, 1966.

Parsons, T. *The System of Modern Societies.* Englewood Cliffs: Prentice Hall, 1971.

Parsons, T. and Platt, G. *The American University.* Cambridge, MA: Harvard University Press, 1973.

Roberston, R. and Turner, B.S. (eds) *Talcott Parsons, Theorist of Modernity.* London: Sage, 1991.

Scheler, M. *Problems of a Sociology of Knowledge.* London: Routledge & Kegan Paul, 1980.

Stauth, G. and Turner, B.S. *Nietzsche's Dance. Resentment, Reciprocity and Resistance in Social Life.* Oxford: Basil Blackwell, 1988.

Turner, B.S. *Citizenship and Capitalism, The Debate over Reformism.* London: Allen & Unwin, 1986a.

Turner, B.S. *Equality.* Chichester: Ellis Horwood, and London: Tavistock, 1986b.

Turner, B.S. (ed.) *Theories of Moderntiy and Postmodernity.* London: Sage, 1990.

Turner, B.S. 'Preface to the New Edition', in K. Mannheim, *Ideology and Utopia.* London: Routledge, pp. xxxiii–lviii, 1991.

Veblen, T. *The Theory of the Leisure Class.* New York: Macmillan, 1899.

Weber, M. *The Methodology of the Social Sciences.* New York: The Free Press, 1949.

Weber, M. *Roscher and Knies, the Logical Problems of Historical Economics.* New York: The Free Press, 1975.

Weber, M. *Critique of Stammler.* New York: The Free Press, 1977.

Weber, M. *Economy and Society.* Berkeley, Los Angeles and London: University of California Press, 1978.

Williams, R. *Keywords, a Vocabulary of Culture and Society*. London: Fontana, 1976.

Willis, P., with Jones, S., Canaan, J. and Hurd, G. *Common Culture. Symbolic Work at Play in the Everyday Cultures of the Young*. Milton Keynes: The Open University Press, 1990.

Wollin, R. *The Politics of Being. The Political Thought of Martin Heidegger*. New York: Columbia University Press, 1991.

Wuthnow, R. *Meaning and Moral Order. Explorations in Cultural Analysis*. Berkeley, Los Angeles and London: University of California Press, 1987.

INTRODUCTION

THE three essays contained in this volume were written largely during the last years of Mannheim's stay in Germany. They are, in a sense, a sequel to *Ideology and Utopia*, his principal study in the field of the sociology of knowledge, for the three essays, too, are concerned with the social derivation of meaning. The present volume, however, constitutes not only an extension and elaboration of the principal thesis of *Ideology and Utopia*, but also a new departure.

I am inclined to regard *Ideology and Utopia* as an attempt to translate a disillusionment with the excessive claims of German idealism into a sociological theory of thought. Mannheim's critique aimed at two aspects of German idealism: the overestimation of the role of ideas in human affairs and the consequent tendency to assume that concepts which emerge in various periods of history inherently evolve from one another in something like a logical continuum. Mannheim's sociology of knowledge sought to outline a method for the study of ideas as functions of social involvements. Once the image of an autonomous evolution of ideas was abandoned it was feasible to explore the relationship between thought and its social milieu.

It is easy to exaggerate the scope of this endeavour, and equally easy to oversimplify its aim. Some critics have felt, for example, that the sociology of knowledge lays claim to a canon of truth and assumes the authority of an umpire between partisans, an authority which sociologists engaged in other areas do not possess. Others have feared that the effort is designed to question the cognitive functions of socially conditioned thinking: for if the sociologist seeks to construe ideas as responses to particular situations he assumes the role of a specialist in the business of deflating all claims to knowledge. Still other writers have found the intrusion of sociologists into the realm of ideation a disconcerting expression of indifference to basic values and truths.

Students of the social sciences and the humanities in English-speaking countries have not generally shared this alarm over the implications of *Ideology and Utopia.* The drift of its argument is more germane to the trend of English and American historiography and literary criticism, a large part of which shows an intuitive sense for social realities. The spectre of relativism as a scientific tool—disclaimed by Mannheim but actually implied in his criticial treatment of varied subjects—holds little terror for generations brought up on Durkheim's 'collective representations', functional anthropology, Sumner's relativity of the mores, James's and Dewey's pragmatism, W. I. Thomas's situational method, and Korzybski's semantics. Quite the contrary, part of the dissent voiced in the United States has been directed at certain vestiges of intellectualism which the reader may be able to detect in some of Mannheim's writings, including the present volume.

What are the basic categories of the sociology of knowledge?

Concepts represent interpretative responses to given situations. We are actually dealing with four variables: (1) the situation, such as a community, a nation, a revolution, or a class, which we attempt to interpret when we respond to it; (2) the individual who is peculiarly involved in the situation and accordingly forms his image of it. Such involvements may include occupational aims, political aspirations, kinship ties, economic rivalries and alliances, in short, a multitude of overlapping group attachments; (3) the imagery which individuals or groups adopt; (4) finally, the audience to which the image is conveyed, including its peculiar understandings, symbols to which it attaches meaning, and a vocabulary to which it responds.

The four factors of ideation must be considered as interdependent variables. The same object is differently conceptualized in different situations. Persons involved in the same situation in different ways will offer different accounts of it and will tend to alter the situation accordingly. Finally, the individual conceives a subject in accordance with the audience which he actually addresses or tacitly anticipates, and both the form and substance of a message vary with the audience with which the writer or speaker seeks to establish rapport. The sociologist must assume the interdependence of these four factors, for the treatment of any one as an independent variable introduces into the study of ideation an uncritical and unwarranted type of determinism, be it behaviouristic, idealistic, or evolutionary. To assume, for example, that a common economic position necessarily results in an identical conception of society is as unwarranted as the converse supposition that the established currency of certain ideas in itself prescribes the views which individuals or groups adopt of their situation.

Nevertheless, an inquiry may confine itself to the relationship between only two or three of the four variables. This is what Mannheim does in the essay on the intelligentsia, in which he correlates certain types of ideation with the social habitat of their authors. His observations on the social origin of scepticism show how far one can get with the help of two variables only. In this work Mannheim deliberately avoids making extended use of the third variable, the historical situation, for reasons I shall indicate subsequently. One may assume that he was aware of the fourth factor, the audience, in the formation of concepts. His remarks on the democratic process and such phenomena as formalism and the operational criteria of truth, contained in the last essay, can be taken as an indication of such an awareness.

Once the inquiry is so delimited the objective is to outline typical relationships between thought and social habitat. The particular involvement of an individual in his society opens to him a certain perspective, an area of social experience, which has its scope and its limitations. The scope of social experience is defined by the insights which the person may gain through his participation in the social process; while the limitations of his vista are set by the blockages which he imposes on himself when he assumes a role and is forced accordingly to make characteristic choices. To trace the limits within which individuals interpret their experience is not the same as to refute their interpretation. An image of society which grows out of a wide range of experience is not invariably more valid than a segmental view. Whether a synthetic conception of the whole contains more 'truth' in some sense than does a particular perspective is a question which the sociologist may not decide without overreaching himself. At any rate, the pragmatic test, by which the resulting action proves a proposition, does not always favour the broad, synthetic view of things.

The present essays show in several regards a notable advance beyond Mannheim's earlier treatment of ideation. In his previous publications ideologies appeared as by-products and reflections of social situations. The frequent use of optical expressions was quite significant: ideologies appeared as particular modes of either *seeing* or *obscuring* things, and each position in the social structure entailed a particular *perspective*. To be sure, the use of optical terms for ideologies constituted a gain over the treatment of social bias as mere distortions of truth. But the proposition that each vista corresponds to a certain role does not offer a clue to the nature of the relationship between 'thinking' and social 'location'. Why, one may ask, does an individual who is identified with several groups adopt the conceptions of one rather than of another?

What Mannheim proposed in *Ideology and Utopia* was a sociological theory of ideation as an introduction to a systematic attempt to discover typical relationships between ideologies and social situations. One may designate the aim of such a pursuit as the natural history of ideas. The natural history of a social phenomenon outlines its typical features without necessarily explaining why they are recurrent. Mannheim's monograph on conservative thinking ('Conservative Thought', in *Essays on Sociology and Social Psychology*, London, Routledge & Kegan Paul; New York, Oxford University Press, 1953) offers a typical illustration. In this study Mannheim described a characteristic relationship between the declining position of landowners and their tendency to perceive the social process in organismic and morphological terms. Attempts of this type can be constructive provided that the established relationships are derived from reliable samples whose scope and representativeness are ascertained. Since, however, historical case studies offer but weak support for generalizations the question of how and why certain roles coincide with particular ideologies becomes inescapable; for without demonstration of the dynamics of concept formation the road toward a progressive verification and elaboration of such hypotheses remains blocked. To accept such blockages is tantamount to admitting that the sociology of knowledge is an area of episodic insights and no field for cumulative inquiry.

Although Mannheim did not ignore in *Ideology and Utopia* the question of how ideas emerge from action he did not attempt to offer an explicit answer. The present work, however, reveals a preoccupation with the social mechanism which intervenes between the roles individuals play and the ideas they espouse. This is where Mannheim's recourse to social psychology is rooted. The reader will notice the frequent use of psychological constructs designed to furnish the missing link. These constructs are offered as tools for uncovering the common roots of ideation and role-playing. These constructs are, moreover, open to verification and empirical elaboration in the contemporary scene, for reasons suggested below. The reader is referred to such chapters as 'The Circulation of Perceptions', 'The Theory of an Immanent History of Thought and Why it Emerged', 'Digression on the Social Roots of Scepticism', 'The Natural History of the Intellectual', and 'Social and Mental Distance'. These and several other examples show a persistent concern with the motivation of ideas.

This increased attention to the dynamics of ideation is inherent in Mannheim's adoption of the nominalist theory of groups, the view that groups have no reality of their own beyond the existence of their individual members. Compare with this the 'realist' undercurrent in *Ideology and Utopia*, that is, the treatment of groups and collective situations as the seats of ultimate reality. The 'realist' seeks to construe the behaviour of individuals from the group or a complex situation which he assumes as given. It is only when the individual becomes the ultimate term of reference of sociological constructs that questions of motivation can have meaning for the analysis of social action. Sociological concepts formed on the level of the group are impervious to psychology.

Mannheim's increasing orientation towards a social nominalism explains another departure from his earlier point of view: *the abandonment of the doctrine which asserts the primacy of the historical frame of reference.* This historical emphasis is characteristic of a large area of the German social sciences, from the followers of Hegel, including Marx, to the historical school of jurisprudence and economics. The historical point of view in the German social sciences entails more than a special interest in historical subjects; it rests on the thesis that institutions may be understood only in the context of their development. Once the inquiry proceeds from complex things and the historical continuum becomes the frame of reference, the study of human relations resolves itself into an exploration of how consecutive changes in the major designs of society relate themselves to the involvements of concrete individuals. Such a procedure favours the 'realistic' hypostasis, for the primary concern of the historian is with the larger collectivities or, at any rate, with those actions with which he identifies the destiny of society. The historical point of view was not confined to the German social sciences. It made its entry—via the evolutionary hypothesis—into British and American sociology as well, but with the decline of Darwinism English-speaking sociologists abandoned the historical frame of analysis. History continued to furnish subjects for sociological studies but not their axis. Not so with a significant section of German scholars.

Two assumptions constitute the common denominator of the historical point of view as it is understood in Germany. (1) Customs are parts of a historical *Gestalt*, hence their proper study requires an understanding of their particular configuration in a given period. (2) Historical configurations are, by definition, unique and subject to change. The student of customs seeks to reconstruct their dynamics, the modifications which customs undergo when they pass from one temporal configuration into another. To interpret an event is to fix its place in the total scheme of development. The focus of analysis is the inclusive whole which in the historical perspective is 'prior' to its parts. Once the uniqueness, the *Einmaligkeit* of a situation becomes the frame of interpretation, the 'realistic' conception of collective processes is axiomatic. Since inclusive structures form the subject of history, its student is understandably prone to view such collectivities as the nations as being more concrete and real than simple structures such as the neighbourhood or the family.

This is not the place to discuss the merits and limitations of the 'realistic' approach to history. We may grant the legitimacy of the macrocosmic interest, and we may appreciate the quest for synopses in preference to the minutiae of analytical generalizations. The policy maker and the military planner, for example, cannot avoid dwelling in the larger perspective of things. But the student who assumes the primacy of inclusive structures and the derivative character of simple phenomena is not in a strategic position to develop hypotheses for the controlled study of motivation. Indeed, questions of motivation entered the fringe and not the centre of Mannheim's inquiry in *Ideology and Utopia*. This was consistent with the book's leaning toward the configurational aspects of the social process:

'Just as modern psychology shows that the whole (Gestalt) is prior to the parts and that our first understanding of the parts comes through the whole, so it is with historical understanding. Here, too, we have the sense of historical time as a meaningful totality which orders events "prior" to the parts and through this totality we first truly understand the total course of events and our place in it.' (*Ideology and Utopia*, p. 189, London and New York, 1936.)

In the essays here presented Mannheim does not make use of this realistic paradigm. More than that, in his methodological sketch, which the reader will find in the first essay, he reverses the order of procedure. In place of the earlier recommended approach from the whole towards its parts he advocates an analytical course which advances from the abstract to the concrete, from simple to complex phenomena. Although Mannheim does not abandon the aim of understanding concrete historical subjects, he rejects the direct and unpremeditated attack on them. Instead he introduces two prior levels of articulation.

General sociology marks the most abstract level of analysis which is concerned with elementary and universal forms of 'sociation'. Simmel, Park, and others have given attention to these forms, such as cooperation, competition, conflict, accommodation, distance, isolation, communication, in-group, and so forth. Such forms are universal and elementary because they are not confined to particular situations and they involve a minimum of sociological assumptions.

Comparative sociology signifies the next level in order of concretion. It deals with relations which, though not ubiquitous, can be construed from elementary forms, for instance bureaucracy, castes, and classes.

Historical sociology constitutes the most concrete level on which involved phenomena may be articulated, such as the British Conservative Party, the French Academy, or the American New Deal. Although such subjects are of a high order of complexity they can be construed analytically, from the categories of general and comparative sociology.

What is new in this methodological model, as compared with Mannheim's previous views, is the deliberate abandonment of the *ad hoc* approach to complex historical subjects, past or contemporary. Such *ad hoc* attempts cannot help being episodical, lacking the essentials of scientific continuity: a common frame of reference and mutual relevance. In the procedure which Mannheim outlines complex structures are not just assumed but are derived from simple ones. It is in this sense that the study of subjects of a high order of concretion may become a cumulative pursuit requiring no improvisation.

The present essays, particularly the second and third, in a sense exemplify the recommended plan. Their subjects, the intelligentsia and the democratic process, are not approached on the historical level. Historical references are interspersed, but they are peripheral to the aim of constructing types and suggesting typical relationships which are capable of empirical verification and refinement. The observer who deals with single phenomena on the level of historical processes can propose only interpretive hypotheses whose scope is limited to a single constellation, whether it is the Renaissance, a Melanesian island, or a middle-sized town in the United States. The reverse procedure which advances from elementary to inclusive structures may, however, yield constructs of more general application.

Mannheim's attempt to construe the social genesis of epistemology is a case in point. His construct, which the reader will find in the second essay, lends itself to an understanding of scepticism in 17th-century Europe, contemporary France, and ancient Greece. The hypothesis, moreover, may be tested and further developed in the laboratory of contemporary society.

This analytical plan has the added advantage that it is free of the temptation to interpret the expressions of individual writers as the unitary traits of a period or a whole culture.

The foregoing discussion was concerned with Mannheim's qualified abandonment of the historical point of view and his consequent adoption of analytical and constructive procedures. This trend is new with Mannheim, although one may find traces of this leaning in his previous works, for example in the essays 'Competition as a Cultural Phenomenon' and 'The Problem of Generations'. (*Essays on the Sociology of Knowledge*, London, Routledge & Kegan Paul; New York, Oxford University Press, 1952.) As mentioned before, this departure gives Mannheim access to the intricate mechanisms which govern the actions and thoughts of the individual. That is why he no longer treats ideas as mere optical phenomena, as socially available vistas, but as motivated responses to given situations. Although he does not discard his previous question of what segment of the social process becomes visible to given groups, his present concern is how and why individuals adopt typical views.

To understand Mannheim's scheme for the interpretation of motives it will be necessary to comment on two terms which are basic to his point of view, namely *structure* and *function*. Since he has not made his understanding of these concepts explicit I hazard a tentative exegesis of the meaning which he gave to these terms in the first essay. To avoid an unnecessary expansion of this preface I shall abstain from cross-references to the current literature on the subject.

An object of a certain complexity is viewed as a structure if it is not taken for granted but construed analytically, that is, derived from items of lesser complexity. Social phenomena in particular are construed from the actions of individuals and groups. A profession for example is structured by the particular methods of selecting members, their training and indoctrination, the control of competition, the enforcement of standards, and so forth. Each of these activities discharges a function in so far as it sustains the profession as a viable organ of society. Function is an attribute of a condition which is indispensable for a given performance or a state of affairs. The sum total of interrelated functions on which a stated process depends constitutes its structure. It is well to remember at this point that the term function in itself does not imply a value. An act which performs a function is not necessarily desirable, nor is the process which requires the performance of the function necessarily desirable.

Once a social process is so articulated three conclusions follow automatically: (*a*) certain actions are required for the existence of a structure; (*b*) some actions are not required but are compatible with it; while (*c*) some are incompatible with a given structure and tend to disrupt it. Professions, for example, require some measure of control over the qualifications and conduct of their members, but most professions permit within their ranks a variety of religious and political affiliations. Again, the family as an institution depends on the effectiveness of taboos on incest, desertion, child-neglect, but it is compatible with nearly all vocational pursuits, unemployment, various consumption habits, and so forth. André Maurois, I believe, cites the story of a Parisian who was seen fishing on the bank of the Seine, practically within sight of the public executions, during the climactic days of the Revolutionary Terror. The sociologist is concerned with structurally relevant actions, namely those which are either required or incompatible, while random activities which neither sustain nor disrupt a given structure do not provide data for the analysis. To be sure, an act is irrelevant not in itself but only with reference to a particular structure. By the same token, every act has some bearing on some structure.

Motives are significant data of sociology in so far as they prompt structurally relevant behaviour. To persist a structure must perpetuate motivations of one type and inhibit others. How and whether certain inducements are engendered or repressed is of basic importance for the understanding of action systems. Random motives as such are of little interest to the sociologist; it is only within defined structures that the question of why individuals act as they do becomes fruitful.

The last two essays provide copious examples for Mannheim's application of this principle of structural relevance to motivations.

The essay on the intelligentsia, the second in this volume, grew out of an earlier interest of the author. His aphorism that the study of the intelligentsia furnishes a clue to the sociology of the mind may serve as its motto. Its governing question is: what conditions permitted the unique development of critical and self-critical inquiry and its culmination in the late 18th and early 19th century, and what circumstances account for its gradual decline? The intelligentsia became the protagonist of critical thinking when it constituted itself as a fluid and open stratum which became accessible to individuals of varied social orientations. What makes this intelligentsia unique among its historical variants is its multipolarity, its mobility, its exposure to a variety of viewpoints, its capacity to choose and change affiliations, and an expanding radius of empathy. By historical standards the periods of a relatively detached and fluid intelligentsia constituted brief episodes between the epochs of institutionally controlled thinking in which closed groups monopolized the public interpretation of things. That Mannheim does not conceal his own preferences and that the uncommitted intelligentsia provides not only the subject matter of this paper but also its point of view adds spice to this original study.

The last paper is the most topical of the three. Its subject bears more closely on the title of the book than does the second essay. The sociology of culture is an extension of the sociology of knowledge, to encompass not only discursive thought but the whole gamut of symbolic expression, including art and religion. It is in this sense that Mannheim attempts to trace the growth of democratic attitudes in epistemology, the modern emphasis on the public and formal criteria of truth, and the growing concern with the genesis of things rather than their intrinsic nature. The broad interpretation of democratic attitudes is indicated by the use of such illustrative materials as pictorial styles, church design, and educational trends. Mannheim introduces the concept of distance as a key category for the analysis of authoritarian attitudes in politics, social etiquette, scientific procedure, language, and æsthetics. 'Distance' is conceived by Mannheim both as a general sociological category, and as a key by means of which the modern trend toward integral democracy can be elucidated. In the progressive elimination of authoritarian 'distance' between élites and masses he sees both a promise and a danger: the promise of a full realization of human potentialities, and the danger of creative freedom being stifled where the masses submit to regimentation. The resources of sociological analysis are mobilized by him in the search for a favourable resolution of this conflict in contemporary civilization.

Some readers may ask themselves what bearing these 'Essays on the Sociology of Culture' have on the agenda of American and English sociology.

Certain components of Mannheim's thinking are traceable to the German preoccupation with broad historical perspectives. The latent conflicts and unresolved problems of 20th-century Germany may partly account for the gravitation of German thinking toward epochal issues. American sociologists have, except for the Darwinian interlude, increasingly devoted themselves to the methodical study of simple structures and, whenever possible, left the bird's-eye view of society as a whole to historians and anthropologists. The German concern with epochal questions has often been the source of insightful but loose thinking for which the American research mind with its predilection for controlled procedures has not developed a marked taste. American sociologists have seen more promise in restricted and progressively refined studies than in an intellectual agitation which penetrates wide territories without an adequate equipment for their mastery. Sociologists in the United States have grown accustomed to feel that timeliness and urgency in themselves do not qualify a subject for sociological inquiry.

Still, one may ask, should the social scientist abstain from dealing with contemporary issues because they are too involved for the working tools he has? Or should he try to bring to bear on these matters his scanty equipment and hope for the best?

This is not solely an academic question, nor merely one of scientific procedure. The German concern with historical synopses sprang from an insecure position in a world which was not altogether congenial to the German political heritage, while the American success at home, a secure international position, and the long habituation to close teamwork have favoured attention to subjects which respond to more stringent scientific procedures. Yet, certain changes are taking place on the American scene. The Cold War and the prospect of world tension for some time to come have brought nearer to the United States and England some of the concerns which explain the German preoccupation with historical dynamics. Historians and political scientists have responded to the altered situation for some time; social anthropologists and sociologists are following suit. It is in this changing atmosphere that Mannheim's middle position between the German and the Anglo-American run of attention has related itself to the thinking of Americans and Englishmen. It appears to me that as these papers reach the American and English reader they do not cross a cultural frontier. They pose questions which have been raised already in America, and the suggested answers seem more germane to its climate of thought than those which Mannheim advanced in his earlier writings.

* * * * *

I take this opportunity to express my indebtedness to Miss Janet Coon and to Dr. Hyatt Howe Waggoner, Chairman of the English Department at the University of Kansas City, for their critical reading of the manuscript and for numerous editorial suggestions. Dr. Paul Kecskemeti has not only contributed the translation and editorial revision of the third essay, but his notes and comments on the other parts of the manuscript have been of material benefit to my own work.

ERNEST MANHEIM

Easter, 1955

PART ONE

TOWARDS THE SOCIOLOGY OF THE MIND: AN INTRODUCTION

I. FIRST APPROACH TO THE SUBJECT

1. HEGEL RECONSIDERED—FROM THE PHENOMENOLOGY TO THE SOCIOLOGY OF THE MIND

HEGEL'S *Phenomenology of the Mind* was one of the most remarkable documents of early 19th-century thought. In this provocative *tour de force* Hegel set out to do nothing less than explore the complete hierarchy of meanings which successively emerged from the history of our world. Nearly a century and a half has passed since this speculative experiment cast its spell over German academic thinking. Hegel's magic has worn off, and the historical situation in which the *Phenomenology* could strike a resonant chord is long past. Yet elements of the work still draw and merit attention. We may still find a living message in the claim that meanings cannot be fully captured by frontal attack, but only through the grasp of their social and historical setting. Today one need not be a Hegelian or a sociologist to accept this thesis; but in Hegel's Germany it was not so. The thesis was part and parcel of a bold attempt to construe history as a goal-directed and all-embracing evolution.

The end of the Hegelian climate of thinking came with the entrenchment of positivistic and empirical habits of thought. Yet the subject of the *Phenomenology* is still with us. It brings some of the problems of epistemology to a common denominator: ideas have a social meaning which their frontal—that is their immanent—analysis does not reveal. Thus, ideas can be studied in the social context in which they are conceived and expressed and it is in this semantic setting that their meaning becomes concrete. In short, the sociology of the mind has fallen heir to the subject of Hegel's speculation.

Hegel's work could not have taken hold in its time had it only reflected a single person's thought. The *Phenomenology* is more than that. It is a timely attempt to synthesize the problems of revolution, restoration, enlightenment, and romanticism. Hegel's system was not mere philosophy, but a climactic expression of the insights of preceding epochs. That is why the *Phenomenology* was able for some time to dominate scholarship in the humanities and the social sciences. The organized study of culture in Germany owed its very impulse to this bold philosophical inventory of the realities of its time. This philosophy was able to relate itself to the most intricate details of departmental research. Never again has philosophy succeeded in re-establishing such a close nexus with reality, nor been able to reassert its supremacy over the departmental concerns with human affairs. With the decay of Hegelianism the integrated study of culture lapsed into a multitude of specialized and self-contained pursuits, and philosophy itself resumed its earlier position within the departmental scheme of learning.

Periodic efforts to reintegrate the humanistic disciplines under the never-redeemed promise of a new philosophical synthesis have alternated with attempts on the part of the specialists to recover the lost connection through a philosophical orientation within each discipline. The failure of these trials is apt to demonstrate the fact that compartmentalized experience will merely yield the type of philosophy which has originally been invested in its conceptual scheme. Neither has philosophy as an academic subject succeeded again in transcending its traditional limitations.

There is, after all, nothing to be gained by the restoration of a lifeless tradition of admitted previous merit. We must learn to face each situation as it arises, unencumbered by venerable habits of thought. Each period poses its own questions. Quite often in our time the experimental scientist and the organizer turn up more relevant material for the understanding of the problems of our age than the strained atmosphere of philosophical self-scrutiny.

What is still alive in Hegel's philosophy is his keen situational awareness rather than the sectarian tradition which followed in its wake. Hegel simply voiced in his own grammar the conscience and available knowledge of his period. Kant and Aristotle merely furnished him with a vocabulary of established currency, but his vision and categories which articulate it were as contemporary as the impact of the revolution on the Prussian monarchy. Nothing, however, was farther from the spirit of the historic Hegel than the Neo-Hegelian necropsy performed a century later.

The object lesson which Hegel and his late renaissance entail for us holds also true for Marx and his school. A critical study which holds aloof from the wrangle over the true meaning of Marxist orthodoxy may yet unfreeze those elements of the Marxist system which still have a diagnostic meaning. Once freed of their dogmatic involvements these components should be of concern to anyone whose preoccupation is with the realities of the present time. A fundamentally new approach to the study of culture may eventually emerge from such beginnings. What is needed is open-minded observation and students whose sensitivity to the pulse beats of the time is not impaired by doctrinal commitments. It was this open-minded approach which allowed genuine sociologists in Germany such as Max Weber, Alfred Weber, Troeltsch, Sombart, and Scheler, to derive significant leads from Marx. Their polemic encounters with Marxism bear the marks of all true controversies which penetrate, rather than bypass, the opponent's position.

2. THE SCIENCE OF SOCIETY AND THE SOCIOLOGY OF THE MIND. DIFFICULTIES OF A SYNTHESIS

The type of sociology here advocated is unlike that which ended the French alliance of historic philosophy with ethnology and moral philosophy. Nor do we propose at present to follow the lead of that phase of American sociology which operates primarily in the field of social disorganization to provide a diagnostic guide for remedial practices in the community. None the less, there are unmistakable signs that the trend I wish to advance is in the ascendant in the United States.

We can well dispense with preliminary inquiries into the academic delimitations of the field, its key concepts, and the methods which other students employ. The questions which give sociology its focus are basically extensions of the problems which a given collectivity faces in a given epoch. Nor do we have to bid for the accreditation of sociology in Germany, with the plea that it is a going concern in all civilized countries. Often ignored, sociology germinated in the ferment of German philosophy and the stir of politics and economics during the early growth of industrialism. It was not the expansion of academic specialization which gave it its early momentum. It had detached itself from philosophy before the decline of the latter became apparent, and had also disengaged itself from the historical sciences before their earlier synthesis got lost in the minutiae of a plodding routine which positivism stimulated during the second half of the 19th century. The decisive impulse of sociology came from the challenge of public affairs. This fact should be remembered by those who feel tempted by the apparition of a haphazardly delimited and prematurely specialized science of society.

What then is the position of sociology in the prevailing scheme of scientific specialization?

It cannot be gainsaid that sociology, like any scientific endeavour, is a specialized pursuit of circumscribed scope. There is no need, at present, to fear the loss of its departmental character, for it operates comfortably within the limitations first defined by Simmel and implicitly confirmed by the American research practice. It is still safe and feasible to outline with Simmel the scope of the field as the 'forms of sociation'. Dissenting formulations, such as those of Leopold von Wiese, Vierkandt, I. W. Thomas, and Park and Burgess, are part and parcel of the healthy expansion of a young discipline. But these delineations mark only one, the first, theme of sociology. Its actual subject, society, exists not only in acts of sociation and the coalescence of men into structured groups. We encounter society also in meanings which likewise join or divide men. As there exists no sociation without particular understandings, so there are no shared meanings unless they are derived from and defined by given social situations. The dichotomy of the two academic realms of analysis, namely Simmel's science of the forms of sociation and the sociology of ideas, does not bespeak two such separate entities in the real world, although the necessities of academic specialization may make their thematic isolation temporarily expedient. There is no harm in such an abstraction so long as it is treated as an artifice. Ultimately, however, the duality of the ideational versus the social realm of things must resolve itself into a single view of the original subject of human reality from which the two aspects of sociology were originally abstracted.

The one major risk of specialization in a derivative field lies precisely in the failure of the specialist to remember the genesis of his particular frame of reference. It is not only the historians of literature, economics, and law who have sometimes succumbed to the temptation of reifying their adopted framework of constructs. Sociologists likewise tend to forget that literature, language, and art in themselves are mere abstractions. 'Society', too, is a construct, for the acts of sociation which constitute society are inseparably fused with those acts in which ideas are conceived and reinterpreted.[1] While sociology conceived as the science of sociation is a legitimate discipline, its key concept, that of sociation, is a mere facet of human reality. Schemes of specialization which isolate certain aspects of reality for the purpose of topical analysis must, at their very inception, bear some sort of a design of the ultimate syntheses which re-establishes and articulates the context of the original subject.

Some interpreters of sociology have, deliberately or unconsciously, tried to make their discipline academically acceptable by following the hallowed principle of specialization at any price, even at the risk of losing sight of the pivotal question inherent in the subject. While the practice has saved some sociologists the censure of colleagues labouring under an acute phase of departmental chauvinism of one or another colour, sociology has come dangerously near to discarding its identity and its primary objective, which is the rational mastery of the universe of human relations. This universe is not tailored to the designs of a compartmentalized academic tradition. Nor will stop signs planted along the borders of a properly accredited field of specialization check the interdependence of men. Those who mean to gain an insight into its problems will not shy

[1] See for example Bart Landheer, *Mind and Society: Epistemological Essays in Sociology*, The Hague, 1952, p. 22: 'In the first place, it is necessary that society as such is a concept, an abstraction.'

away from following a given clue into contiguous areas. The needs of our time may well bypass the implicit methodology of those who urge departmental self-sufficiency. This is not to say that the contextual type of inquiry will supersede specialization in the realm of science. Quite the contrary: the division of labour has become an elementary condition of learning. This admission, however, does not warrant by any means the fatalistic acceptance of the thesis that the sociology of the mind is too large a subject for any legitimate attack. The necessity of defining the focus of inquiry cannot everlastingly condemn the social sciences in their entirety to voluntary blindness to problems which straddle the agreed borders of two or more disciplines. There must be, and indeed there is, a growing sensitivity to those configurations of reality which the segmental view conceals.

We are faced then with the question of how to develop within, or if necessary from, our present state of fragmented knowledge an integrated view of human relations. We must learn to see discrete facts in their relationships, and to fit segmental vistas into a concrete perspective. The question points to the problem of the sociology of the mind as the counterpart of the science of society. Inasmuch as society is the common frame of interaction, ideation, and communication, the *sociology of the mind* is the study of mental functions in the context of action. It is from this approach that we must expect one of the possible answers to the needed synthesis.

To concede the necessity of such an approach is, however, not the same as to admit its feasibility. Will not, after all, the proposed scheme open the door to unmitigated dilettantism and a spurious type of catholicity? Will not sheer opinion and guesswork take the place of scientific method? Such misgivings cannot be lightly dismissed, for they are shared by many who are prepared to realize that ultimately every scientific method must transcend its self-imposed sectional limitations. These qualms can be met in so far as they stem not from a principled rejection of the needed synthesis, but from fear of its consequences. It is only the sworn partisans of a departmental fetish who cannot be persuaded, for there is no hope for those whose preoccupation with matters of procedure as such has made them blind to concrete objectives.

No discipline can successfully make the rules of procedure for another one. The method of inquiry in a wider and differently defined area will have to grow out of effective practice in it. Eating is the proof of the pudding, not its preparation.[1] Let it be said, however, for the sake of those who are troubled by the spectre of improvisations, that the proposed type of inquiry has a manageable and limited compass. The sociology of the mind is conceived as an integrated view of social action and of mental processes, and not as a new philosophy of history. Nothing like an all-embracing historical teleology is advanced, nor is a closed system of disguised dialectical sequences advocated, still less a morphological scheme of culture cycles. Such attempts at synthesis have had their day. The business of the social scientist is to follow or devise communicable rules of cooperative procedure rather than to play the lone hand of the visionary. Integration is no less an occasion for team work than analysis, although the division of labour of the first type will have to differ from the latter. Synthesis may be expected to grow only from observations made with a view to integration. To argue that the business of integration must be adjourned until the pertinent facts are assembled in the respective fields is to misjudge the nature of the synthetic procedure. Integration does not begin with the completed accumulation of facts, but rather with each elementary act of observation. The problem is not one of psychology; the question is not how one person may absorb the wisdom and experience of many. Nor is polyhistory the objective. What is needed is continued experimentation with the procedures of cooperative research, with methods of condensing knowledge around new foci of interest.

To condense a bewildering volume of information to manageable proportions is to make available, sift, and refine pertinent data for successive operations. The present neglect of these intermediate steps accounts for much of the waste of effort sanctioned by our parochial organization of research. Potentially fruitful research ventures terminate somewhere in

[1] The universal norms of scientific inquiry, such as the communicability of procedures, the minimization of assumptions, and the avoidance of covert assumptions pertain to the public and cooperative functions of scientific procedure in general, while methods are specific in as much as they are distilled from actual operations in particular areas.

no-man's-land for want of coordination. A vast portion of the sociological output has no cumulative character because it lacks the design for relevance to subsequent use and because of the time-honoured reluctance to put together what the specialist has taken apart. To repeat, integration is not merely a final adjunct to the fact-gathering routine; it embraces the whole process, beginning with the research design for relevance and proceeding to the condensation of the pertinent material assembled regardless of its departmental pedigree. The prerequisite of a cumulative core of generalizations in the social sciences is a growing body of *negotiable* knowledge, that which has meaning in diverse fields of inquiry and is amenable to use in new and subsequent frames of reference. Continuity and advancement in such fields as economics, anthropology, political science, communications, art, and literature are not assured as long as their *subjects* are treated as independent and mutually impermeable entities.

The growing interdependence of life demands of the student of human affairs an increasing facility in seeing things in their relationships. This will not be the fruit of intuition, but of a thematically focused division of labour. If the still dominant order of specialization may be termed vertical, the needed type will have to be horizontal. It must centre around concrete subjects, rather than one single aspect of many, loosely aggregated items of information. For example, the horizontally specialized student of a certain literary current will have to come to grips with the careers and mobility of the literati who espouse it, the incentive system under which they work, the nature of the public to which they address themselves, the channels of communication available to them, the social orientation of their patrons, and the social and political divisions in which they make characteristic choices. In short, while the vertical division of labour relieves the specialist of a full account of his subject, the alternative method of specialization converges on given topics from a multitude of directions in which pertinent relationships may be located. This is not to undertake the impossible, namely to reconstruct the infinite detail which makes up a concrete phenomenon. The aim is a condensed account of those relationships which are relevant to the generalizing approach to a chosen subject. The adoption of this type of procedure does not end specialization of the departmental type; it merely superimposes on it a plane of operation of a different tilt. Basically this is also the plane of operation of the policy maker, the party leader, and the industrial executive. They, too, have learned how to reach decisions on the basis of a condensed view of a complex situation and they know how to use and guide the specialist for a given purpose. We shall not pass the preliminary stage of the social sciences, the stage of elemental analysis and segmentation, unless we learn to work with the findings of others, regardless of their field of accreditation. Short of that we shall continue the unwholesome practice of having to derive the elements of a concrete perspective of things from those specialists who are unconcerned with relationships and having to leave the synthesis to the extemporizations of the philosophers of history.

The business of keeping *en rapport* with an increasingly complex reality necessitates experimentation with legitimate methods of interdepartmental research. Unquestionably, the use of secondary sources, however critical, entails a wider margin for error in the social than in the older natural sciences, mainly because of the greater interpretive involvement of the data of the former. Some correctives may be obtained through the identification of the particular viewpoint which has governed the interpretation of given data. Only experience can disclose additional ways of minimizing the factor of inexactitude. No blueprints or prefabricated rules of procedure are at hand to guide such an undertaking. Closed systems are mostly the upshot of a retrospective view of an achieved order of things, while the present state of the social sciences offers no semblance of a field of consolidated research procedures.

3. TENTATIVE NATURE OF THE INQUIRY. ITS INITIAL OBJECTIVE: A CRITIQUE OF THE FALSE CONCEPTS OF SOCIETY AND MIND

The following essays do not constitute chapters of a compact system. An attempt at the sociology of the mind can hardly hope at present to advance beyond the initial stage, and no prospect of a unitary grasp of the subject looms on the immediate horizon. All that seems practicable today are single tentative steps towards a sociological illumination of history and a better understanding of our own actualities. The subject of these inquiries will not reward an impetuous attack, for this can promise no more than a set of haphazardly conceptualized observations or, worse still, the enshrinement of a bygone imagery. There is no substitute for the piecemeal advance towards our objective and for the gradual refinement of the tools of inquiry.

Montaigne called his essays 'Attempts'. The sociologist in particular will appreciate this expression of a prudent and frank acceptance of the fragmentary view of things. In situations such as Montaigne's, one does not gain a new insight without first clearing the ground to remove the obstructions to a wider vista. Critical analyses must provide the initial steps which may free the elements of a new perspective from their entanglements with older, untenable habits of thought. Only continuing self-scrutiny and the periodical review of what appears to be newly gained ground may guard against the temptation of forcing new experience into the mould of outworn systems. Students who place the search for genuine answers above the 'ques for certainty' will not accept panaceas and summary formulas in lieu of the piecemeal grasp of a problematic situation. This is the reason for the fragmentary character of the works of Max Weber, Dilthey, Sumner, and W. I. Thomas, and it should also hold true for the present efforts. This is not to disclaim their ultimate orientation towards a sociology of the *mind* which should eventually provide the wider frame of reference for our earlier inquiries in the sociology of *knowledge*. It was from these earlier studies, including *Ideology and Utopia*, that the thesis of the existential involvement of knowledge emerged, that is the proposition that the relationship between particular conceptions of reality and given modes of involvement in it is capable of scientific articulation. The following inquiries are undertaken in the hope that the previous arguments may eventually develop into the wider proposition of the existential involvement of the mind, as the frame of reference for the sociology of the mind.[1] At present only scattered pieces of this larger framework are visible, mainly on

[1] The reader will find a preliminary outline at the end of this introductory chapter.

occasions when it collides with earlier points of view and whenever further progress in the historical inquiry depends on a renewed methodological introspection. Even though today empirical studies are far more important than methodological reflections, one need not make a fetish of facts. For raw facts yield no answers unless relevant questions are directed towards them. To repeat, the aim of the following considerations is not to construct an inclusive system. The advance towards the stated objective can only proceed step by step, from the elementary to the complex. A preliminary clarification of the principal concept of this essay, however, will have to precede the subsequent phases of the study. The main argument of this introductory chapter, therefore, will be concerned with the appropriate uses of the concepts of history, society, and mind, and with the critical review of their interpretations in earlier periods of German sociology and philosophy.

II THE FALSE AND THE PROPER CONCEPTS OF HISTORY AND SOCIETY

I. THE THEORY OF AN IMMANENT HISTORY OF THOUGHT, AND WHY IT EMERGED

It is common observation that, in spite of the free flow of ideas across political frontiers, certain themes are recurrent in the organized thinking of each country. These limitations of intellectual diffusion not only illustrate the social footing of thought, but also furnish a cogent reason for paying distinct attention to the initial milieu of a research endeavour. To present a proposition merely in the affirmative and without its antithetical import is to bypass its point of departure. Close scrutiny might reveal the polemical origin of all affirmations, including those which are formulated without overt regard to their antitheses. Since the sociological interest in the mind originated in Germany, the present argument will be advanced with reference to the prevailing German controversy about the subject at hand. Attention will be focused not so much on individuals as on current modes of thought, particularly on certain habitual misconceptions which still encumber the terms 'society' and 'intellect'. The priority given here to the controversial aspects of these categories should not imply a purely negative estimate of the German preconditions for the sociological exploration of mental phenomena. Quite the contrary. German humanists from Hegel to Dilthey not only uncovered a wealth of material, but also provided a fruitful frame of inquiry. The frames of reference of Dilthey's *History of Human Consciousness*, his *Critique of Historical Reason*, and Scheler's *Philosophical Anthropology* need no excuse for their existence. The fact that the German approach bears the stamp of its philosophical origin can well stand up to criticism, whether it comes from abroad or from a misunderstood positivism of the German variety.

And yet, German humanistic learning has partly lost and partly never really possessed an essential view of things which Americans and Europeans elsewhere were able to capture: the realization of the social character of man's thought and action, the familiarity with social history, and, most important, the capacity to see action and thought, trivial or sublime, in their proper perspectives. The exaggerated emphasis which certain historians and philosophers placed on the 'great personality' and his 'solitary destiny' is a case in point. We do not mean to disparage a grand gesture or a sincere pathos which such epithets express, but we question the standards of comparison from which these appraisals stem. Men who are not conversant with the social dimensions of individual achievement, who see only the finished products of mental processes and do not know how they come about, are not really in a position to distinguish the individual component of creative achievement from the social. One cannot gain a true historical perspective without an awareness of the social setting of historical events. The crux of the problem, however, is not how to sight the social dimension of events, but rather how succeeding generations were able to ignore it.

One cannot blame the sociological inhibitions of German humanism on Hegel, for he was a keen observer of the social actuality of his time. The shocks of the French revolution, the decline of the old German empire, and Napoleon's interlude did not fail to make their imprint on Hegel's understanding of history and his share in the political and intellectual reconstitution of Prussia. Hegel's concept of the 'objective mind' tells the story of his appreciation of the social, notwithstanding the spiritualistic and supra-rationalistic construction of his system. But what successors distilled from his work is a mirage of self-propelling ideas and a sublimated version of history narrated in a social vacuum. And yet, no critique of the unfortunate doctrine of the immanence of thought history can ignore Hegel's own role in the genesis of that perennial *leitmotiv* of German historical thinking.

The thesis of the immanent evolution of ideas is predicated on the assumption of a self-contained intellect which evolves by and from itself through pre-ordained sequences. In the following pages this conception will be analyzed in four steps. The first two should uncover the rather trivial circumstances which condition the metaphysics of the doctrine. At this point the author accepts the risk of making light of matters sublime, but for once the attempt will have to be made to review that inflated conception of mental phenomena. The genesis of this distortion will be traced back to certain attributes of scholarly existence. The third and fourth phases of the analysis will deal with the religious premises of the subject.

The first step. A mere glance should be sufficient to locate the long list of devotees of the doctrine in the teaching profession. The protagonists were mostly philologists, historians, and philosophers who formed their convictions, as almost everybody else does, within that particular segment of the universe in which their daily lives took their habitual course. It stands to reason that an existence which is some steps removed from the theatre of events tends to be contemplative and therefore subject to certain delusions about the nature of reality. The clash of parties, interests, and opinions in the larger arena may in the perspective of contemplative aloofness easily become transfigured to a mere controversy of alternative schools of thought. While the men who daily face the rough and tumble of life employ thought as a tool for coping with situations that arise, the denizens of the academic sanctuary invoke thinking as a medium in which to reconstruct and visualize accomplished facts. While the mental functions of the practitioner both originate and terminate with his problems, the cogitative processes of the scholar are sparked and nourished by the thoughts of others. And while the functionary and operator directly encounter social situations, the scholar faces the appearance of an intellectual continuum of mutually productive ideas. It is the generalization of this intramural illusion which evokes the notion of an all-inherent and self-begotten intellect.

We might expect to be told at this point that surely scholars also have a private life which must check their professional delusions, that surely they, too, would employ thought in their daily affairs as a problem-solving function. Indeed, that must be the case in the extracurricular moments of life; but it is in the nature of such detached and yet highly interdependent existences that their traditional *esprit de corps* may effectively inhibit the interpenetration of the private and the professional view of the world. The academic enclave is, however, not the only one to occasion self-perpetuating delusions. The 'rentiers' of the pre-war period—the recipients of fixed incomes from independent sources—likewise entertained views in which accepted ideals of a 'good life' co-existed with the contrary facts of this tainted world. The depression made a revision of that bifocal outlook inevitable, and gradually daily and private experiences overruled the axiomatic conception of the world order as it should have been. We continue to witness the decomposition and transformation of these social strata and we may study the concomitant shift in their mentality. But the lesson will be lost on those scholars whose sense of security rests on the tradition of scholastic self-sufficiency. The open view demands periodical reorientation and self-scrutiny, and it offers little reassurance to the cloistered individual. An apprenticeship with the 'makers' of history might well serve its philosophers. Whatever the intellectual compass of the men at the helm may be, they can ill afford to follow a deceptive chart. Action exposes an illusion quicker than contemplation.

Thus, the position of the scholar entails a potential source of bias. No doubt, leisure and detachment are prerequisites of learning; but the bias of thinking in a lifelong state of aloofness must become cumulative if the derived solutions need not ever pass the pragmatic test of reality. An intellectual production which does not have to meet the demands of concrete situations can hardly fail to escape the pitfalls of incestuous reasoning, that is, the tendency to idealize its subject. The antidote for such bias will be found neither in a refined methodology nor in a more copious use of source material. The corrective must come from the consistent effort to understand thought in its situational setting. In short, the solution lies in the open perspective of sociology rather than in the closure of hermeneutics.

Thus far the German approach to historical matters has alternated between tracing political events and tracing sequences of thought. The middle ground between these two interests has seemed either impervious to analysis or not rewarding as a field of research. Lame attempts at 'cultural history' have fallen wide of the mark. While Burckhardt's portrayals were of an artistic genre, his successors sank into the mire of anecdotal detail. Lamprecht's intuitive grip did not reach down to the real nexus of things. The materials which these studies brought to light are significant, but they have only limited bearing on the essentials of history. The intermediate realm of history has, on the whole, remained unexplored, chiefly because access to it has continued to be blocked by the predominance of political history and the preoccupation with the evolution of ideas.

The observer whose sole concern is with the grand sweep of political occurrences will hardly appreciate that the things which take shape in daily routine may be of equal significance and, more important, that they also have structure. But as German state lore barred the approach to sociology, so the refined scholasticism which was invested in the history of ideas also proved a stumbling-block for the rise of a concrete psychology. A sense of man's changing attitudes and circumstances, well understood in France ever since Montaigne, has not really evolved in Germany, perhaps with the notable exception of Nietzsche. German idealism has remained immune to insights into man's motivations. They have been deemed trivial by comparison and peripheral to the maelstrom of events on the level of the state and in the realm of ideas. The reverberations of Hegel's philosophy and Ranke's historiography bypassed the intervening field in which concrete individuals interact and try to make the best of their circumstances. Marx and Lorenz von Stein might have proved suggestive of the missing dimension of German historicism if it had not been for a sanctioned tradition of the scholastic disregard of things real.

The second step. The illusion of the immanent flow of ideas receives additional support from the manner in which the humanist encounters his source material. The works of the past appear to the scholar as pictures in a gallery—an array of discrete entities. The temptation to construe this array as an organic and continuous growth is well-nigh irresistible to those who confine their interest to the historical records of creative expression. What is ignored in this imagery are the intervening areas in which men act and react as social beings. Thus, the idealistic delusion is rooted in nothing more profound than the conceptualization of the two-dimensional scheme in which the library and the museum present their exhibits. The missing third dimension, the social, will hardly be discovered in this perspective. Actually there are no such things as artistic evolution or literary history as such; real are only those singular situations which generate an urge to represent an aspect of life. Expression of thought and perception are in themselves mere fragments of reality and their complete chronology is, by the same token, not history, although there is no harm in such constructs as art history, so long as they are used as classificatory devices created for convenience. It is their reification which is the ultimate hazard of all book learning.

Third step. While the argument of the preceding steps dwelt on the trivial aspects of scholarly existence, the present phase of the analysis must concern itself with a subject more sublime: the religious origin of the German concept of 'Geist'. It was Luther, in particular, who transmuted the religious conception of the spirit into secular philosophy. Earlier the medieval Church enunciated the antagonism of the spirit and the flesh, but the void between the realm of the spirit and human life became absolute only in Luther's radical dualism: 'For that which is not of the Spirit or Grace liveth not' (Luther *On the Freedom of the Christian*. 1520). The oversublimation of the spirit and related concepts in German humanistic literature is attributable to the continuing influence of Luther's dualism.

Fourth step. The immanence theory has still another root in German religious teaching, namely in the doctrine of *spiritual freedom*. This idea, too, was elaborated by Luther: 'It is then plain that no external thing of whatever description can give him' (viz. man) 'freedom or faith. For faith and freedom, as opposed to rancour and subjection, are not corporeal and external.'

A secular version of this doctrine became the cardinal thesis of German idealism. Luther's 'freedom' (from temptation) came to mean indetermination; his conception of spirituality (man's communion with God through faith) developed into the doctrine of the self-evolving, sovereign intellect, while, on the negative side, Luther's moral conception of bondage evolved into the philosophical thesis of determination in the physical realm. 'Thought or knowledge possess themselves in absolute freedom.' '. . . freedom as such is the ultimate basis of all consciousness.' (Fichte, *Bestimmung des Gelehrten*, 1794). Understandably, this dualistic conception has effectively inhibited the rise of any milieu theory and the deterministic and the sociological approach to intellectual subjects. For such 'externalisms' cannot gain a rationale from a philosophy which is predicated upon the absolute freedom and indeterminateness of the mind.

It may seem, at this point, that our last two steps followed the idealistic precept of explaining one idea from the currency of another. Indeed, the affinity between Luther and the immanence theory cannot be properly understood apart from the social setting in which the over-extended concept of freedom evolved and found acceptance in Germany. This process was motivated by the thwarted aspirations of the German peasantry and the middle classes of the 18th and 19th centuries. The contrast to the Puritan mentality is striking. The social outlet which the Calvinistic sects found and their opportunity to act upon their religious convictions with tangible success reconciled the Puritan with the real world as a proving ground: the sober pragmatic view of life did not clash with the Puritan motivation. The rise of a parallel development in Germany was, on the other hand, inhibited by the rigid structure of the territorial states and the early identification of the Lutheran church with them. Lacking a concrete socio-political focus for their thought and action, the educated German middle classes made their accommodation to the bureaucratic state and spiritualized the idea of freedom to mean intellectual indeterminism. This introverted concept of freedom has become the keystone of the immanence theory and one of the main academic barriers to a sociological approach to history, thought, and politics.

Digression on Art History

The immanence theory did not remain confined to the major and minor systems of German philosophy. The theory has attained far greater importance through its application to nearly all branches of historical inquiry. But in no area of research has the full sweep of the doctrine been put to a more thorough test than in the history of art. It was here, therefore, that the untenable position of the theory became first evident.

Inherent continuities were first sought and construed in the media of style and form. In a way, stylistic evolution and art for art's sake rest on analogous conceptions. Both affirm the autonomy of form and its primacy over the contents of art. The application of these principles to the concrete material of art history eventually had to expose those aspects of art which the stylistic approach left out of consideration, for example the religious objectives of the early painters and sculptors. It became evident, moreover, that the works of art of later periods also manifest essential elements of their author's *Weltanschauung*, and that this *Weltanschauung* has some bearing on the historical placement of the art object. Dvořak's work marks the transition from the stylistic interpretation of art to the wider conception of art history as an aspect of the religious and philosophical modulations of ideas.[1]

Since Dvořak it has become current parlance that the stylistic approach must be broadened to a cultural analysis of art. The diminishing promise of an overspecialized view of the subject has, quite naturally, encouraged attempts to overcome the limitations of one specialism—alas, by the addition of others. Art historians now began to look for analogies between contemporary works of art and expressions of thought. While this departure from the lineal construct of a stylistic evolution did open a novel perspective of research, the new cross-referential use of additional historical material did not escape the limitations of the earlier procedure. The works of the past were still envisaged as they must appear in the libraries and museums, as discrete entities, although presently they were spoken of in

[1] Compare Max Dvořak, *Kunstgeschichte als Geistesgeschichte*, Munich, 1924.

one breath, and assembled in a single universe of discourse. It was now assumed that there must be discoverable relationships between contemporary works of sculpture, painting, literature, and philosophy, but their demonstration was left to nothing more concrete than an intuitive morphology. That the various constituents of a matured culture possess a certain cohesiveness was well understood, but their synopsis was left to interpolation. Hamann's and Hausenstein's studies show a tentative expansion of the synoptic view into the social realm.[1] Dehio's great work does not lack references to the social situation in which the artists performed.[2] Yet, these insights furnished only incidental background material and have not matured into principles of articulation.

The tacit abandonment of the immanence theory undoubtedly widened the scope of these studies. Still, they had not advanced to the cardinal questions of art history: whose mentality is recorded by given art objects? What is their social identity? What action, situations and what tacit choices furnish the perspectives in which artists perceive and represent some aspect of reality? If works of art reflect points of view, beliefs, affirmations, who are the protagonists and who are the antagonists? Whose reorientation is reflected in the changes of style? Such questions do not arise within the fragmentary view of art objects. The conceptual vacuum between them will be only concealed, not bridged, by such traditional constructs as 'the spirit of the time'. Only society as a structured variable has a a history and only in this social continuum can art be properly understood as a historical entity.

2. FALSE POLARIZATION OF THE ATTRIBUTES 'MATERIAL' AND 'IDEAL'

A second fallacy which, much like the immanence doctrine, has encumbered German reflections on history, is expressed by the polarized conception of the *ideal* and the *material* realm of things. Once again one cannot help asking why a basically

[1] Compare Richard Hamann, *Der Impressionismus in Leben und Kunst*, 1923, and *Deutsche Malerei im neunzehnten Jahrhundert*, 1914; Wilhelm Hausenstein, *Vom Geist des Barock*, 1920, and *Barbaren und Klassiker*, 1923.

[2] Compare Georg Dehio, *Geschichte der deutschen Kunst*, 3 volumes, 1919–24.

simple subject could be so persistently misconstrued. How was it possible to doubt the social character of the mind and to ignore the mental involvements of social behaviour? To cogitate an abstract intellect without concrete persons who act in given social situations is as absurd as to assume the opposite, a society without such functions as communication, ideation, and evaluation. It is in this strained dichotomy that the term 'material' was conceived as the reverse of a disembodied spirit. What does the term 'material' actually mean?

There was among Hegel's philosophical successors a so-called 'left wing' which applied to itself the epithet 'materialistic', to express their opposition to the idealistic trend of thought. Strauss, Feuerbach, and Marx, each in his own way, voiced the common creed of this antithetical school. Their opposition had little to do with Büchner's much better known scientific materialism. Their confusion is responsible for much of the muddle which beset the controversy of idealism versus materialism.

The materialism of the left-Hegelians injected into the political literature of the mid-century the conundrum of who are the makers of history—outstanding individuals, or the masses. To have meaning and to be answerable, the question should be rephrased to mean: Are isolated individuals the authors of history, or socialized and interdependent persons? Individual stature and collectivities are neither incommensurable nor are they antipodes. Personal eminence is attributed to an individual who shows an unusual grasp and mastery of an unusual situation. While the 'great men of history' do not transcend the social realm of things, no sociologist can reasonably doubt or ignore their existence.

When events are, however, viewed in retrospect or from a distance the temptation grows stronger to attribute the known results of an unrecorded chain of actions to a known person who formed the last link, in other words, to ascribe the unknown to the known. Much of the historical hero worship gains support by the haze which covers the relevant detail. Vierkandt's early study, *Die Stetigkeit im Kulturwandel*, 1908 (continuity in cultural change) offers an insight into the cumulative character of most great inventions.[1] They are, for the most

[1] Compare also W. F. Ogburn, *Social Change*, 1923.

part, the sum total of less well-known inventions which eventually become synthetized by a final step. To know the antecedent steps is not to belittle the last, synthetic feat, but only the whole process will furnish a yardstick for the appraisal of the concluding act. To conceive an act in complete isolation from any other act is about as extreme as to assume that anyone may speak a language which had no previous currency in any human group. To speak at all is to alter and develop an existing language. The difference between the street-corner conversation in the local slang and the linguistic innovations of poets is one of degree. It makes, therefore, little sense to attribute ideas only to great individuals and to reserve the epithet 'material' for multitudes. Nor does, for that matter, the thesis of the material determination of ideas convey a proposition capable of an empirical test.

The hypothesis of the so-called historical materialism is, however, of an entirely different character. While the expression bears the imprint of its polemic origin, it is but another name for the economic interpretation of history. Whatever its merit may be, the insistence on the primacy of the economic 'substructure' over the ideological 'superstructure' does not posit the primacy of matter over ideas, but the priority of one type of social interaction (the economic) over others. Both species of action involve ideation, communication, as well as biological needs and a material apparatus.

The materialistic interpretation of history, so understood, may mean one or all of these three things. It may first imply the claim that the functions which meet the basic, biological wants of man have a greater urgency and are less amenable to postponement and sublimation than are those which meet the so-called secondary needs. Second, economic activities have a more limited scope of variability than others, and, therefore, it is the latter which are subject to the 'strain of consistency' with the former. Finally, economic activities have an absolute continuity and in that sense they form the primary basis of social integration. These propositions can be intelligibly discussed without recourse to the unrewarding antinomy of mind and matter.

3. THE FALSE CONCEPTS OF HISTORY, DIALECTICS, AND MEDIACY

History has become increasingly identified with a comprehensive and dynamic view of reality. What makes a narrative historical is not its past tense, for the historian may be at work already before the dust has settled. Nor is historiography achieved through a mere chronicle of dramatic events. The growing interdependence of society and its accelerated shift have given us new criteria for reporting and interpreting change. History will be considered for the present purpose an *explicit* account of change narrated *comprehensively* as a *continuous* process. The following annotation should shed some light on the meaning of these terms.

Change is made *explicit* if sufficient account is taken of the operative forces to make the course and outcome of the process cogent. There is a certain parallel between the historical and the dramatic presentation. The resolution of a genuine drama must be compelling once the dramatic situation is fully exposed. The action must inherently follow from the exposition and no *deus ex machina* may decide the outcome. The historian must likewise unravel the train of events from a stated configuration of factors which constitute the historical situation. He must, in other words, advance the deterministic approach as far as the facts will warrant. The measure of explicitness is, of course, relative to the scale and format of the report; a miniature sketch may present a sharper and more convincing outline of a given subject than a wealth of unstructured detail painted on a large canvas.

The Mesopotamian annals of court events and the Polynesian genealogies of chiefs do not constitute history, for they lack *continuity*. The substance of history—whether we call it life or reality—does not occur intermittently but as an unbroken stream of actions. Some of these are discrete, such as rebellions, discoveries, battles, legislative acts, and literary events, while others are continuous, such as activities which provide for food, shelter, health, education, safety, the maintenance of order, and so forth. The whole complex of these functions constitutes a structure because their relationships show a recurrent pattern which is characteristic of a given society. It is only through the articulation of these permanent functions that the continuity of life becomes manifest and that the discrete events may be understood as elements in the historical continuum. What makes an account of change continuous, then, is not a 'complete' record of events—if such is at all possible—but the narration of events in the particular context of continuing functions.

Historical reality can be understood only as an inclusive framework of interrelated activities. Inasmuch as reality is the substance and subject of history, *comprehensiveness* is one of the criteria of the recount. The historian may, however, view his subject in any particular perspective he chooses. He may restrict his focus to any single aspect of life, such as law, administration, literature, or economics. He will then select for presentation those facts which bear on his specialized interest, but he will place them in the comprehensive framework of those continuous functions which give life duration. The subject remains the same—life—although the focus of selective attention may vary. In short, any array of discrete events such as successive inventions or conquests may furnish the descriptive material for the report, but what makes it historical is the comprehensive framework within which the selected material is presented.

History is then not a substantive, but an attribute of an evolving collectivity; it is not only a record of change, but also an account of that which changes. History conceived without its social medium is like motion perceived without that which is moving. Dilthey still used the expression 'socio-historical reality'. Before him Hegel likewise spoke of evolving collectivities which he construed as the 'Volksgeister' (literally: folk spirits). Whatever the weakness of such a flatulent concept may be, at least it offered a frame of reference of some sort for Hegel's evolutionary deductions. His successors abandoned the attempt to centre history around the 'Volksgeister', partly because of the volatility of the term, and partly because of the apparently shrinking scope of national histories in an era of mounting class conflicts. It was thus that the concept of history pure and simple, as an entity *sui generis*, and used without reference to any collectivity, began to assume a substantive meaning. The 'historicity' of things has even become the subject of a special ontology developed without regard to the social subjects of change. German philosophical literature abounds in personifications of history as a productive force, as a catalytic agent or as an inexorable power. Here again we encounter the notion of a preordained course of events of which society is the passive object and scene rather than the author and performer. This reluctance to face social reality as the matrix of change also explains the overworked dichotomy of nature and history or the natural versus the historical sciences. The more realistic Western practice of contrasting the natural with the social sciences has, on the whole, not gained acceptance in German literature.

The same disembodied notion of history has also bedevilled the 'dialectics' of the post-Hegelian reflections on history. Dialectic in Hegel's version is the course in which the mind creates and resolves contradictions through its successive phases of self-realization. Since thought is identified with reality, and the evolution of the mind with the historical process, dialectics govern both emergent thought and the tangible course of universal history. Now Hegel's dialectic is wholly consistent with his system, nebulous as it may be in much of its architectonic detail; since the evolving mind is the spark and substance of history, the historical process must also reflect the dialectical development of the mind and the antithetical emergence of all its concepts. Since the abandonment of Hegel's system, however, it has become customary to speak of the dialectics of history *per se*, without any thought of what it is that moves or evolves in the stated antithetical forms. Actually what is dialectical is not history but given social situations which reveal inconsistencies or contradictions in the social structure. This autho , for instance, has attempted to analyse antithetical impulses in group competition and in the conflict of generations.[1] (To recognize actual antagonisms is, however, not the same as to postulate their dominance and continuous evolution throughout history. We shall soon return to a fuller discussion of Marx' class conflict theory of history.) The seat of contradictions is not the mind, nor the foreordained rhythm of history, but concrete social situations which give rise to conflicting aspirations and, hence, to antagonistic interpretations

[1] Reprinted as chapters 5 and 7 in Karl Mannheim's *Essays on the Sociology of Knowledge*, London and New York, 1952.

of reality: the persistent evasion of its analysis once again proves to be the source of mystification.

What then does sociological analysis mean?

The initial problem of sociological analysis—as, indeed, of most branches of scientific inquiry—is how to bring to bear single observations on a structured field which exceeds the scope of individual experience. There are, of course, simple structures which are amenable to direct experience. The pecking order in a chicken yard or the rivalries in a play group may be identified in a single exposure. Now, knowledge of a subject which cannot be encompassed in one act evidently requires a series of acts chosen not at random, but according to a scheme which fits the structure of the field. The problem is one of strategy. It is a question of selecting vantage points of consecutive observations so that they will bear on one another and ultimately disclose the design of the field. Now, all analyses take their departure from certain random encounters, that is, from some immediately apparent aspect of the subject. Subsequent considerations derived from additional exposures to the subject will, however, modify the interpretation of what was first perceived. Its new meaning is no longer based on direct, *ad hoc* experience, but is 'mediated' by subsequent phases of the analysis. Thus, the inquiry progresses from the direct and immediately given view of the field to its derivative aspect or, to use Hegel's classical term, to 'mediate knowledge'.

'. . . to understand an object is . . . to grasp it in its determinate or mediate character. . . .' (Hegel, *Encyclopädie der Philosophischen Wissenschaften*, 2nd Edition, § 62).

Even day-to-day encounters with people often enough necessitate progressive reinterpretations of previous experience. I meet a stranger in the dentist's parlour. He inquires about my age, marital status, income, posi ion, training, and he makes unfavourable comments on my qualifications for my position and on my social manners. At this point I am ready to demand his credentials, when a third person intimates by gesture that my partner is intoxicated. That changes my first diagnosis of the man. My earlier observations were not altogether incorrect, but in the new context their meaning has changed. Such is the typical course of sociological analysis of complex structures. Now, sociology is a field of scientific inquiry inasmuch as the structure of its subjects does not become apparent in the random context of day-to-day encounters. The analysis usually advances, therefore, from simple to complex sets. The simple ones are those which are immediately apparent, while the complex structures become patent in the course of consecutive steps which redefine the previous data of experience. A field is complex not in itself but in regard to given acts which are focused on it. A field is complex if its design is not revealed by any of its parts or segments and if the whole field does not enter the focus of a single act. The complex, therefore, is grasped in a series of interrelated acts. That the attribute 'complex' is relative to the act in which a subject is encountered has been clearly seen by Hegel:

' . . . it is common experience that truths which are evidently derived from most complicated and mediate considerations may present themselves directly in the consciousness of those who have become conversant with knowledge of such types. Solutions which are the results of involved analyses will present themselves directly to the mathematician as well as anyone well versed in the science; every educated person has within his ken immediately present a number of general viewpoints and principles which are derived from repeated reflexion and life-long experience. . . . In all these instances the immediacy of knowledge does not exclude its mediate character, but direct and mediate knowledge are so interlinked that the first is even a product and result of the second.' (Hegel, *ibid.*, § 66.)

What Hegel describes in these passages is, by and large, true of analytical progression in all empirical sciences: at certain stages the data of immediate experience assume a new, derivative, meaning as they become redefined in each newly discovered universe of discourse. That each induction and each generalization pertains to a corresponding set of assumed or perceived circumstances, that is, to an implied universe which is subject to revision and expansion, is one of Hegel's lasting contributions to scientific methodology. In more recent times de Morgan[1] and Zalai[2] have demonstrated the systematic connection between each induction and its corresponding

[1] De Morgan, *Syllabus of a Proposed System of Logic.*

[2] Bela Zalai, 'A filozófiai rendszerezés problémája', *Szellem*, No 2, Budapest, 1911.

sphere of notions. In the physical sciences it was often the apparent exceptions from established generalizations which demonstrated the limits of a given universe of induction and which made the assumption of a more inclusive universe necessary. It was thus that Einstein's theory of relativity not only explained and confirmed Newton's laws of universal gravitation within the limits of low velocities, but it also accounted for certain crucial exceptions not explained by Newton's laws. In like manner Newton's gravitational laws both confirmed Kepler's first law concerning the eliptic orbit of a planet and accounted for the deviations which Kepler's law did not cover.[1] In each of these revolutionary advances in physics, the new hypothesis both controverted and partially confirmed earlier generalizations, while at the same time it uncovered new phenomena which had not been apparent in the previous context of experience. Einstein's general theory of relativity, for example, made the so-called Einstein shift effect predictable.

It appears then that the consecutive revisions and extensions of the scientific universe of generalizations bear some resemblance to Hegel's dialectics. Three features, in particular, suggest the analogy: the qualified affirmation of the previous hypothesis, the abandonment of its sphere of generalization, and the establishment of a wider sphere of accountable relationships. What, however, is here missing of Hegel's dialectics is the speculative unity of thought and reality, that is the introspective identity of subject and object which forms the cornerstone of Hegel's panlogistic system. How is this striking difference between Hegelian reasoning and scientific procedure to be explained?

The aim of science, as it has crystallized in the course of the last 600 years, is to expand the scope of accountable experience in verifiable steps involving only assumptions on which agreement among the informed is secure. The stringency of scientific procedure is based on its communicability, on its shared and minimized assumptions, and on its public criteria of evidence. 'Scientific' is, therefore, primarily an attribute of procedure and not of truth. What makes Hegel's method of reasoning peculiar is his aim to reinterpret rather than to expand a given historical range of experience. His system is

[1] Homer H. Dubs, *Rational Induction*, Chicago 1930, p. 278.

intended to be an apotheosis of the social and political order of things as it had evolved up to Hegel's time. '. . . Since philosophy is the exploration of that which is reasonable (*vernünftig*), it is therefore the grasp of things contemporary and real . . .' (Hegel, *Grundlinien der Philosophie des Rechts*, Preface). This identification of reason with actuality explains the monistic character of Hegel's deductions. All this is in the nature of a rational theology which endeavours to reconcile faith with secular thought. If Hegel's conceptual edifice is a rational theology of the political and social order of his time, Marx' is a canon of the revolution. At the end of the cavalcade Hegel resolves, Marx confirms and expands the contradictions which are disclosed earlier in the argument. While in Hegel's crowning synthesis all previous antinomies come to a rest, Marx' system culminates in the diagnosis of an irreconcilable class conflict which he sought to imply with the aid of the dialectical method of public interpretation. But neither Hegel's nor Marx' terminal diagnoses are simply discovered, in the manner in which the Grimm brothers detected the Indo-European language family or Mendeléeff arrived at the periodicity of atomic weights. Rather both syntheses represent the fully developed versions of the author's initial points of view. The untenable character of the present social order is as much a volitional premise of Marx' as is the finality of the state of 1830 an axiom of Hegel's system.

Thus, the primacy of volition over cognition is an implicit cornerstone of Hegel's system and a conscious axiom of Marx'. In fact, the Marxian dialectic has become a strategic device for widening the daily frictions of an evolving world economy into major crises, a device for giving these frictions an air of historical fatality. It is from this volitional premise that Marxism became both an ironclad system and a technique of arriving at fixed conclusions from varying points of departure. That, in versatile hands, this strategy is capable of an unlimited application was demonstrated not only by the founder and master, but more recently by the erudite refinements which Lukács and his followers have introduced into the Marxian interpretation of philosophy and literature.[1]

The foregoing references to Marx and Hegel were made to

[1] Compare George Lukács, *Geschichte und Klassenbewusstsein*, Berlin, 1923.

call attention to the dogmatic use of mediate categories. It would be a mistake, however, to discard these devices merely because of their speculative misuse by two masters of wishful interpretation. Although the danger of their abuse by men who place justification above the exploratory effort cannot be denied, mediate categories are indispensable tools of social inquiry once they are stripped of all mysticism. For a perspective of human affairs cannot be derived from direct and, necessarily, piecemeal observation. The basic deficiency of the positivistic reaction to speculation is its failure to provide for a method of inquiry into fields which are not accessible to direct approach. The private or unmediated and fragmentary view of a nation's economy contains as many distortions as did the heliocentric concept of the universe. It is this failure to transcend the immediate and fragmentary scope of observation into the realm of objective structures which still hamstrings the social sciences of our time. Too often the student of the humanities merely amplifies the distortions which originate in our daily and haphazard encounter with things partially observed. The primitive practice of personifying incidentals and of reifying casual perceptions will continue to deprive sociology of its promise so long as we proceed to base the main body of our generalizations on the immediate approach. Thinking in mediate terms, therefore, is by no means the same as departing from the realm of verifiable experience into the rarified air of speculation, but is rather an advance from the fortuitous and subjective view to objective analysis, from isolated fragments to the whole, and from raw observations to the grasp of structures. It is in these progressions that we substitute defined situations and relationships for the labels which we used to attach to haphazardly enountered phenomena.

We may, at this point, anticipate an objection by some of those readers who so far have not dissented. They will wonder whether the foregoing argument does not bog down in a mystification of the 'social' in precisely the same way in which the concept of history has been reified in recent philosophical parlance. What in particular is meant by 'society' and the social context of action? For one thing, they do not imply a super-individual entity existing above and apart from the individual; only the acts of sociation of various orders are all that is given. But neither is the category of the social confined to a narrow range of phenomena, as are, for example language, law, or religion. The interactive process encompasses a variety of such aspects of culture, and it necessarily involves the mind. One cannot separate the social from the mental domain of behaviour. It is senseless to pose questions such as whether the mind is socially determined, as if mind and society each possessed a substance of its own. The sociology of the mind is not an inquiry into the social causation of intellectual processes, but a study of the social character of those expressions whose currency does not reveal, or adequately disclose, their action context. The sociology of the mind seeks to uncover and articulate those acts of sociation which are inherent in, but not revealed by, the communication of ideas. The blindness to the action context of ideas gains support from the fact that ideas remain communicable and seemingly understandable long after the social situation which they helped to define or control ended. Actually ideas take on new meaning when their social function changes, and it is this relationship of meaning and function which the sociology of the mind elaborates. This approach does not seek to relate two discrete sets of objects—the social and the mental—to one another, it merely helps to visualize their often concealed identity.

4. THE MEDIATE CHARACTER OF ROLES. THE SOCIAL CIRCULATION OF PERCEPTIONS AND COMPLEMENTARY SITUATIONS

If communicated ideas cannot be properly understood apart from their functional context, the psychology of the individual must remain even more enigmatic without an understanding of the whole complex of his social situation. This is the proper subject of social psychology. The observation of collective reactions is only part of its business. The primary aim of social psychology is the understanding of how individual perceptions dovetail with the *social circulation of perceptions* among those who constitute a social situation. Just as the whole complex of the division of labour can be understood only as an interactive process, rather than as a multiple of individual performances, so also must the social psychologist envisage the social interdependence of individual perceptions. The direct and short-circuited approach to the person is likely to remain abortive.

The split personality for example is not always the product of early experience. Discrepant behaviour is sometimes the acute response to a contradictory situation. Persons who are in the thick of the economic struggle often appear hard-boiled at one moment and tenderly affectionate at another.[1] The co-existence of these two unrelated traits in the same person stems from his two opposite roles, namely the competitive, which fosters hard-fisted attitudes to others, and the private and familial which inhibits competitiveness. In a society which minimizes the economic functions of competition we should expect more homogeneous and integrated personality types, provided of course that such a society did not re-establish the necessity for competition in other fields of interaction.[2]

The polarity of the familial versus the economic role is only one pair of roles of the many which the individual may assume. As a rule, preliterate societies do not create such complex situations for their members as does contemporary society. The diversification and differentiation of the contemporary person seems to be a consequence of his multipolar situation.[3] By comparison, the dominant personality type of simpler societies is more clear-cut and rigid, for it is derived from fewer roles. The fact, first observed by Simmel, that in contemporary society most goals must be approached through a concatenation of intervening ends explains the modern prominence of self-control and endurance as essential requirements for social success.

[1] Compare this author's essay 'On the Nature of Economic Ambition and its Significance for the Social Education of Man', in Karl Mannheim, *Essays on the Sociology of Knowledge*, ed. Paul Kecskemeti, London and New York, 1952.

[2] Marx alluded to the situational character of the person: 'It is evident . . . that the complexity of the individual depends on the complexity of his relationships.' And: 'Indeed it seems . . . that individuals create one another physically and mentally, but they do not create themselves'. In 'Die deutsche Ideologie', Part I, *Marx-Engels Archiv*, vol. VII, ed. Ryasanow, p. 286.

[3] Marx had a keen appreciation of the social dimensions of personality: 'The foregoing makes it clear that the real wealth of the individual depends entirely on the real wealth of his relationships.' Marx and Engels on Feuerbach, Part I of 'The German Ideology', p. 286; *Marx-Engels Archiv*, vol. VII, ed. Ryasanow.

Such considerations require certain revisions in the popular image of man. Personality traits such as thoughtfulness, ruthlessness, or the domineering bent are not attributes of the individual as such, but rather aspects of his behaviour in particular relationships. What may appear to be a pervasive personality trait could easily prove a dependent variable of specific associations. Unselfishness in the primary group is not the same as selflessness in the larger society, and the militancy of the warrior is not the same as the pugnacity of the competitive business man. In short, personal attributes, such as bravery, timidity, loyalty, or selfishness are working abstractions which in the last analysis have meaning only within well-defined areas of behaviour. It is not adequate to speak, as some psycho-analysts still do, of drives in general, on the one hand, and of society as an agent of repression and sublimation on the other. What is needed is an increasingly precise observation of the variously structured areas of interaction.

To repeat, it is misleading to speak of the social determination of the individual—as though the person and his society confronted one another as discrete entities.[1] Yet, once this is said it must be remembered that the various components of the person are differently—and sometimes inconsistently—socialized.

While the foregoing discussion focused on the relationship between the person and the areas in which he acts, the present argument is concerned with phenomena which I propose to call (a) *the complementary social situation* and (b) *the social circulation of perceptions*. The first is involved in a shared situation which elicits inverse perceptions in the participants. The second expression, the circulation of perceptions, refers to the interaction between partners. A few examples will serve to clarify the meaning of the two categories.

The sociologically informed student of personality is not likely to attempt to explain certain dominant traits of an individual solely in terms of his attitudes and dispositions. Certain neuroses or inferiority feelings, for example, often develop in response to a contrary disposition of a partner—the husband, the mother, the teacher, the playmate, the class-

[1] A conclusive criticism of this dichotomy will be found in the first chapter of C. H. Cooley's *Human Nature and the Social Order*, New York, 1912.

mate, or the business associate. Marriages often create such a functional polarity. For example, the husband who freely spends money often evokes thrift as the complementary trait in his wife. Nothing would be gained by diagnosing a trait so evolved as an attribute of the total personality. Such a disposition, when viewed apart from its complementary function, will not help to predict future behaviour, for the woman who is penny-wise in her domestic situation may prove to be a careless financial manager of her social club. Thrift in our example is a complementary trait and is confined to only one social situation. The man's free and easy approach to pecuniary matters and the woman's acceptance of the compensatory restraint are merely the economic aspects of a complex division of roles: the man uses prerogatives which reaffirm the woman's subordination and her restricted choices in the marital situation. Such patterns of circulating responses are, however, not confined to economic matters: they may also enter into the wider realm of social values. If we visualize the host of displacements and sublimations which operate in each of such circular responses, and if we consider their social ramifications, we begin to realize the insurmountable difficulty which an individualizing psychology faces. What is needed to find a pattern of continuity in man's behaviour is a mediate approach which takes account of the partnerships in which man forms his compensatory habits and perceptions.

Our emphasis on the social and functional aspects of personality should not be interpreted as an implicit denial of the individual realm of existence. Nor does our insistence on the sociological perspective mean that the individual is less real than his relationships. No doubt personality can be understood only as a continuing process of integration. A person's conscious self is probably the result of persistent efforts to preserve its organization and to restore its disturbed equilibrium. Such efforts involve compensatory acts of varied types. Inferiority feelings usually furnish an impetus to seek compensation within or outside the field of felt inadequacy. The objective of such efforts, as indeed of most responses in which vital emotions are engaged, is to preserve the unity of the self. In short, one can admit the autonomous structure of the self and yet maintain that the conception of the individual as an isolated entity must lead to a distorted view. One of these distortions may be traced back to a historical source, the humanistic movement of the 18th and 19th century and its exaggerated image of the autonomous individual. The development of personality cannot be conceived entirely as a process of intrinsic growth; for certain dispositions often do evolve, as we have seen, in response to a new demanding situation. Thus a young person who is suddenly transplanted from the shelter of his family into the arena of occupational competition may evolve a militant attitude towards people n place of his earlier gentle demeanour.

Nor is the integration of the personality and its organization entirely a product of nuclear growth; it is also the upshot of the person's multiple participation. The individual is, in almost any culture, a member of a variety of groupings. It is this multiple involvement which ordinarily prevents the preponderance of a single attribute. This may account for the familiar fact that the personality of an individual who is involved in only a few situations is easier to describe than that of a man of the world whose self is formed in more varied types of relationships such as the family, political club, friendships, occupation, salons, learned societies, numerous speaking acquaintances, and so forth. It is no accident that the idea of the balanced personality did not originate in the guild or in a society of specialists, but in the intimate associations of 18th and 19th century aristocracy with the literati of the time. This idea is bound to fade away in a society of specialists in which the experts take the helm.[1]

The historical example just cited illustrates the circumstances under which a new model emerges. A social stratum takes on a new structure when it encounters a new situation and evolves a new way of life. The new ideal which is born in this encounter gives added impetus and direction to the beginning reorientation. The sociological view of this change may appear to ignore the role of individual choices or to reduce them to a mere shadow of social functions. Suspicion of this is often nursed by the fear that political freedom is inconsistent with social interdependence. This suspicion is unwarranted. Political,

[1] For the sociology of the humanistic paradigm see H. Weil, *Die Enstehung des deutschen Bildungsprinzips*, Schriften zur Philosophie und Soziologie, Bonn, 1930.

like any other institutional, accommodation evolves out of the needs and the elements of a solution which are inherent in a situation. Its concrete analysis does not minimize the scope and value of liberty. The area within which a person realizes his measure of freedom is not the absolute space of the universe; rather it is outlined by the needs of the group to whose challenge he responds. This challenge-response relationship, however, is neither a case for pure determinism nor is it void of elements of determinacy. We are free to make choices and to work out our own solutions within the range of given alternatives and available means.

A last example should illuminate the complementary nature of perceptions when they originate in reciprocal relationships on a social scale, and not only in individual partnerships. Here again we must note that the complementary perception of a known situation is not necessarily manifest, and it is not always apparent whose complementary perceptions we share. The present example relates to the often discussed companionate marriage and the corresponding changes in the forms of sexual attraction. The sexual partnership which the companionate type of marriage realizes is considerably more sober and unsentimental than the romantic ideal of triumphant love which overcomes the tempting trial of a long waiting period. Although the particular form of marriage which seems to be gaining ground is not necessarily monogamous in the long run (for it often becomes a successive polygamy), it does have the characteristics of a genuine partnership based on a multitude of joint interests of which the sexual is but one. This unromantic association lies somewhere in the middle between the overspiritualized love of early romanticism and the wholly despiritualized sexuality which has sustained prostitution in the West. How can one account for the rise of this new type of relationship between men and women?

Since the existence of prostitution (which in Western history may be traced back as far as Solon) sexual love has taken two forms: the tender and individualized *eros*, on the one hand, and the unsublimated and aggressive type on the other. Each of these two patterns usually involved partners of different social types. The tender and intellectualized *eros* has its history. In certain strata of Greece it was the ranking hetaera, and particularly the boy, rather than a man's own wife, on whom this *eros* centred. Equally long, on the other hand, is the history of the pariah concubine or prostitute. Both served to gratify the masculine appetite. We find towards the end of this long period of dichotomized sexuality the well-bred 'Biedermeier' girl[1] who dedicated herself to waiting for the man of her dreams; and the prostitute who answered the polygamous and de-spiritualized drives of men. The two female roles reflect the social differentiation of eroticism on two levels: the 'Biedermeier' girl responds to the sublime form of the male *eros*, while the prostitute becomes the caretaker of its physical aspect. The two complementary roles are parts of the same man-centred life situation. While women of different strata played opposite roles, men maintained, in characteristic cases, a split attitude towards sex which encompasses both its aspects. Men are capabie of adaptations to either of the two extremes of sexual attraction. It is clear that what may appear to be a masculine trait is actually the personal manifestation of a structural cleavage in a historical society.[2] To explain these manifestations we have to trace their social distribution. In earlier periods of Western custom the male approach to women varied with their social type, and it was the latter which actualized one of the two potential attitudes to the opposite sex. We have also noticed that with the advent of a middle solution a significant change in the approach to the opposite sex is taking place in both partners. With the passing of the ascetic waiting period, love is less often and less typically perceived in its former over-spiritualized form, and yet the evolving type of *eros* is anything but pure sex. The apparent middle solution not only affects women, but gradually also modifies the dichotomous approach of men to women.

The transformation which has, in large measure, taken place resembles what economists call the process of redistribution. The sexual discrepancy between men and women (which may be attributed to biological factors) used to impose a social

[1] In the first half of the 19th century the fictitious name of Gottlieb Biedermeier came to symbolize the world of the middle classes, puritan or philistine as the case may be.

[2] The cultural variability of the sexual division of roles is well illustrated in Margaret Mead, *Sex and Temperament in Three Primitive Societies*, London and New York, 1935.

burden on women, mostly on pariahs or prostitutes. With the declining polarization of the feminine role and the advent of a middle solution, the burden which was formerly placed on a more or less professional minority is increasingly shared by the majority of women. The new type of partnership entails a decreasing, though not vanishing, 'spirituality'. The reader need not interpret the present outline of this development as its advocacy. This is not the occasion to classify the Biedermeier form of love as a highly repressed variety, commercialized sex as a brutalization of the female partner, and the companionate association as the sound middle solution. The aim of this digression into the subject of sex was to call attention to the fact that not only individual but also group experiences may become complementary, and that the roles which we live and directly experience may be in reality nothing but the inversion of the unknown roles of unknown individuals.

5. TOWARDS AN ADEQUATE CONCEPT OF SOCIETY

The preceding examples should illuminate the principal thesis that mental processes have a social dimension and hence the sociology of the mind is but a systematic attempt to articulate the social character of mental processes. This was demonstrated on three successive levels of complexity. On the level of the first example (the dual character of the economic man) the context was more directly apparent than on the second (womanly thrift as a complementary phenomenon to the pecuniary irresponsibility of the husband) and, particularly, on the level of the third example (the variations of sexual partnership) which illustrates the circulation of perception on a collective scale.

Two conclusions must have emerged from the foregoing considerations. First, immediate perceptions are in themselves incomplete and often accessory phenomena which do not explain themselves. Second, the referential character of perceptions significantly depends on their function and social habitat. They may be ignored only at the price of misreading the particular meaning of given perceptions. Once this is clear one can no longer compartmentalize human manifestations into a social and a meta-social realm. The theories which pose such a dualism are argued in somewhat the following fashion. The significant creations of art, philosophy, and literature are supra-temporal and supra-social in so far as their meanings transcend the time and situation of their origin; while the small events of the daily routine, the details of social intercourse, and the made choices which reveal a current taste, are the legitimate subjects of sociology. This theory is germane to an earlier venture known as *Sittengeschichte* (history of custom). Not that sociologists should not, and would not, pay attention to the humbler details of life, but if the earlier attempts at a *Sittengeschichte* taught us a lesson, it is that an aggregation of remarkable details of daily life does not necessarily add up to more than an assortment of *curiosa*, unless each of the items is selected with a view to a structural scheme. The oddest thing in this whole procedure, however, is the tendency to concede a social character to the minor details of daily currency, and to deny it to the momentous events or the 'representative' manifestations of culture. Another variant of this plus-or-minus view of human affairs is the juxtaposition of the petty wisdom which rules the weekday struggle for existence and the gilded classics which exalt us on holidays. We need not look too far to recognize several other members of this family of opposites, to wit, the finite and the infinite, the personality and the group, and the individual and the mass.

Let us, at this point, anticipate the objection that much of the foregoing is but an exercise in the application of economic patterns of interpretation to history and thought—witness our repeated references to the division of labour, functional differentiations, and so forth. The objection is justified, for, indeed, we do not hesitate to perceive thought matters in categories derived from economics. One need not conceive economics as an all-inclusive field, or share the bias of an economic determinism, to realize that the most fundamental social categories were first elaborated in the field of economics. It is one of those disciplines which were first to free themselves from theological constrictions, which early began to evolve a secular view of things, and early discovered the structured character of society. In our view, economics is not the substructure, but a particular concretion of sociology. We believe, for example, that competition is a social process and a sociological category, although it was first visualized in its economic setting. One may admit the distinctive character of economic competition and yet emphasize the common social aspect of competition in all its variations. The sociological application of this category to thought is by no means tantamount to an over-extension of the framework of economics. If there is to be a hierarchy of frameworks, that of sociology is more inclusive than that of economics, and it proves so particularly in its application to communicated ideas. This claim does not contradict the observation made earlier that economic relationships in their entirety have a greater continuity than others, and that they tend to set the pattern for human relationships in a variety of spheres of interaction. One may well acknowledge this and still insist that economic behaviour is but an aspect of social action.

The examples cited above should have also demonstrated that ultimate reality (or existence on the level of ontology) attaches only to the individual and only he constitutes the ultimate unit of social action—and yet, social action cannot be understood without its group setting. We can resolve the seemingly insoluble controversy between the nominalists and the universalists if we concede to the former that the individual is the seat of reality and the reality of groups is derivative, and insist at the same time that the group approach to the individual is more effective than the direct. To recognize that the individual is the focus of reality is not the same as to construe the self as an isolated entity: to understand his behaviour one has to know the constellations in which he acts.[1]

6. A PRELIMINARY OUTLINE OF THE STEPS TOWARDS THE SOCIOLOGY OF THE MIND

The aim of the following considerations is to visualize the social dimension of the mind rather than to reify its concept and to deduce it from a hypostatized concept of society. Although we shall have to continue to concern ourselves with sociological abstractions, what we propose is not a scholastic exercise, but a method for discovering the action situations, the group structures, and the choices which, in one or another

[1] For a nominalism of a more clear-cut type than that advocated here see Bart Landheer, *op. cit.*, pp. 22, 28, 30.

way, are involved in meaningful utterances. The sociology of the mind has a universal application to thought history in as much as social situations are tacit components of all mental acts, no matter what academic disciplines or socially established divisions have custodial care of them.

First step. Recorded expressions of thought, sentiment, or taste are scrutinized for their inherent or intended meaning, while all inquiries into their intrinsic validity or verity are adjourned until the third step.[1]

Second step. The whole gamut of social relationships in which these utterances are conceived and made is traced and established. Particular attention is given to the choices and the order of preferences which are implicitly manifested by the actions of the participants in the given situation.

Third step. The content analysis of the utterances is resumed in the restored context of the original interaction, and their complete situational meaning is reconstructed.

Easy as it is to offer a nutshell description of the method of analysis, its effective application requires a certain imaginative realism and a sense for complex relationships which the earlier approaches to thought history have ignored. Even more needed are both a capacity for reconstituting the total concept of things and the willingness to relinquish a synthetic vision if it does not happen to fit the facts. The patient assembly and critical use of data must supplement and check the play of intuition. Valuable as this faculty is, the mastery of the empirical case study method and, in some cases, of statistical sampling procedures are preconditions of sound analysis. Facts must be established and verified and factors isolated before the attempt can be made to fit them into a hypothetical pattern. True, facts in themselves do not speak a language and do not reveal structure unless an experimental pattern is applied to them. It is the hypothesis which provides the question and it is its ultimate fit which suggests the answer. The cultivation of disconnected facts and the assembly of episodic detail will not provide us with an insight into their interrelationships. Bricks and mortar without the intervention of the mason and the

[1] For a more detailed discussion the reader is referred to the essay 'On the Interpretation of "Weltanschauung" ', in Karl Mannheim, *Essays on the Sociology of Knowledge*, London and New York, 1952.

architect do not constitute a building, nor can a historical structure be reconstituted from its elements without a design which dovetails the pieces into a meaningful configuration. The test of historiography is whether it shows a pattern which fits the facts and whether it is able to explain their relationships. The mere enumeration of what is known of an event will not answer the question of why it happened as it did.

7. THE THREE TYPES OF SOCIOLOGY AND THE CORRESPONDING LEVELS OF THE SOCIOLOGY OF THE MIND. STRUCTURE AND CAUSALITY

We may now return to our earlier question: What is the specific subject of sociology as distinguished from that of the sociology of the mind? The latter proposes to elaborate, as we have seen, the social dimensions of communicated meaning. The answer is implicit in the thesis, voiced earlier, that 'society' does not exist as an independent entity. The social dimension of things is universal and does not constitute a separate domain comparable to that of art or religion.

Groups consist not only of cooperative and competitive relationships. Nor are they fully described by the mutual awareness of their members. The unconscious is as much a dimension of the social as is the conscious. Even before we become conscious of a 'we' situation we already share certain ways in which we see things or remain blind to them. The common preconscious approach to certain objects is as much a phase of the socializing process as is the learning of the vernacular or the concerted stipulation of the family budget. Some sort of a meaning, whether conscious or unconscious, is involved in all social relationships, and the two—meaning and group relationships—occur in a merged state.

And yet, things which are merged in reality may be perceived separately. Abstraction is a tool of inquiry. We may well make the thought process as such or the underlying group structure the subject of our attention. We may legitimately narrow our focus as long as we do not reify the boundary line which we find convenient for the delimitation of our inquiry. For it is one thing to narrow our focus to one aspect of the subject by withdrawing our attention from another, but it is a different thing to declare the vacated area irrelevant to the occupied one. The first act in itself does not create a mere phantom; it only designates a principle for selecting items for subsequent elaboration. In short, abstractions do not necessarily distort reality.

We have already dealt with fruitful abstractions. Competition was a case in point. Acts of competition have their concrete setting, be it economic, erotic, or political. There is no competition *in abstracto* and yet, in whatever setting competitive acts are performed, they have certain functional characteristics in common. This is the level of abstraction on which *general sociology* conceptualizes behaviour; its subjects are the acts of sociation conceived in relative isolation from their historical incidence. General sociology construes rather than describes its subjects, and it proceeds typologically from elementary to complex phenomena. Elementary are those acts which enter into all or many relationships, while complex are those phenomena which present combinations of elementary acts. This was the level of abstraction on which Simmel projected his plan of a 'formal' sociology and on which others are making legitimate attempts to trace social behaviour back to elementary (that is: sub-historical) acts of sociation. I refer to Park's and Burgess' work as the most fruitful of all, little known though it is in Germany. One may regret, perhaps, their somewhat narrow conception of the field of general sociology and its confinement to the most elementary processes. The general theory of sociation should be supplemented by a comparative study of historical phenomena. Max Weber's *Wirtschaft und Gesellschaft*[1] offers in this regard a significant model, inasmuch as he follows up the prefatory presentation of his general sociological system of categories by *comparative* historical treatises which elaborate the historical ramifications of those categories. Another noteworthy feature of this work is the manner, reminiscent of theoretical physics, in which complex structures are successively evolved from the more elementary acts of sociation. Thus, we find in this work not only a discussion of domination, but a

[1] Now translated in selections by T. Parsons under the title of *The Theory of Social and Economic Organization*, New York, 1947, and by H. Gerth and C. W. Mills, *From Max Weber, Essays in Sociology*, London and New York, 1946.

systematic coverage of its historical variations construed from a minimum of elementary relationships.

The next level of analysis—next in order of concretion—is the *historical.* Its aim is the constructive grasp of the singularity of historical structures. Max Weber did not advance to this level of approach, mainly because within his individualistic and nominalistic frame of reference he had no access to singular historical phenomena. He rather construed these as particular combinations of elementary relationships. Witness the three volumes of his *Sociology of Religion*, and particularly his *Protestant Ethics and the Spirit of Capitalism.*[1]

What we propose is not the causal analysis of the discrete events of history, but an understanding of the broad structural changes which become manifest on the various levels of social interaction. This is the manner in which Marx, in his own way, conceived the historical character of capitalism, and it is thus that Sombart studied the subject. The character of these approaches differs from the purely historical in so far as they visualize unique events not as events, but as components of singular structures in the process of change.

It is unnecessary to juxtapose the causal and structural types of analysis as opposites. We advocate an intermediate view which does not exclude either procedure. Both may be embodied in an approach which proceeds from single components and their immediate causal relationships to the structural complex. Instead of describing the successive steps of such a procedure let us state its methodological assumptions which, at this point, we take for granted:

(a) General sociology constitutes a legitimate frame of reference: its categories take, by virtue of their general scope, precedence over the categories of historical description. On this level the singular phenomena of history are construed as particular combinations of suprahistorical tendencies, as they are observed on the level of general sociology.

(b) Single causes become compounded and integrated into collective processes.

(c) Such a composite of causative impulses must be understood as a structure whose behaviour is not fully described by the

[1] Translated by T. Parsons, London, 1930.

actions which compose it. Causal relationships compose, but do not account for, the dynamics of complete structures.

(d) The dynamics of change may at times take an antithetic course and invert a given trend. This is the meaning of the observation that some historical changes are dialectical. Change through opposites, however, is by no means a universal feature of history, but only one of its possible courses. The apodictic generalization that history necessarily and invariably proceeds through structural inversions is part and parcel of the dogmatic aspects of the Marxist view. The thesis that capitalism is the dialectical opposite of feudalism is as questionable as the corresponding prognosis that the trend of capitalism points towards its antithesis. What the student of social change may learn from Marx is not his political and propagandistic casuistry, but the structural approach to change and to the dynamics of history.

In summary, sociology may be developed in its three dimensions, namely as general, comparative, and structural sociology.[1] The sociology of the mind is inherently potential in each of these three types. Meanings and symbolic acts may be studied on each of the three levels. We can for instance approach the subject of *Gemeinschaft* (community) as the locus of sympathetic attitudes through each of these three avenues. We may trace the communal types of relationships to their artistic and legal expressions; we may elaborate a typology of their historical or anthropological variations as they occur in known types of communal situations; and finally, we may narrow our frame of reference to the concrete legal or artistic manifestation of singular *Gemeinschaft* structures. In short, the sociological study of symbolic acts (or, to use the well-established term: cultural sociology) derives its threefold universe of discourse from the same sources from which the three approaches to human relations as such stem. The choice

[1] Talcott Parsons envisages similar, though not identical, levels of analysis: 1. that of the individual actor; 2. of an interactive system; and 3. of systems of culture patterns. 'Each implies the others and therefore the variability of any one is limited by its compatibility with the minimum conditions of functioning of each of the other two.' *The Social System*, London and Glencoe, 1951, p. 27.

between these avenues may not be always free, but an awareness of which of the three approaches is feasible in a given instance is essential for the proper outline of a research objective in the area of cultural sociology.

III. THE PROPER AND IMPROPER CONCEPT OF THE MIND

1. A SECOND REVIEW OF ITS HEGELIAN VERSION

Let us insist at the outset that Hegel's concept of the mind is still basic to the undertaking here proposed. We shall, therefore, have to refer back to Hegel as we develop our views on the subject of this chapter, without attempting anything like a dogmatic interpretation. This renewed departure from Hegel may seem surprising. The reader may wonder what relevance Hegel may still have to a contemporary once he has thrown overboard the immanent conception of ideas, accepted an individualistic ontology, and rejected the hypostatized notions of mind and society.

What makes Hegel's original point of view still worth remembering is his collectivistic, and potentially sociological, understanding of ideas. It was Hegel who set the pattern for the structural view, and it was he who sensitized later German sociologists and humanists to the total context of historical things. Much as some German philosophers of history succeeded in short-circuiting this constructive impulse by inconsequential armchair speculation on God and world history, the original pattern entails more than such speculation. The spurious dichotomy of the immanent evolution versus the social history of ideas was the upshot of a split in the ranks of Hegel's successors. Such a dichotomy was alien to Hegel's thinking.

What is constructive in the original endeavour is the pattern it sets for the discovery of the overall relationship of things which the microscopic view conceals. American sociology operates, in comparison with German, on a more solid empirical basis, but it lacks the synthetic bent, the overall perspective, and a tested model of dealing with inclusive structures. German sociologists have not developed a tradition for controlled elementary observations, but it is part of their heritage to posit fruitful structural hypotheses and to envisage their subjects in a broader perspective. The two practices will have to merge if sociology is to master both the simple and the complex, and the techniques of isolation and integration.

The rapprochement of the two tendencies will remain impracticable, however, as long as we think in such antithetic terms as the generalizing method and the configurational (or singularizing) approach. Such is still the accepted custom—established since the romantic movement and the rise of German historicism, reinforced by certain phases of the Marxist influence, and continued through recent historiography. This questionable polarization of the field bespeaks a presumptuousness which is the common pitfall of all dogmatic commitments to a certain methodology. Such preconceptions do not augur well for profitable work.

2. THE GENESIS OF THE MIND CONCEPT

We shall presently attempt to recapture step by step the tenable portions of Hegel's thought, beginning with the collectivistic features of his mind concept. It did not make its appearance with the suddenness of a pistol shot. We may grasp the long evolution of the concept through successive periods of social history if we recount its varied and shifting meanings. Today we are in a position to discern a few stages of this evolution, largely as a result of Hildebrand's research summed up under the caption 'Geist' in the Grimm brothers' German dictionary.[1]

[1] Compare R. Hildebrand, 'Geist' in the series *Philosophie und Geisteswissenschaften*, ed. E. Rothacker, Halle, 1926. In keeping with the style of a dictionary article, Hildebrand arrayed in chronological order the various meanings of the term 'Geist', together with pertinent quotations. To present the essentials of that historical shift we have altered the original sequence, particularly since Hildebrand did not aim at a sociological analysis of meaning. A critical examination of the material demonstrates the interesting fact that older stages of the evolution are often expressed only in recent documents—a fact which corroborates the observation that the recent forms of a word meaning do not necessarily displace the older ones. The two may coexist and thereby perpetuate both phases of a historical metamorphosis. Once we are able to date these meanings and to locate the implicit social perspectives which originally gave rise to their currency we enter the field of the sociology of meaning.

Originally 'Geist' did not have its present connotation of an objectified and socialized set of meanings; it rather denoted something transcendent and ecstatic. Hegel's term still reflects both significations: the socially shared and objectified heritage which the word 'culture' expresses, and a gripping and ecstatic experience whose roots go back to early religion. The German use of the expression 'Geist' in preference to its synonym 'culture' betrays the same ambivalent interpretation of culture as a cumulative patrimony and as a state of spiritual exposure. That German philosophy seeks to retain both connotations of the term constitutes at once a liability and an asset. The ambivalent use of the term 'Kultur' is unquestionably responsible for a good deal of fuzzy thinking. Another stumbling-block of German philosophy is its carry-over of a primitive ontology which is implicit in the subjective reading of 'Geist'. This ontology in effect acts as a deterrent to a fresh and independent approach to human matters.

Let us examine more closely the primitive metaphysics which the term 'Geist' perpetuates. We may trace it back to its early form in which spirit is still coterminous with breath.[1] Soon this material image of breath becomes associated in a primitive animistic manner with the seat of life,[2] and reality takes on a double character which we may still recognize in the philosophical ontologies of our time. Within the world of sense perception and in its place a second world of essentialities emerges. The two realms are, however, not discrete and mutually exclusive; they are rather conceived as the double aspects of each and every physical object. Breath, for instance, is both the puff of air that it appears to be and also the essence of life. Spiritualism is the upshot of a lengthy evolution in which the distance between the empirical world of things and the transcendent realm of essentialities became increasingly articulated. Religious élites often play an important role in the rise of such a spiritualism: they tend to translate their ascetic aloofness from the affairs of daily life into its ontological devaluation. With the ascetic rejection of the world of daily activities the spiritual realm becomes the seat of reality. At this point things spiritual become real and they are no longer mere attributes of breath.

[1] Compare Hildebrand's references, p. 2. [2] *Ibid.*, p. 3.

The two phases of the process are still present in Luther's thinking: he refers interchangeably to breath and spirit, but he also uses 'Geist' to denote spirituality only. Luther voices the first version when he says: 'Heaven was made through the word of the Lord and His armies were created by the spirit of His mouth'; and even clearer: 'they perished by the breath of the Lord and by the spirit of His wrath'.[1] We encounter, on the other hand, the non-material conception of the spirit as a separate entity in the following passage: 'For all that is not of the spirit and grace is dead.' Here 'spiritual' is coterminous with divine, transcendent, and the opposite of the finite.

None of these conceptions bears the slightest relationship to such things as culture and reason. These connotations evolve much later. It would be a mistake, however, to assume that the act of partaking of the spirit was construed as a solitary, individual experience. We incline towards such an interpretation since our intelligentsia elaborated a subjectivistic and inner-directed aspect of religion. In its archaic forms spiritual exposure was understood to be a single act of collective participation and it was a simultaneously shared spirit who communed with man.[2] Its collective nature was, of course, not that of a common cultural possession such as language and science are; it was rather something like a collective seizure. This communal ecstasy also provides the background of the primitive acclamation through which archaic groups (in their ancient or modern setting) express unanimous decisions. In a ritualized form the practice has survived in certain religious bodies. It is said, for example, that elections should be held 'per viam inspirationis Sancti Spiritus'. It is this spiritual communion of cardinals which elects the Pope: 'no doubt, the Holy Spirit speaks clearer in the assembly than to single men.'[3]

The distinctive character of these conceptions of the spiritual is the collective empathy in which it appears. In spiritual matters the primitive person does not act and commune distinctly as an individual; in these regards he is more highly socialized than the contemporary. A complex mass society offers less opportunity for collective ecstases, but it widens the scope for the institutional transmission of culture. We encounter culture, therefore, as a solidified and objective heritage which

[1] Compare Hildebrand's references, p. 70. [2] *Ibid.*, p. 30. [3] *Ibid.*

is individually accessible. The channels of cultural transmission are, of course, open in primitive society, too; after all, selective continuity is the essence of all culture, but the rational organization of the transmissive process is more peculiar to large and complex societies. Only in this sociological perspective can we understand the modern reinterpretation of the spirit concept to mean something akin to reason. This tendency became dominant with the enlightenment and its substitution of 'mens' for spirit.[1] Hildebrand emphasizes that prior to Adelung no dictionary makes mention of the thinking intellect.[2] But soon voices are raised in protest against the rationalistic and objectivistic interpretation of the term, coupled with attempts to link it to earlier traditions in which the concept was not restricted to the reasoning capacity.[3] Goethe gives expression to this view: 'in music we come to anticipate such a future, for there it is nothing but spirit and without it there is no future (as there is no past either).'

The genesis of Herder's conception of 'Geist' is as complex as Hegel's. But while Hegel's 'Geist' is a 'higher' type of thought Herder's is a higher type of sympathetic vision: 'thus our art critics try to employ all their erudition and wit to deprive us of the sweet moments in which we behold and follow the spirit of others.'[4] We notice that 'Geist' here involves not only cognition, but also volition and activity. But while the rationalistic current rejected the earlier ecstatic components of the term and more and more equated it with conscious reasoning, the classics and romantics revived the earlier non-conscious and supra-rational elements of *Geist*. In this literary reaction against the calculating mentality of the Age of Reason we encounter *Geist* as the animus of history and as a 'higher' type of reason which also involves contemplation, volition, and action. All these ingredients are peculiarly fused in Hegel's well-articulated concept. It is Hegel's characteristic synthesis of the classic and romantic view which provides the background for Hildebrand's summary: '. . . we must emphasize that in our 19th-century usage 'Geist' involves not only our thought but also that which lives and acts in us and animates and guides us, and they were also

[1] *Philosophie und Geisteswissenschaften*, ed. E. Rothacker, Halle, 1926, p. 93.

[2] *Op. cit.*, p. 96. Adelung defines spirit as 'a corporeal substance capable of thought and volition.' *Ibid.*

[3] *Op. cit.*, p. 98.

[4] *Op. cit.*, p. 99.

involved in the earliest connotations of breath of life, gasp, and signification.' Here we have the description of a concept of culture which implicitly covers its rational interpretation as an externalized and available heritage, but it also retains the early image of collective and dynamic acts. It would be a mistake not to see the promise which this tradition, so characteristic of German philosophy, entails.

3. THE SUBJECTIVE AND OBJECTIVE MANIFESTATIONS OF THE MIND. THE SOCIAL GENESIS OF MEANING

Having dwelt on the archaic and subjective connotation of 'Geist' as it presents itself in Hegel's work, we turn now to its modern aspects. One of the recurrent themes of German philosophy is the dissociation of knowledge from the act of knowing. We find, indeed, that experience tends to detach itself from the acts in which it originates and to become accessible independently of them. This objective aspect of the act is well elaborated in Hegel's philosophy, notably in his distinction between the subjective mind on the one hand, and the objective and absolute on the other. The modern distinction between the subjective or temporal act and the intended or detachable meaning is foreshadowed in Kant's and Bolzano's theories, but we find it more incisively outlined in Hegel's system. It was he who envisaged most clearly the collective and social character of meaning.

Meanings attain their first social significance through their dissociation from the original act. As soon as a meaning emerges from the subjective perception which brings it to light it relinquishes its previous singularity and becomes a common focus. We are concerned here with the difference between thinking and thought, or the act of doing and the deed. Deed, or an accomplished action, is to be considered here as the realization of a collective conception, in the manner in which the maker of an effigy gives expression to a common image. (We find here a close parallel to Durkheim's 'collective representations' which, by the way, raise the interesting question of how much Hegelian thought went into the coinage of this noteworthy category. At any rate, the strength of the Durkheimian approach to the problem of collective meaning is partly attributable to the philosophical perspective in which he outlines the problem.) An objectified meaning is a product of sociation. We objectify not only thought, but also emotions, moods, and whatever filters 'out' of the closed circuit of singular experiences. No doubt the impetus to objectify meanings is eminently social and no consciousness can evolve in an unsocialized individual (if by consciousness we understand the sum total of directed acts which resolve themselves into intended meanings). Meaning, therefore, is a sociological term and it is inseparable from some phase of sociation. It is not our concern with identical objects which brings us into a social nexus, but the identical meanings which we jointly attribute to objects; we encounter one another not in things but through their significations. We conceive meanings, however, not only in communicative acts, but also in solitary moments. We perform an act of sociation already in an isolated state of contemplation. Thus, cognition and communication are inseparable functions. Organisms which cannot communicate are also incapable of objective concepts. Human contacts which are established upon a biological impetus do not in themselves constitute associations unless they transcend the initial impetus.

To what social needs and situations are we to trace the objective bent and the strain of reflexivity? This question is basic to the sociology of culture. We must sharply distinguish between the two acts. It is one thing to make a solitary experience intelligible to others, and another to reflect on it, to give an account of it to oneself, and thus to transmute the known into knowledge. The two impulses come from different social situations which bear on these alternative ways of rethinking an experience. Acts of reflection have been linked to what is sometimes termed a modus of deficiency, namely a social hiatus in the act of communication. The term alludes to certain gaps in a collective experience which makes its meaning deficient and therefore incommunicable, as a result of which the original objective impulse becomes retroverted and reflexive.

Bolzano's theory of meaning ignores the social function of significations; it posits an absolute antithesis between the isolated individual and the conscious realm of concepts. In so doing, he blinds himself to the fact that meaning is not an abstract entity, but a concrete function of common experience.

One may well concede Bolzano his separation of the subjective act from its objective meaning without accepting the implied thesis of the disjunction between meaning and the (collective) experience from which it stems. Once the myth of a detached realm of significations is rejected, meaning becomes a natural subject of sociological inquiry.

The question, raised even by Max Weber, of how we move from individual experiences to an objective meaning or to the sociological point of view, is a topsy-turvy version of the real question of how we get from the concrete social meaning of things to Max Weber's individually intended meaning and to the conception of an abstract sphere of detached significations. Indeed, we must ask how it comes to pass that for certain purposes we ignore the social character of the actor (the individual) and his acts. Let us attempt to reconstruct the social context of the first question, namely how percepts derive from the original acts of perceiving.

The original seat of meaning is, presumably, the cooperative situation. The identical manipulation of identical things opens up certain common avenues of approach. A log may be a potential canoe, spear, raft, or fuel—depending on the needs of those who intend to use it. It is the joint actions in given or potential situations which fix the common or variable view of a thing. Once a common approach to the thing takes hold, it only needs a common symbol to attain an objective import. The common appellative is therefore not an abstraction and not a derivative of individual significations, but the primary form in which each individual comes to attach meaning to the object.

Linguistic studies in primitive communities furnish us with documentary evidence of the collective genesis of certain meanings. The appearance of the solitary genesis of concepts is the final upshot of a work differentiation (to which Simmel devoted a significant book) which diversifies the possible approaches to the same thing, and which presents an object in varying perspectives. Such a complex situation entails a diversified view of things, but not as yet the loss of a common universe of experience. The import of things is still concrete as they are still the objects of a common approach. The common frame of reference disappears only when two or more groups or cultures exist side by side, each having its own approach to things, and the individual is in a position to choose between them. Country and city or crafts and commerce may become the sources of such diverse points of view. The passage of the individual from one to the other, and his freedom of choice between them, describe the primary situation in which the person finds several approaches to the same object available. This is also the seat of relativism and of the sceptical point of view; this marks the origin of the antithetic conception of the particular and the general aspect of things. The twilight appearance of objects is inherent in the interpenetration of several discretely structured communal groupings. The same twilight situation makes it possible for the individual to evade certain rules of behaviour. We see here the rise of a profane society from the sacred. Carl Mennicke once observed that primitive communities do not make provision for ethical escapes: the only alternative to conformity is repression, which is another way of saying that the formation of complexes is a complementary phenomenon of the sacred. A complex society with its pluralistic ethics provides for escapes, but it also occasions neuroses. The discovery of psychology significantly coincides with the general accessibility of escape mechanisms, for it is only in a free and uncommitted situation that one's own spontaneity and one's own reasons for making certain choices come into focus.

The contemporary adolescent faces a similar marginal situation when he is about to begin to live his own life outside the parental home. The manifestations are the same whether individuals or whole strata of society face crossroads. What is it that is peculiar about the Sophists and Socrates (as we shall see later) if it is not their reorientation from a feudalistic agrarian way of life with its mythological world towards the more fluid order in the coastal city of artisans and tradesmen? The experience of a new world full of escapes, the realization of the ambiguous face of things, and the discovery of the subjective domain of perception in place of the older collective outlook—these are the elements of a new and puzzling situation which made Greek logic as the codification of a detached and unchannelled thinking possible in the same way as psychology emerged from a similar bewilderment centuries later. This is also the genesis of what is called abstract and formal thinking. It is the product of interchangeable social roles in which the person is free to relinquish common approaches and is forced to replace collective understanding by the abstract common denominator of the fleeting individual views of reality. As the concrete universe vanishes, the polarity of the isolated individual and the generalizing reason (later the abstract consciousness) makes its appearance. In sum, both the Greek period of enlightenment and the modern Age of Reason derive their common features from the dissolution of a feudal order and its succession by a mobile, urban society in which the relationship between group and thought is no longer directly apparent. Only the romantics endeavoured to devalue the significance of these changes by the projection of a wish dream of the past into the future.

4. THE SUPRAPERSONAL CHARACTER OF MEANING

The strength of the Hegelian *Geist* concept lies, as we have seen, in its grasp of the social dimensions of meaning, and it is this fact which makes the distinction between the subjective act and its objective counterpart, the socially relevant meaning, possible. But this is not all. We are still groping within the solipsistic realm of appearances so long as we do not look beyond the objectivity of significations. For on this level we are still dealing with nothing but individual meanings, communicable though they may be, and we are not yet cognizant of their relationships. Thus, when we try to approach history on this plane we encounter a sequence of discrete expressions which lack historical continuity. In this nominalistic perspective (in which only individual perceptions are real) we cannot come to grips with such events as the evolution of American Common Law from the English, the Japanese assimilation of Western technology in the 19th century, the growth of the Prussian state from Frederick II to Bismarck, or the Protestant revolt against the medieval Church. We cannot reconstruct social changes from the mosaic of individual utterances and we cannot account for an event of the past or the present without even having a name for its milieu.

Our previous insistence that the individual is the primary

locus of reality need not make us forget the fact that human relations, however complex, are also real. (To be sure, the group does not absorb the individual and the person does not completely assimilate and reflect his society, but there are common areas in which the actions of the individual become socially and historically relevant and, conversely, group structures become the primary determinants of the actions of single persons.) What Hegel's *Geist* implies—beyond the discernment of objective meanings referred to—is the collective framework of history which we have to know to understand its continuity. The problems and alternatives which the single individual faces in his actions are presented to him in a given social framework. It is this framework which structures the role of the person, and in which his actions and expressions take on a new sense. It transcends those meanings which the individual 'intends' when he cogitates or conveys an experience. As soon as we speak of structured behaviour or thought we are moving on this second level of objective significations: we seek to grasp the meaning of meanings by attempting to reconstruct the context of individual action and perception.

5. CRITIQUE OF THE ENTELECHY AS A CONCEPTUAL MODEL

In an effort to isolate the constructive elements in Hegel's work from its speculative phases we directed attention to his concept of the 'objective mind' and its social components. We have seen that mental phenomena have a structure and a supra-individual dimension. But as soon as that is said we face a potential perversion of this view, which bears the signature of Hegel himself. The distortion is inherent in the tendency to treat structured meanings as unfolding and self-realizing entelechies. It is not easy to expose the fallacy of this view, for it contains a grain of truth, although the false perspective in which it is presented and the confusion it has created overshadow the light which the conception spreads.

To illustrate Hegel's questionable procedure, one would have to construe the evolution of the baroque as a process which unfolds the intrinsic potentialities of this style in the very same order in which the single artists actually realized its incipient possibilities. Such an approach to a historical process is not interpretive but exegetic; it merely fits scattered pieces into a construed, unitary pattern. One might rightly contend that the evolution of the baroque is not fortuitous and that it does not lack a certain consistency, but it would be absurd to claim that the actual course of baroque history is logically preordained. The regional mutations of this style and its varying interpretations by individual artists should dispel any notion of a predetermined and irreversible evolution of the baroque. One may concede the grain of truth contained in this panlogistic conception, namely that given sets of ideas and styles more or less set a limited range for its variations. One may even defend the thesis that each additional concretion of a pattern consecutively narrows the scope of its mutations. But the notion of a preordained course of unfolding meanings fails to take account of two additional circumstances: the incidence of catastrophic events (such as invasions) which may recast the setting in which a current of thought evolves; and the given scope within which an artist or an organizer is free to create new structures.

Let us turn to a concrete example. The ultimate decline of Rome was probably foreshadowed at the outset by the character of its slave capitalism. That such a social system has both potentialities and limitations is true enough; and we may say, therefore, that the actual history of Roman society was potential in its incipient structure. But that does not mean that the actual course of events was predictable. Certain cross-currents which were present in the early milieu of Rome could have arrested the growth of slave capitalism at an early stage. The external resistances to Roman expansion could have matured centuries before they eventually took a decisive form. No sociologically informed historian could retrospectively predict Hannibal's defeat without an account of certain circumstances which were external to the structure of republican Rome. Turning to modern history, capitalism has taken on different characteristics in France, England, Germany, and the United States. Resources, the geo-political milieu, and migration played an important part in the diversification of the culture and politics of these countries. The common elements in their economic structure reveal nothing which could account for the obvious differences. What perverts the structural view of change into a doctrine of total determinism and predestination is the misconception of structure as a principle which inexorably unfolds itself. This emanatistic view beclouds the role of the milieu—geographical, historical, and social—and obscures the scope of individual variations. What the concept of structure does entail is not a telic process of self-realization, but a given range of successively limited choices. But choices they remain, however narrowing their limitations may become. To ignore the role of leadership and to deny the catalytic function of single persons is a distortion of the sociological interest in the collective setting of events. It is one thing to apply the sociological method to the study of Fascism and the rise of world revolutionary movements; it is quite another to forget the roles of Mussolini, Marx, and Lenin. We may be well aware of the limitations which narrow a leader's radius of action, but we cannot appraise his achievements or shortcomings without seeing both the alternatives he faces and the initiative he takes.

6. THE EXPLANATORY AND THE EXPOSITORY PROCEDURE. THE STRUCTURE OF EVENTS

The malpractice of presenting the structure of things as their source of emanation is responsible for the *expository* approach to the history of thought in lieu of the *explanatory*. Once we conceive change as a goal-directed process through which a preexisting scheme comes to its inexorable realization, we narrow our focus down to the basic design which seems to map out the place of each event as it occurs in a predetermined sequence. What we attempt thereby resembles the performance of a person who pores over a jig-saw puzzle. He seeks correspondences between the basic design and the single pieces as he fits them together. His procedure is expository in the same sense in which we try to understand the meaning of single sentences in the context of a whole speech. We assume thereby that history has a preordained design. Once this assumption is made, the problem is how to unravel the intrinsic plan which unfolds itself, and it becomes superfluous to wonder about the causal relationships of single events.

This religious type of historical exegesis sets the pattern for Hegel's philosophy of history, as it has also become the tradition of German historiography and certain phases of German sociology. Even attempts to construe history without a divine plan still reveal the influence of that tradition. But once we abandon a presentation of history as a succession of retribution and rewards we have to discard the expository method. Or must we? Not entirely, for we still retain the structured meaning of historical change. The fact that the positivistic type of historical research is inconsistent with a broad teleological interpretation does not mean that we must perforce restrict our approach to the fragmentary and microscopic view of events. We need not apply teleological hypotheses to history to realize the structured character of change. As soon as we try to outline a phase of history as a concrete set of alternatives we envisage history as a totality, as a configuration. We cannot gain such a perspective without the expository intent of fitting fragments into a larger pattern.[1] But this is not the same as the Hegelian method of tracing a phase of history back to its universal design. We are not looking for the telic meaning of events, but for their structural setting.

[1] Sapir arrives at the same conclusion with reference to the patterns of linguistic development: 'Language exists only in so far as it is actually used. . . . What significant changes take place in it must exist, to begin with, as individual variations. This is perfectly true, and yet it by no means follows that the general drift of language can be understood from an exhaustive descriptive study of these variations alone. They themselves are random phenomena, like the waves of the sea, moving backward and forward in purposeless flux. The linguistic drift has direction. In other words, only those individual variations embody it or carry it which move in a certain direction. . . . The drift of a language is constituted by the unconscious selection on the part of its speakers of those individual variations that are cumulative in some special direction. This direction may be inferred, in the main, from the past history of the language. In the long run any new feature of the drift becomes part and parcel of the common, accepted speech, but for a long time it may exist as a mere tendency in the speech of a few. . . . As we look about us and observe current usage, it is not likely to occur to us that our language has a "slope", that the changes of the next few centuries are in a sense prefigured in certain obscure tendencies of the present and that these changes, when consummated, will be seen to be but continuations of changes that have been already effected. We feel rather that our language is practically a fixed system and that what slight advances are destined to take place in it are as likely to move in one direction as another. The feeling is fallacious. Our very uncertainty as to the impending details of change makes the eventual consistency of their direction all the more impressive.' (Edward Sapir, *Language*, New York, 1921, p. 165 f.).

We must ask at this point whether the structural interpretation of change leaves room for causal inquiries. The question foreshadows the answer: the alternative is not stringent, and the two procedures are not mutually exclusive. Social structure is the order in which causal sequences recurrently operate within a social system.

For example, modern capitalism can be understood as a system of interlocking operations, such as production, distribution, the price mechanism, the credit system, the competitive stimulation of demand, the recruitment of the labour force, and so forth. We do not have to know what motivates the director of the Mint to know what money is, and we need not inquire into the reasons of spending to know what inflation is. We may very well grasp the principles which govern the flow of capital from one industry to another without paying attention to the relationships between the individual stockbroker and his client. These operations form a system which, though unplanned, has a functional scheme which we can reconstruct without searching for its author. We have to assume that it is the result of an adaptive process which has taken its course through numerous causal sequences of the trial and error type. The important thing is, however, that the system is functioning as if it had a blue-print. More than that, the underlying plan of the system not only outlines functions and roles which must be performed, but it also allocates motivations for the needed performances. Thus, to the investor on the commodity market local price differences present an opportunity for profit, but at the same time he performs an economic function by equalizing the price level of grain.[1]

The *causal* perspective of this operation makes it clear to us *why* the investor performs his role, but it is the functional scheme which shows us *how* he may perform successfully and *what* his scope of action is. The sum total of causal motivations does not explain the complete structure: in fact, not all actions for which inducements exist are necessary for the functioning of

[1] The social system 'must have a sufficient proportion of its component actors adequately motivated to act in accordance with the requirements of its role system . . ." (T. Parsons, *The Social System, op. cit.* p. 27.) See also T. Parsons, 'The Position of Sociological Theory' in *Essays in Sociological Theory, Pure and Applied*, Glencoe, 1949, pp. 7, 11.

the capitalistic system. Not only does almost everybody do a good many things which are irrelevant to the operation of that system, but there are social enclaves, such as isolated communities, nomadic gypsies, feuding clans, which were bypassed by the economic developments of our time. Their scheme of life is no part of the 'blueprint' of our social system. We shall have to distinguish between structurally *relevant* and *irrelevant* actions and motivations.

7. THE QUESTION WHETHER THE WORLD HAS STRUCTURE

The distinction just drawn has a bearing on subsequent considerations. History is made up of events, and an event may or may not be relevant to a given structure in which it occurs. Does that mean that certain occurrences are intrinsically irrelevant? Freud uncovered the unconscious system of meanings and thereby disclosed the relevance of things hitherto considered trivial, such as lapses of memory and slips of the tongue. They proved to be relevant within a previously unrecognized context. Actually we can never decide with complete finality that an occurrence is no part of any system, for its irrelevance to known systems does not preclude the possibility that it is intrinsic to an undiscovered structure. The term relevance merely denotes that an event is foreshadowed by the design of a *known* system. We must be prepared to anticipate that apparent structural inconsistencies may resolve themselves in a system of wider scope which transcends our present ken. This raises a problem of which Hegel had a keen appreciation.

One may, perhaps, interpret Hegel's panlogistic theory as an attempt to construe the universe as an incarnation of logos or, in our more pragmatic terminology, as a completed structure which is, in its entirety, open to rational comprehension. This ambitious theory presents us with a fruitful working hypothesis which we may accept without harm. Let us, for a moment, argue the point in the fashion of the scholastics. If the world is intrinsically nothing but a jumble of discrete things, it will refute the panlogistic hypothesis, but we may then still try to find in this overall chaos limited areas into which we can carry some conceptual order of our own. But the apodictic rejection of the hypothesis of an ordered universe may close our view to a possible design if the world should have one. In short, we do not stand to gain by throwing a potential tool of exploration unseen and untested overboard. Such expectations have proved fruitful in certain areas—witness Quesnay's *Tableaux Économiques*.

In our present view the world does not appear as a single and completed structure, but as an aggregation of partially structured orbits. Again, let us cogitate this fact in the manner of the scholastics. It may be that the world really is an aggregation of partial orders. It is also conceivable that the universe has a completed structure, but we do not yet discern it. The third possibility, however, is the most engaging of all, namely that the human universe is structured differently and to varying degrees in subsequent phases of history. If that were the case we should have to vary and differentiate our structural criteria. Max Weber appears to have had such a differentiation in mind in his essay on *Protestant Ethics and the Spirit of Capitalism*, in which he stressed the primacy of religious motivations in the early history of capitalism, while he conceded the decisive role of an economic determinism in an era of full-fledged capitalism. In extension of this train of thought, we may assume that from the point of view of an evolving system a large portion of the events which take place in an early phase of the development is merely coincidental and unstructured, but as the new order evolves it permeates an increasing area of social behaviour.

8. THE CAUSAL ACCOUNT AND THE EXPOSITORY EXPLANATION RE-EXAMINED

The previous discussion gives a new perspective to our earlier question concerning the role of the causal versus the interpretative analysis of history. These two approaches are usually construed as opposites. Although many students have followed their better judgment in rejecting the necessity of a choice between such an alternative, the question has yet to be faced and answered. Max Weber defined sociology as an expository (or interpretative) explanation of social behaviour. This synthesis of the two methods, the explanatory and the expository, is basically fruitful, although Max Weber's actual application of this synthesis does not completely fill the need. Be that as it may, he clearly realized the necessity of combining the expository and the explanatory procedure.

Let us first of all insist that the essential problem of an expository account of historical phenomena does not revolve around the intentions of the participants. That men have motivations and perceptions about their actions may be taken for granted, and we may readily concede that these perceptions can and should be understood. What makes the problem somewhat complex is the fact that individual actions are, regardless of their motivations, part of a structured whole and must be interpreted as such. Is it the causal type of explanation which will accomplish that or is it the structural account? Actions have, apart from their underlying intent, an objective meaning which is inherent in their structure. This meaning reveals itself through expository analysis, but it is also accessible to causal explanations, so that every occurrence appears in two distinct—though interrelated—perspectives. In the causal view we seek to *construe* an event through as many of its determinants as we are able to isolate. The final construct is largely an approximation of the actual event, and when the approximation is close enough for a given purpose we say the event is *explained*. On the other hand, we *interpret* the same occurrence if we detect its function in the equilibrium of the whole system in which it takes place. The conception of the system as an equilibrium is merely a heuristic device and is equally applicable to changing as well as to static structures. The function of an event is its necessary role in a system or, more specifically, it is the particular manner in which the heuristically assumed equilibrium of the system is conditioned by that event.[1]

The two aspects, the causal and the functional, are interrelated. The functional design of a performance outlines the scope within which the play of causative agents is relevant to the structure of the system. For instance, the investor's acquisitive bent is structurally relevant in so far as he performs the function of equalizing prices. Inasmuch as the price equilibrium

[1] For a similar use of the category of equilibrium see T. Parsons and E. A. Shils, *Towards a General Theory of Action*, Cambridge, Mass., 1951, pp. 107 f, and 120.

The reader is referred to the excellent discussion of 'function' in Robert K. Merton, *Social Theory and Social Structure*, Glencoe, 1949, pp. 21–81.

depends on that function, the free play of investors on the commodity market is structured, while the same motivation may also find an outlet in structurally irrelevant fields of activity (e.g. collecting antiques). Both types of activity are motivated and causally explainable, but only one may be interpreted in functional (in this case: economic) terms.

Two things must be clearly understood at this point. First, the performer need not be aware of the functional meaning of his actions and he is rarely motivated by it. Max Weber's oversimplified conception of the 'meaning' of action—as an intended or unconscious aim—prevented him from realizing the objective or functional meaning of behaviour. One may well assume such a meaning without construing it *à la* Hegel as a goalward drift of events. Second, the structural interpretation of behaviour does not obviate the causal. Quite the contrary. The equilibrium of a system depends for each of its functions on free play of the trial and error type. The motivations which underlie this free play are for all practical purposes fortuitous, and yet their incidence is essential for the maintenance of the equilibrium. It was Hegel's shortcoming that he construed his objective meanings not only teleologically, but without regard to the causal process, and it is for these two reasons that he could not rise above the exegetic perspective of history.

9. THE STRUCTURAL AND THE RANDOM CONCEPT OF CAUSATION. THE PROBLEM OF MULTIPLE CAUSATION

We still face the problem of how the causal explanation of events relates to their functions. To be sure, *what* constitutes a historical or social fact can only be understood through its function. We identify such things as clans, nations, castes, or pressure groups not causally, but through their structural setting. There are many impulses which are at work in the formation of families: the quest for companionship, security, sex, and economic considerations, but it is primarily its child-rearing function which defines the family. Its performance may be consistent with varying combinations of impulses, but certain of its functions must be willed and carried out in order to sustain the institution. Certain incentives are indispensable, while others are merely compatible. In a way, each institution selects the impulses on which it depends for its performance.[1] A minimum of incentives such as the wish for companionship and offspring, the capacity for sharing experience, and self-restraint are necessary for the continued existence of a monogamous union. Impulses not necessary for the functioning of the monogamous family may be nevertheless consistent with it.

These considerations explain to us two things. First, given structures depend on specific causative agents, and their absence may bring about the decay or modification of those structures. A lowered level of economic aspirations is inconsistent with a high rate of capitalization. A saint would be an anomaly on the Stock Exchange or in the intelligence service. Pareto claims that the domestication of élites disqualifies them for their role, while monastic organizations may be able to accommodate traits of competitiveness, but they do not require them.

Second, we may now elucidate the familiar observation that a given phenomenon may be explained on several concurrent levels of causation. We may then speak of a redundant determination. Lynching, for example, has been explained as an inverted expression of a collective guilt feeling, as a phase of an intensified competition for scarce opportunities, as a defence reaction of a threatened social order, and as an extreme case of social distance. How can we account for such a causal redundance? The answer suggests itself if we remember that events are actuated by an overflow of chance impulses. Some are functionally required, others are not. Now, when we interpret the functional meaning of an event we take account of the required motives and ignore the irrelevant ones, namely those which are functionally adventitious. We forget the multilateral sources of action and are baffled when we encounter them in excess of the functional minimum. We have the feeling that the phenomenon is over-explained. But the impression is unwarranted, for we merely face different selections of the same chance aggregation of motives. What makes us feel uncomfortable is the fact that we have not discovered the difference between the required set of causal agents and the abstract classification of random motives which we thus bracket

[1] See T. Parsons, 'The Motivation of Economic Activities', *Essays in Sociological Theory*, *op. cit.*, pp. 206 ff.

together without regard to their functional relevance. It is so when we assemble separately the psychological, sociological, economic, and political 'causes' of the same occurrence. We are confused by the fact that a thing has more than the functionally necessary causes.

10. HISTORIOGRAPHY AND THE STRUCTURAL VIEW

That the causal and the interpretative approach to social events are equally important cannot be questioned once it is clear that given structures require particular causal agents for their existence and that a structural change cannot take place without a corresponding shift in the necessary motivations. The interpretive method helps to visualize the objective or functional meaning of an occurrence and the particular scope within which random motivations operate—relevantly or irrelevantly. The sociologist is, of course, primarily interested in the required minimum of the relevant motives.

We must view social change both as a set of caused events and as a structured process. We may, for instance, seek to determine what circumstances caused the repeal of the English corn laws and we may also explore the meaning of this event in the context of the English industrial revolution. Although we deal merely with two aspects of the same thing, the two procedures open up different perspectives. The first, which reveals the causal sequence of events is the historical perspective, while the latter is the structural. Historiography, when it is true to type, seeks to reconstruct occurrences in the concrete setting of their determinants, while the structural approach bypasses the causal mechanism of change and converges on its functional design. Usually the two methods are complementary, and hardly any study of consequence ignores entirely either aspect of the social. Yet the aims of the two methods are clearly distinct: the causal method reconstructs events in their temporal sequence, while the structural interest focuses on the patterns which operate in a functional system. The latter is the aim of sociology, notwithstanding the fact that it may deal with historical facts. The sociologist is what he is because he identifies concrete structures where other students of human affairs see discrete phenomena or homologies.

II. THE MATRIX OF WORKS AND OF ACTION

So far we have not differentiated between various types of structure. But, by way of illustration, we have referred to such diverse examples as capitalism, the price system, and the baroque. They are all concerned with the structure of various things, and this common denominator up to a certain point justified our practice of dealing with such divergent things on the same plane. Now we have to turn our attention to two distinct areas in which we encounter structures.

Capitalism is a particular context in which persons *act*, and the structure of capitalism designates a system of patterns which govern the relevant actions of the individual. Baroque, on the other hand, is not a matrix of action, but a common pattern of certain accomplished *works*. When they are properly arrayed they reveal a unitary trend toward a known terminus and a common type of configuration. The difference is patent: in the first instance it is actions which make up a structure, in the latter it is works; and it would be as incongruous to speak of a baroque action framework as it is to regard feudalism as a pattern of completed works. The baroque style does not exist *per se*, apart from a multitude of creations which express it, while feudalism exists only in a fluid state of interlocking actions.

The second difference lies in the significance of motives for the understanding of action. While we may not always take account of the incentives which spark an activity, they are, by their very nature, germane to its structure. The profit motive is as inseparable from the entrepreneurial system as are honour and loyalty from the feudal. We view works of art and science, on the other hand, not in a fluid state, not in the act of creation, but as its terminus. One may, of course, detect motivations in every act, but they bear no relationship to the fabric of the finished piece. The hiatus between the objective meaning of a theorem or an art object and the motives of the author is considerably more radical than it is between the motives of an action and the meaning of the deed. This is the same as to say that work structures, in marked contrast to actions, are hardly illuminated by their causative agents.

The third difference between the realms of action and work

pertains to their respective context. The total context of actions forms a system in which usually there is ample room for both willing and reluctant participants. A common style or a current of thought, on the other hand, can only take shape if it finds individuals who somehow adopt and express it. Such expressions as an 'economic style' (used by Sombart) are basically metaphors. In speaking of the structure of art we mean a configuration which takes shape through a succession of works; and we may speak of a structure of thought in reference to the pattern which evolves through a series of completed formulations. The structure of action, on the other hand, outlines an order of interdependence. It is this distinct aspect of actions which permits us to construe them as parts of an equilibrium.

12. THE DISCOVERY OF THE STRUCTURAL RELATIONSHIP BETWEEN ACTION AND WORKS

Naturally we are primarily concerned with social action, and this is also the key subject of sociology. As we have already pointed out, the social is not an aspect or phase of things comparable to aesthetics or law, but is the framework of behaviour. This framework, however, comes in sight on two levels. First, in the perspective of sociology as the science of sociation, and second, in the vista of the sociology of the mind. This twofold perspective corresponds to our distinction between action and work structure.

The structure of action is derived from its group involvement, from the ways in which the performance of one depends on the performances of others. Now, to reconstruct the order in which roles interdepend, we need not take account of the images which the participants form or follow as they play their respective roles. But as soon as we seek to interpret these images in the context in which roles are assumed our frame of reference shifts to that of the sociology of culture.[1]

We are now dealing with roles not directly, but only in their derivative form, as they incarnate themselves in accomplished works. We recognize that a formed imagery conveys elements of the situation in which it is conceived. Moreover, such creations not only reflect their incipient milieu but also reveal the

[1] Sociology of culture or of the mind are used interchangeably.

concerted volition, the action consensus of some who belong to that milieu.

IV. AN OUTLINE OF THE SOCIOLOGY OF THE MIND

It has been the aim of our discussion up to this point to sight the problems which must guide present German sociology. In this attempt we have sought to separate the constructive elements of the heritage of German thought from its dead ballast of looseness and falsehood. We have used Hegel and Marx as symbols of this two-faced tradition which easily lends itself to a distortion of history, but which also carries the promise of significant solutions. We have hoped to show that the preconditions of German sociology make it a peculiarly fertile ground for the growth of a sociology of the mind.

Once the efforts made in various fields of German scholarship mature to a correlative study of social and mental processes, phase by phase, period by period, we should be in a position to identify, at one glance, the social aspirations which are invested in given expressions of thought. We have to study the mechanism by which social action and thought processes permeate one another. One need not fear, as some do, that this endeavour ultimately resolves the realm of thought into nothing but sociology. On the contrary, the proposed approach should add a third dimension to the flat and lifeless perspective in which scholastic doctrinaires have presented the creative works of man. While other lands have advanced the sober analysis of social behaviour, the contributions of German scholarship should make it possible to elaborate the significance of the social process for the objective creations of culture. The promise of a heritage may sometimes balance accomplishments already available. But to capitalize a heritage one has to live in it and at the same time be sufficiently distant from it to see what in it is relevant to the present and what is not. It may be well worth heeding a tradition, not for the sake of its venerable character, but because it stems from past situations which may arise again. One may be alert to the leads which come from the past and yet currently review and sift its patrimony. It is with this aim in mind that we have attempted to separate the dead wood from the live tissue in Hegel's work.

We have, so far, sought to gain workable concepts of history, society, mind, and structure. The remaining portions of this prefatory essay will be concerned with an outline of the proposed type of study.

No sociological system of the mind will be attempted. Systems are too often substitutes for new observations and convenient pigeonholes in which to bury unexplored material. But it may not be idle casuistry to attempt a preliminary sketch of the areas in which the objective manifestations of culture may become, and have already been, distinct objects of sociological exploration. The outline is tentative, but it has its bearing on the subsequent essays in this volume.

1. THE SOCIOLOGY OF THE MIND ON THE AXIOMATIC LEVEL. THE ONTOLOGY OF THE SOCIAL AND ITS BEARING ON THE HISTORICAL CHARACTER OF THOUGHT

This is the perspective in which the essay on 'The Problem of Generations' was conceived. Nothing metaphysical is meant by ontology, but merely a collocation of the basic data of the historical thought process.

The historical character of thought is evidenced not only by the individual consciousness, as it appears from within, phenomenologically as it were, but also by the fact that men cogitate as members of groups and not as solitary beings. The thought of individuals is historically relevant in so far as the groups to which they belong continue through time. The transmission of group understandings from generation to generation is an interpretative as well as a selective process. Each act of transmission sifts, interprets, and selects certain elements from past experience. One cannot properly visualize this interpretative process without the concurrent social selection which takes place as a new generation accepts or modifies the accumulation of the old. The transmission of thought is basically a phase in the succession of generations. It is the analysis of this succession which illuminates the continuity or discontinuity of thought. This raises our first question of how *traditions* originate.

(a) First, we have to distinguish between the mental traits

of *amorphous* and *discontinuous sociations* on the one hand, and *continuous* ones on the other. Here one would have to show how the perpetual formation and dissolution of small groups within the larger society decide the nature of tradition as it crystallizes in the succession of generations. One should further throw light upon the social significance of the impulsive formation of short-lived small groups which do not create traditions, and the bearing of such fluctuating associations on the mentality of the larger society. One should further consider the fact that common understandings in a society exist only to the extent that certain groups are able to assure their continuity through time and space.

(b) This brings us to the sociological aspects of *continuity in time and space*. The continuity of historical time (which, needless to say, is not that of chronological time) depends on the nature of communication in given societies. Not only individuals but also societies can regress to an earlier mental climate if a representative group is displaced by another which has preserved a previous social orientation. Historical discontinuity often results from the disruption of communication between successive élites. Discontinuance in space occurs, on the other hand, when contemporaneous groups break contacts and henceforth act and react in a self-contained fashion. Without these elementary facts we may not understand either the single or multiple stream of thought through history. Such factors as group closure and mobility significantly shape the flow of ideas in space and time.

The category of innovation is as basic to the social ontology of the mind as is tradition and its disruption. How do new things break through the 'cake of custom'? The familiar reference to the genius is not sufficient. To repeat, one need not ignore the role of leading individuals to consider the psychology of the pioneer secondary to the sociological question of what situations provoke new collective expectations and individual discoveries. The answer is almost implied in the question: innovations arise either from a shift in a collective situation or from a changing relationship between groups or between individuals and their groups. It is such shifts which father new adaptations, new assimilative efforts, and new creations.

The reverse phenomenon, the *stereotyping process*, likewise points to constellations which are open to elementary analyses.

(c) Continuity, discontinuance, regression, the stereotyping process, innovations, and the single and the multilineal stream of transmission form the basic sociological categories of mental processes. They constitute the irreducible elements of complex phenomena. Let us add to this array one more category: the *historical dynamics of thought*. It, too, will have to be understood as a social process. By dynamics, we mean the common strain of a large number of events. One may speak of dynamic change, rather than of mutation, if such phenomena as continuity, discontinuity, innovation, and stereotypization become interdependent parts of the same social process.

On the present ontological level we are concerned with dynamics merely as a derivative of the basic forms of sociation and not with concrete, historical processes. Why is it, one may wonder, that mental processes are dynamic, have a common drift, and occur in a directed stream, rather than in a dissociated and random form? Once again we have to trace the phenomenon back to its social matrix.

The relative closure of groups, which is attributable to their provisions for security and to the division of labour, prevents an unlimited mobility of the individual. That this is so is evidenced by certain marginal situations: the disruption of continuity in the medium of thought and sentiment tends to coincide with the dissolution of the groups which sustained the linear trend; their waning cohesiveness is reflected in a growing freedom of choice and a generally weakened norm-consciousness. That thought history takes the form of compact sequences is attributable to the closure of the most communicative groups of a society to alternative impulses.[1]

The relative impermeability and closure of groups explain

[1] On the level of general sociology Max Weber offers a good example of the opposite consequences which the same event may have when it takes effect in differently structured societies: '. . . the opportunity for the mass production of cotton goods, created by the mechanical utilization of the crop, had opposite effects in Europe and America; in Europe cotton provided the impetus for the unionization of free workers—the first major union was organized in Lancashire, England—while in America cotton became the basis of slavery.' Max Weber, *Wirtschaftsgeschichte*, München and Leipzig, 1923, p. 84.

the fact that thought processes are not uniform through space and time and that they occur in distinct configurations. An evolutionary and dynamic trend continues as long as the sustaining group stays cohesive. Within such a continuum the sequences are so interrelated that one cannot be properly understood without the other.

The preceding sketch provides some fragments of a social ontology of the mind. We attempted to trace such basic phenomena as continuity, discontinuity, and dynamics to the elementary forms of sociation. If the sociology of the mind is to become an area of rational study such elementary relationships must be established before concrete analyses may be attempted.

2. THE SOCIOLOGY OF THE MIND ON THE LEVEL OF COMPARATIVE TYPOLOGY

From the elementary factors of sociation, which are not in themselves historical but furnish the mould for the historical process, we advance now to their concrete, empirical variations. And yet we have not abandoned the abstract perspective of the social process, even though we seek to identify the lineaments of elementary groupings in their historical incidence. In other words, we focus on the general aspects of the particular as we attempt to reduce empirical configurations to a rational typology construed from a feasible minimum of variables. Such a typology should ultimately provide us with a canon of variability, a guide to the derivation of complex phenomena from simple ones. That canon should bear equally on the *processes of sociation* and *motive formation.*

With the increased emphasis on the variability of elementary phenomena we approach the third level of analysis: the sociological study of individuation in the medium of history.[1] Here, as also on the previous levels, the method of approach is the same whether we study social action or the objectified documents of culture. It is essential, however, to bear in mind that the transition from the general to the concrete and particular view of social groupings is not abrupt, but takes us through an intermediate field of complex phenomena whose

[1] Compare Karl Mannheim, *Die Gegenwartsaufgaben der Soziologie,* Tübingen, 1932.

typology is an indispensable tool for the mastery of historical structures.

3. THE SOCIOLOGY OF THE MIND ON THE LEVEL OF HISTORICAL INDIVIDUATION

Let us repeat that the sociological grasp of historical change will, in the long run, depend on a prior elaboration of the elementary groupings through various levels of complexity. It is only through this gradual progression towards concrete structures that we equip ourselves for the business of dealing with historical configurations.[1] For every intermediate phase of the typology which we may bypass, we ultimately pay the penalty of having to regress to the *ad hoc* attack, to improvisations in which intuition is likely to play a major role. One can, of course, always take historical facts at their face value and array them without the appropriate sociological apparatus, but such an impromptu venture, equipped only with common sense, will stop short of the structural grasp of the material. Most of the short cuts to the dynamics of history suffer from the common maladies of abrupt and unpremeditated diagnoses. One of these maladies is the tendency toward unreliable interpretations and unverifiable verdicts. The other is the temptation to hypostatize *ex post facto* the inner necessity of a past turn of events without prior examination of the alternative solutions which were potential in one phase or another of the development. This is how history has often been construed in the grand sweep, as the realization of pre-existing ideas, as the resolution of epochal issues, or as the fulfilment of an inexorable destiny. Comte, Hegel, Marx, and Spengler demonstrate these pitfalls of an abrupt and ill-equipped attack.

The essays on 'The Problem of the Intelligentsia' and 'The

[1] Kurt Lewin expresses a similar view in his paper 'Field Theory and Experiment in Social Psychology,' *American Journal of Sociology*, May, 1939: 'It cannot be the task of sociology or psychology to elimate the historical side of their problems. On the contrary, a field-theoretical approach cannot avoid taking into account the historical character of every fact and its specific historical setting' (p. 892). But 'questions of . . . a systematic type of causation will have to be answered experimentally before the dynamic aspect of "historical" problems of origin can be treated satisfactorily.' (p. 892 f.)

Democratization of Culture' hold a middle ground between general sociology and the historical type. These studies are not conducted on the historical level, and they do not confine their subject to any period. The second essay, for example, treats the process of democratization comparatively, as a trend which prevailed in a number of known situations—in the ancient world, in the period of the French revolution, in the late medieval city, and in preliterate societies. The first essay is likewise conceived on this intermediate level. It, too, deals with a complex situation, that of the intelligentsia, but still on the level of variability. Any student of the dynamics of thought will have to come to grips with the variable role of this stratum. A sociological study of merit is still not available on this subject, in spite of the extensive literature which deals with it. Let it be said that in this essay the author's ambition was not to tap untouched sources, but rather to offer samples of the rich store of relevant material which has accumulated in various fields of specialization. Although the approach followed in both essays is still general and comparative, the typology used is no longer elementary and abstract, but of a complexity which at times approximates to the historical view. Still, the author has not attempted a premature historical synthesis, particularly since the present need calls for studies on the intermediate level of complexity.

The following outline, which will conclude this essay, offers a summary sketch of the sociology of the mind as the author conceives it at the present.

V. RECAPITULATION: THE SOCIOLOGY OF THE MIND AS AN AREA OF INQUIRY

The primary aim of the sociology of the mind is the study of mental processes and their significations in their social context. The subject is envisaged on three levels.

A. THE AXIOMATIC VIEW

Attempt at a social ontology of the mind with a view to its historical character. Analysis of the basic constants of sociation which condition continuity, tradition, discontinuity, and the dynamics of thought.

The problem of continuity may be approached under the following three aspects:

(a) *Amorphous and discontinuous sociations as the bases of discontinuity, and the lapse of tradition in the stream of mental processes.*
(b) *Continuous contacts in space and time as the bases of concurrent and historical traditions.* The phenomena of continuity; interruption, regression, single and multilineal traditions. The succession of generations, stereotyping, and innovations.
(c) *The contingency of dynamics.* The relationship between group closure and the incidence of compact periods of thought. The significance of the initial situation.

B. COMPARATIVE TYPOLOGY

An attempt to elaborate the concrete variations of elementary social processes and to identify their corresponding variations in the realm of thought.

C. THE SOCIOLOGY OF INDIVIDUATION

I. *The Genesis of Structures.*

(a) The relationship of social motivations to thought structures.
(b) The significance of social groupings for the genesis of standpoints. The relevance of structured situations to concept formation.

II. *The Dynamics of Structures.* Social change and its significance for the concrete dynamics of thought.

PART TWO

THE PROBLEM OF THE INTELLIGENTSIA:

AN ENQUIRY INTO ITS PAST AND PRESENT ROLE

1. THE SELF-DISCOVERY OF SOCIAL GROUPS

We live in a period of growing self-awareness. It is not any fundamentally new faith that sets our age off from others, but an increasing consciousness and preoccupation with ourselves.

What is the nature of this contemporary consciousness? Man in earlier periods lived in an atmosphere of beliefs without the urge to take stock of himself. He lived without caring to know how. He accepted faith, knowledge, and action as we accept life itself. Man of an earlier age lived timelessly and without the need to reflect on the conditions of his existence. To us articulateness has become essential. We want to name not only the known but also the unknown. The urge to think, of course, is not new, but the aim of earlier thought was self-assertion and reassurance, and it was in this quest for security that man accepted himself and his beliefs unconditionally.

The trend of modern thought points in another direction. Its aim is not assurance and not reconciliation with the given conditions of life. The person whose circumstances change does not perceive himself in fixed and definitive terms.[1] His outlook can never become compact, for it breaks out of any set frame before it can finally crystallize around a well-formed image of

[1] We do, from time to time, witness collective reactions against social mobility by those whose station in life has become fixed; but they do not form a representative type of our industrial society.

the world. Neither has stout self-sufficiency remained an ideal. Self-containment is an ideal of a soil-bound society, while the representative type of our age has the characteristics of a Proteus who perennially transcends and reconstitutes himself, and whose foremost motives are renovation and reformation.

The individual who fitted the medieval mould sought to relive an old-established role. The new type, as first formed in single examples since the dissolution of the compact view of the Middle Ages, is a perennial seeker of new horizons. He seeks to peer behind each new truth and in the process he discovers again and again the adventitious nature of particular situations. While the stationary type accepts each condition as a timeless order of existence, the dynamic seeker dispels false absolutes and deliberately dwells on the finite and conditional realm of things. But as he ventures beyond the area of an established world-view he faces at each turn the perennial problem: how can he who knows about his own conditional existence reach and carry out unconditional decisions?

Different as man in various ages may be, he posits similar questions about himself: he wants to know how to think of himself in order to act. Some conception of the world and the self, unspoken though it may be, accompanies every move we make. The question, Who are we?, has always been asked, but it is always through the medium of different objects that such questions are faced. Man hardly ever wonders about himself unless he is confronted with things or situations. If someone asked me who and what I am I should be at a loss for an answer, but not if I am questioned about what I am in the eyes of A or B. We understand ourselves primarily through the views of others. The decisive question, however, is who is the other in whose perspective we see ourselves?

What holds true for the individual applies almost identically to groups. They, too, have a 'reflected self', to use Cooley's expressive term. The history of collective self-interpretations, which is not the subject of this essay, is in a sense the evolution of consciousness, and each phase of this development is characterized by the nature of those others in whose image men view themselves. The longest of these periods is marked by man's attempts to understand himself *vis-à-vis* a personal God, a relationship which varied from the master-servant situation to that of father and child. Each of these relationships expressed an existing social paradigm and a set of actual norms whose ultimate guardianship rested with a personal God.

The waning of this unitary world view of the Middle Ages marks the beginning of a long search for a new guardian of new norms. It was after various intermediate solutions that the Enlightenment arrived at the new guarantor of a new order: reason. We may, in retrospect, qualify the timeless norms of reason as the rules of the competitive order of the middle classes. One should not, however, draw the outlines of this order too narrowly, for it includes the courts of absolute princes and the newly constituted bureaucracy.

The next absolute emerged after the defeat of the French revolution and the subsequent restoration, namely 'history'. It was through the deification of history that the opponents of the middle-class revolutions were able to prove that the absolute reason which these revolutions enthroned was merely one of its possible variations, all of which are the creations of history. This is not the occasion to show how in this rearguard action the philosophy of rationalism abandoned its absolute claims by conceding their temporal character, or how it retreated to a more abstract and formal conception of reason. But even in this secondary and formalistic version rationalism could not hold its ground against the rise of new and substantive affirmations.

As reason itself appeared to be a function of history the basis of self-interpretation shifted again. No point of view could be defended any longer on the ground of its intrinsic rationality, for only history could legitimize—or invalidate—a political claim. It appeared more desirable to be on the side of the *Weltgeist* or to be the exponent of the next phase of history than to be a prophet of timeless truths. Historical pragmatism took precedence over revelation. Some wished to identify their viewpoint with the ultimate verdict of history, while others preferred the sanction of the next stage. Among the notable formulations are: 'Every epoch is near to God'; 'World history is a world tribunal', and even more poignantly: 'God sides with the strongest battalions'. These expressions of historical self-vindication, coming as they do from Ranke, Hegel, and Marx, are all couched in the language of historical pragmatism.

The ground on which men sought to understand and to assert themselves shifted once more when the historical argument gave way to the sociological.

The sociolgical interpretation superseded the historical by virtue of its more basic question: Whose work is that perpetual shift which creates new norms and revokes old ones, and whose history is it? Indeed, on second thought it must be plain that the word 'change' may have meaning only as the verb of a sentence which states that something changes. When used as a subject history becomes a mythical and incomprehensible entity which takes the vacated place of God the creator. Although some philosophers of history still occupy themselves with the nature of historicity, the obscure verbalism of post-Hegelian vintage has given way to a train of thought which may be summed up in the following simple postulates:

(a) Men are the real authors of change, not history.
(b) The shifts of the 'intellect' are the mutations of the human mind.
(c) It is not the mind of the isolated individual which changes but the perceptions of sociated persons.
(d) The history of the human mind expresses the consecutive tensions and reconciliations of groups.

We deal no longer with verbal substitutes but with the observed actions and periodical perplexities of men. Thus, the ground for the self-interpretation of man has shifted once more. No longer does he see himself in the mirror of a personal God, reason, history, or a *Weltgeist*, but in the perspective of his social pursuits. Now, one may ask: Is this sociological panorama not another passing view, to be succeeded by better ones? Maybe, but so far no other method has superseded the sociological, and no other attempt has proved more basic. We cannot fail to note that in the succession of interpretative endeavours each is more inclusive and basic than the last, and each new solution both embraces and resolves the earlier. This is truer of the sociological frame of reference than of any other, so much so that wherever the discussion is free and open, sociology has become the inescapable ground of self-validation for radicals, moderates, and conservatives alike. No one today who is unable to gain a sociological and historical understanding of himself can find his bearings in the present state of affairs. Two further observations seem to follow from this.

A. In each epoch men arrive at some form of self-evaluation which is more or less adequate to the mastery of their circumstances. It is usually individual pioneers who first adapt their views to a changed situation in order to restore some measure of consistency between their actions and thoughts. Gradually, others, who at first resisted the new views, follow suit as their situations likewise change.

B. One need not see a symptom of decay in the gradual displacement of the earlier personality trait of stalwart contentment by the newer strains of self-scrutiny, self-revision, and adaptability. The new traits evolve in response to an increasingly dynamic world which has added an urban way of life to the rural, an industrial to the agrarian, and a bureaucratic to the feudal. The pioneer has become a central figure in this shift, for he accepts it for what it is and is ever ready to review his position in a changed order.[1] In this effort sociology proves a superior tool because its working hypotheses leave fewer facts out of account and fit more of the relevant circumstances than do others. The hypotheses of a world governed by a vengeful ruler was adequate to a situation in which nature produced the essentials of life. The dependence on the whims of rain and wind is appropriately expressed by a *Weltanschauung* to which fate or an implacable God are basic. Agriculture is one of the first concerns in which technology begins to displace fate. The shift from the digging stick to the tractor marks an accelerated shrinkage of the domain of unpredictability, and in the course of this displacement the assumption of an inscrutable and all-pervading will loses its relevance to an increasing number of situations. In this new state of affairs a synopsis which reconciles man's thought of the universe with his chronic perplexities no longer fits the need. At this point the cultivator gives precedence to a detailed plan of action over a reassuring conception of the cosmos.

The criteria of an adequate self-evaluation change similarly in the realm of social organization. A general synopsis which

[1] See in this connection David Riesman's observations on the passing of traditional motivations and the consecutive rise of the 'inner-directed' and the 'other-directed' character. *The Lonely Crowd*, New Haven, 1950.

harmonizes thought with social behaviour is adequate to a relatively stable and simply structured society. As long as man's social relations are mainly of the primary order in which conformity, obedience, and the practice of reciprocity assure the necessary performances, the hypothesis of a preordained plan presents the attainable optimum of an ethical orientation. But a changing society and a dense and specialized population cannot function without a working plan, understood at least by some, which is able to explain and guide even the minor details of the necessary performances. If today we ask ourselves who and what we are we mean to rediscover our place in the existing social order.

Our age is characterized not only by a growing self-awareness but also by our capacity to determine the concrete nature of this consciousness: we live in a time of conscious *social* existence. This process of self-clarification began from below. To be sure, the middle classes had early in their history some sort of a sociological orientation and, in a sense, one can spot sociological insights in the political thinking of the patriciate which ruled the city states of the Renaissance. We may say the same of the princely chancelleries of the territorial states, and neither should one ignore in this connection the sociological significance of such writers of the restoration period as de Maistre. But only in the thinking of the proletariat did the sociological point of view become all-inclusive. The proletariat was the first group to attempt a consistently sociological self-evaluation and to acquire a systematic class-consciousness.

Social consciousness is no longer a privilege of the proletariat; we find it also in the upper classes, and it evolves more and more in every discernible grouping, including those created by differences of age and sex.

What then is the typical origin of group-consciousness? It begins with groups attempting to take stock of their position in a new situation. Women, for example, are relative newcomers in the company of such groups. It is no mere accident and no fad that inquiries concerning the nature and position of women, youth, the aged, and the middle-aged have been proliferating in greater numbers than ever before. Each of these groups sought to redefine its place in society, but in this endeavour it was not only forced to take stock of itself but also to deal critically with a set of ready interpretations. Women used to accept the male definition of their role; more than that, women used to see themselves as men saw them. The awareness of this fact marked the beginning of feminine group consciousness. A collective definition, such as the masculine interpretation of womanhood, is not a mere hypothesis, a replaceable theory; it is rather the source of collective habits and actions. As a group, therefore, reviews its own definition supplied by an other, it begins to revise its relationship to the other group. We only have to recall Ibsen's *Doll's House*, presenting for the first time in modern literature the clash of two conceptions of womanhood. A new self-evaluation, such as Nora arrived at in Ibsen's play, rarely succeeds without the confirmation of like-situated and like-intentioned individuals.

The same is true, *mutatis mutandis*, of the German youth. It produced a host of philosophical theories, all of which reacted to a current conception of youth conceived by an earlier generation. In these earlier views youth was defined in a merely derivative role, as a preliminary stage to maturity. This is precisely what the various youth proclamations assailed in asserting the autonomous value of being young. The social impetus of this emanicaption movement came from the Industrial Revolution which offered unprecedented opportunities to adaptable young men with initiative, in preference to older men with set views and work habits. In a stable society of farms and artisans the guardians of tradition, the mature and the aged, are the public interpreters of the social order which they construe in their own favour, while an industrial society places an increasing premium on youth and lowers the currency of accumulated wisdom.[1] (It would be interesting to explore the question whether the declining usefulness of the

[1] Let me quote an interesting observation of Max Weber's which bears on the problem: 'Age is originally the seat of honour. The aged are, apart from their experience and the prestige which it confers, inevitably the holders of an honorific status in communities which in all their concerns are solely oriented toward tradition, convention, and customary or sacred law. For the aged know tradition, they are the most effective arbiters in disputes, and their recommendations, their prudence, their "placet", or their belated endorsement are taken as guarantees *vis-à-vis* the supernatural powers that the decisions reached were correct. Among persons of similar economic position the elders are simply those most advanced in

older age groups necessarily undermines their ideological role. To answer this we should have to ascertain what constellations enhance the social scope of the older generations and, conversely, which situations favour the young. The dynamics of the Industrial Revolution is only one of several factors.)

Social consciousness does not always coincide with the ascendency of groups, for the conscious reaction to social change is a modern phenomenon. This is, as we have already pointed out, characteristic of all strata and not only of the proletariat, although its self-awareness was the first and most poignant of these manifestations. That such aspirations are successful only in our time may be attributed to various circumstances, but it is evident that so long as a group is dominated by another it accepts and lives the role which is imposed on it, as a matter of course.

Two factors make such a social self-awareness possible. First, contemporary society has evolved a great variety of controls which take the place of coercive power as the main guarantee of super- and subordination.[1] Second, contemporary society has assumed a large share of the educational and disciplinary control which primary groups and communal organizations used to exercise.

Let us turn to the first factor. If we ask ourselves why it is

years in the household community, the clan or the neighbourhood. The relative prestige of age as such varies considerably. Where food is scarce those past the age of physical usefulness are considered a burden. Chronic warfare weakens the position of the old in relation to those of military age, and it often stimulates a democratic consensus of the young *vis-à-vis* the prestige of the old. This is also the case in periods of economic and political changes of a revolutionary character, whether peaceful or violent, and also in periods of weakened religious controls, in which sacred traditions are at an ebb. Age, on the other hand, is held in high esteem wherever experience is an actual asset and wherever tradition remains a vital force.' Max Weber, *Wirtschaft und Gesellschaft*, 1st ed., p. 609, Tübingen, 1922. See also Kingsley Davis' remarks on the situation of Western youth: 'The Sociology of Parent-Youth Conflict', *American Sociological Review*, August, 1940, pp. 523–535.

[1] David Riesman describes an advanced stage of the process which crystallizes a multitude of mutually balancing pressure groups, veto groups as he calls them, 'each of which has struggled for and finally attained a power to stop things conceivably inimical to its own interests and, within far narrower limits, to start things.' *The Lonely Crowd*, Garden City, N.Y., 1953, p. 247.

that class conflicts in antiquity and the later antagonism between masters and journeymen did not occasion class-consciousness, we have to look to the circumstances under which a later industrial society produced free workmen and free contractual partnerships.

Success on the free competitive market demands a continuous awareness of social change. The necessary adaptation to these shifts requires immediate responses and independent judgment free from conventional or mythological delusions. The individual who must live by his wits and seize his opportunities as they arise no longer feels committed to a prescribed way of life. The immediate effect of this new state of affairs is an increased rationality, first in economic behaviour, then in certain derivative situations, and finally in the conceptualization of one's own interests. These situations teach men to orient themselves from their own point of view and to disregard traditional ideologies of an alien stamp. This is the first step towards social self-awareness. It evolves first individually, but it takes on a collective character as like-situated individuals discover the common elements in their position and arrive at a common definition of their roles. The resulting group ideologies arise in disregard of traditional sentiments, as they relate to blood, regional ties, or caste honour.

The second factor which favours group consciousness is the modern practice of educating the person in a socially neutral atmosphere, while its absence in the traditional type of education inhibited the rise of a new and independent group orientation. It has often been pointed out that journeymen could not acquire a class awareness of their own, even in times of their economic decline, so long as they lived with their master's family. This common primary group situation of masters and journeymen or apprentices perpetuated the latters' loyalty to the guild and their hopes to join the ranks of master craftsmen. This very situation blocked the rise of that class resentment which later led the proletariat to its self-centred conception of society. The evolution of a feminine group consciousness shows distinct analogies. It began at the very moment when women entered vocations and made the competitive situation on the market the basis of their careers. This marked the beginning of the conflict between the traditional and patriarchal interpretation of the feminine role and the views which working women formed of themselves.

Let us sum up the argument presented so far.

1. Ideologies coexist in an antagonistic relationship to one another. The most radical form of this antagonism consists of the unspoken assumptions and the suggestive framework of thought by which dominant groups inhibit the independent self-awareness of subordinate strata. Since these latter groups do not find an adequate outlet for their social impulses they usually resort to repression and sublimation, to use Freud's terminology, while those in control are freer in so far as they are able to react in accordance with their own conceptions of themselves. This is also characteristic of the state of affairs between men and women inasmuch as a male-dominated society grants men a large measure of freedom of expression, while it confines female conduct to a more rigid precept of feminine propriety. The male control of feminine expression need not be confused with the more general proposition that one cannot live in a group without some measure of inhibition. The question is whether a group creates its own inhibitions or must accept them from another.

2. A significant trend of modern society (of which more will be said in the subsequent essay on *Democratization*) may be seen in the fact that each group tends to evolve its own perspective and to feel uncommitted by the public interpretation of the existing order.

3. This is also the reason for the well-observed, but unexplained, phenomenon that democratization in its first stage does not produce equality and universal like-mindedness, but accentuates group divergencies. Indeed, we witness the continued growth of nationalism rather than cosmopolitanism.[1] The

[1] The democratic process occasioned this same manifestation as early as the late Middle Ages. Witness the development of regional styles in Bavaria, Swabia, Franconia and other provinces. Dehio correctly alludes to the social roots of this development (without adopting, however, the sociological point of view) as follows: 'After the international currents which dominated the 14th century, the 15th strikes us as an eminently German century. . . . This was due to the fact that art struck roots in new strata untouched before. Art became more national because it became more

democratic process which enhances the general capacity for self-determination primarily integrates people in like situations and it awakens consciousness of kind on a national scale before it expands group consciousness to a global dimension. Nationalism is in this regard a phenomenon parallel to feminism and the German youth movement.

2. OUTLINES OF A SOCIOLOGICAL THEORY OF THE INTELLIGENTSIA

The rise of the intelligentsia marks the last phase of the growth of social consciousness. The intelligentsia was the last group to acquire the sociological point of view, for its position in the social division of labour does not provide direct access to any vital and functioning segment of society. The secluded study and the dependence on printed matter afford only a derivative view of the social process. No wonder that this stratum remained long unaware of the social character of change. And those who became eventually sensitized to the social pulse of the time found their way towards a sociological evaluation of their own position blocked by the proletariat.

This was not an accident, nor did it happen by design. The proletariat had already perfected its own world view when those latecomers appeared on the scene, and that world view had the same hypnotic effect as had earlier ideologies which dominant groups used to impose on subordinate strata. It was quite natural that the proletariat placed itself in the centre of its world view. All groups which grope for a social orientation first attempt a self-enhancing interpretation of society, and

popular: This is the double meaning of its increased *popularity*. Our initial observation that the 15th century was an eminently German century must be qualified by a second observation: it was the century of the *third estate*. The burghers supplied its impetus and its patterns, in marked contrast to the aristocratic and universal art of the climactic period of the Middle Ages.' G. Dehio, *Geschichte der deutschen Kunst*, 2nd ed., Berlin—Leipzig, 1923, Vol. II, p. 132. The second stage of the democratic process which began in the period of the French Revolution and at the end of the revived feudalism of the territorial states, again coincides with nationalism as a momentous force of integration—in opposition to the mere ideological cosmopolitanism of the enlightenment. Nationalism in this new phase expanded its scope from the regional to the national—both in its cultural and political aspects.

this bias corrects itself only on a higher level of reflectivity—a level which we approach through the sociology of knowledge. Subsequent strata, therefore, had to come to grips with the entrenched ideology of the proletariat before they could understand themselves. This process closely parallels the earlier emancipation of the proletariat from the ideologies which previously inhibited its class-consciousness. As the scattered groups of the intelligentsia set out to find their sociological bearings they began to interpret themselves within the framework which the proletariat evolved for itself. This accounts for the suddenly lowered self-esteem of the intelligentsia; its former conceit now gave way to subservience.

The earlier conceit of the intellectual is partly explained by the fact that so long as he was the only accredited interpreter of the world he could claim in it a significant role, even though he acted mostly in the service of other strata. The history of the intelligentsia is full of instances of its self-importance, from the imperiousness of priestly strata and their rivals, the prophets, through the poets laureate of the humanists to the historical visionaries of the enlightenment and the romantic philosophers who pronounced the verdicts of the *Weltgeist*. True, we know of the long uphill struggle which raised sculptors, architects, and painters from the ranks of craftsmen and servants to the respected position of artists, largely since the late Middle Ages and the Renaissance. These, however, were exceptions. Just as some painters for highly placed patrons would not forget to portray themselves in some corner of an allegorical picture, so did also philosophers reserve for themselves a preferred niche in their *Weltanschauung*. The pundit's faith in his own mission, however, lasts only so long as he holds the key to the secrets of the universe, so long as he is the thinking organ of other strata. His presumptuousness ends when he encounters the commanding world view of another group. The servility of some modern free-lance intellectuals stems from a feeling of helplessness which overcomes him when he, the magician of concepts and king in the realm of ideation, is challenged to establish his social identity. He discovers that he does not have any, and he becomes keenly conscious of this.

We have to acknowledge the imposing consistency with which the proletariat reinterpreted the social universe. One must ask, on the other hand, to what extent this new point of view has forced an alien and inadequate self-appraisal on the intelligentsia. Let us review Marx' conceptual apparatus as he tailored it to the needs of one stratum.

A. What is the axis of a proletarian sociology? It is a class sociology and it operates with only one sociological category: class. Within this narrow framework a phenomenon is either class or non-class. This technique of prejudging a subject has often been employed before in order to undermine an opponent's self-assurance, by confronting him with an alternative within which he cannot assert himself. To use an analogy: a woman who is made to see herself in the alternative of housewife or harlot will be unable to associate herself with any of the additional roles which the emancipation movement made possible.

This is one of the most sublimated but also the most spleenless methods of forming an ideology. It is not a calculated stratagem. It confuses the opponent only because it springs from an aggressive and unreflected self-assertion. The proletariat itself had once been the passive object of this very method of ideological control. And so the intellectuals, inexperienced in sociological thinking, have come to face the alternative, class or non-class, to discover their own nullity; for since they are no class they surely must be a social non-entity.

This abrupt loss of self-certainty took two typical courses.

The first was the choice of those intellectuals who joined working-class parties. It was not an alliance of equals, but a self-effacing willingness to play the role of the proletarian functionary, precisely as some predecessors had championed the cause of earlier ruling classes.

The second course was most clearly exemplified by Scheler. He unhesitatingly adopted the most radical reappraisals of his time and, as if guided by a demon, moved from a religious and historical philosophy towards a sociological orientation. Having experienced the impact of social forces on thought he fell under the spell of an intellectual nihilism, and near the end of his life he envisaged a book on 'The Impotence of the Mind'.

Sociological thinking need not drive the intelligentsia to defeatism and self-derision. A man merely has to be ready to depart from imposed interpretations and to think from his own point of view—as nowadays every group must—in order to find his place in the changing order of things; one may form political alliances, but with a consciousness of one's own position.

It should have become clear that the intelligentsia is by no means a class, that it cannot form a party,[1] and that it is incapable of concerted action. Such attempts were bound to fail, for political action depends primarily on common interests which the intelligentsia lacks more than any other group. Nothing is farther from this stratum than singlemindedness and cohesiveness. A government official, a political agitator or disaffected writer of the radical type, a clergyman, and an engineer have few tangible interests in common. There is closer affinity between the 'proletarian' writer and the proletariat than between the rest of the intellectual types mentioned. It is common knowledge, on the other hand, that the renegade intellectual sons of the bourgeoisie or the aristocracy react differently from other, socially less mobile, members of their own strata. Beside their own varied class interests, intellectuals carry into their vocational situation a special motivation and a particular attitude which the sociologist cannot fail to identify.

The intelligentsia is an interstitial stratum and the proletarian sociology, centred as it is around the concepts of class and party, could not but assign to this classless aggregation the role of a satellite of one or another of the existing classes and parties. Such a conception naturally conceals the peculiar motivations of the intellectual, and it is apt to paralyze his self-appraisal. It is quite understandable that the politician has little use for the peculiarities of such politically nondescript existences, for he deals with clear-cut tangibles which join or divide people. He can afford to think exclusively in political terms and to ignore politically irrelevant groupings. The sociologist, on the other hand, is a diagnostician of social phenomena and it is his business to differentiate.

One may sum up the essential characteristics of this stratum as follows. It is an aggregation between, but not above, the

[1] For an account of such attempts in France compare H. Platz, *Geistige Kämpfe im modernen Frankreich*, Munich, 1922, particularly chap. VII; also E. R. Curtius, *Der Syndikalismus der geistigen Arbeiter in Frankreich*, and V. Hüber, *Die Organisierung der Intelligenz*, Leipzig, 3rd ed., 1910.

classes. The individual member of the intelligentsia may have, and often has, a particular class orientation, and in actual conflicts he may side with one or another political party. Moreover, his choices may be consistent and characteristic of a clear-cut class position. But over and above these affiliations he is motivated by the fact that his training has equipped him to face the problems of the day in several perspectives and not only in one, as most participants in the controversies of their time do. We said he is *equipped* to envisage the problems of his time in more than a single perspective, although from case to case he may act as a partisan and align himself with a class. His acquired equipment makes him potentially more labile than others. He can more easily change his point of view and he is less rigidly committed to one side of the contest, for he is capable of experiencing concomitantly several conflicting approaches to the same thing. This proclivity may occasionally conflict with the class interest of the same person. His exposure to various facets of the same issue and his easier access to other and diverse appraisals of the situation make him feel at home in a larger area of a polarized society, but they make him also a less reliable ally than is the person whose choices rest on a smaller selection of the many facets in which reality presents itself. As a matter of political experience intellectuals are less often tempted to vote the straight ticket and to plead as they always have done or their fathers used to do.

We cannot explain these things if we accept the expedient simplifications of the party functionary or a class sociology, and yet a common awareness of these seemingly elusive facts is indicated by the customary distinction between the 'educated' and 'uneducated'. The average person senses as great a difference and social distance between these two categories as between rich and poor or employer and employee. This is also well expressed by the incomparably greater self-consciousness which people feel about their lack of education than about their lack of means. Such differentials do not become apparent in a class-centred frame of sociological reference.

Let us re-emphasize at this point that intellectuals do not form an exalted stratum above the classes and are in no way better endowed with a capacity to overcome their own class attachments than other groups. In my earlier analysis of this stratum I used the term 'relatively uncommitted intelligentsia' (*relativ freischwebende Intelligenz*), which I accepted from Alfred Weber, without any thought of an entirely unattached group free of class liaisons. The epithet '*relativ*' was no empty word. The expression simply alluded to the well-established fact that intellectuals do not react to given issues as cohesively as for example employees and workers do. Even these show, from case to case, variations in their responses to given issues; still more do the so-called middle classes, and least uniform is the political behaviour of the intelligentsia. The natural history of this phenomenon is a topic of this essay and of an earlier study.[1] After this reminder, it should not be expected that the critics will again conveniently simplify my thesis to the easily refutable proposition that the intelligentsia is an exalted stratum above all classes or that it is privy to revelations. In regard to the latter my claim was merely that certain types of intellectuals have a maximum opportunity to test and employ the socially available vistas and to experience their inconsistencies. I shall come back to this later.

3. HOW SOCIAL GROUPS ARE IDENTIFIED

To determine the social locus of the intelligentsia we shall have to re-examine first those sociological procedures which operate exclusively with the concepts of class and class interest. But first we shall differentiate between *class position*, *class*, *and conscious class*.[2] The first designates the location of the individuals and groups in the social order. Earlier we have pointed out that the term 'social position' is more inclusive than 'political position'. Social location is a general term of reference to the continuing exposure of individuals to like influences or to the same opportunities, inducements, and restrictions. A common social habitat does not necessarily create like interests; for example, the common minority position of different ethnic groups in itself can be conceived without the involvement of

[1] *Ideology and Utopia*, pp. 136–146, London and New York, 1936.

[2] Geiger's methodological observation is here highly pertinent: 'The question of the correct class concept is in itself meaningless. A class concept becomes inappropriate only when it is derived from the standard of one group and is applied to another.' Theodor Geiger, *Die Schichtung des deutschen Volkes*, p. 1, Stuttgart, 1932.

group interests.[1] The term 'location' may even be widened to include such phenomena as generations and age groups.[2] *Class position*, on the other hand, does imply a certain affinity of interests within a diversified society which selectively allocates power and distributes differential prerogatives and economic opportunities.[3]

To advance from the concept of position or location to the concept of class we must first familiarize ourselves with the positional character of behaviour. We understand man primarily through his behaviour and motivations, and these, in their turn, depend on his orientation in a given situation. We speak then of a *positional behaviour* if a person's conduct reveals his reaction to his location. The term *positional orientation* must not be construed deterministically, since a given position permits more than one type of reaction. At the same time a behaviour is positional only if it is guided by the impulses which are latent in a location, as contrasted with a child or an insane person, neither of whom discerns his position or responds to it. A location has an objective and a subjective component. The objective character of a location can be defined without regard to the behaviour of its occupants, for a position simply exists, no matter how and whether one responds to it. Although a position is actualized and becomes discernible only through the behaviour of its holders, they may exist in it without responding to it in a predictable or typical manner.

The most important form of positional behaviour is that which is solely guided by the economic interests of an individual as they are actualized primarily in the market. Now we may speak of a *class* if individuals act uniformly in accordance with their like interests and like position in the productive process.

[1] The difference between class-position and conscious class is clearly seen by M. Sherif and H. Cantril: 'It requires leadership and organization to transform a loose numerical class into a compact psychological class. It is therefore important to bear in mind the distinction between objective and subjective class differentiation.' *The Psychology of Ego Involvements*, New York, 1947, p. 145.

[2] Compare this author's essay on 'The Problem of Generations', *op. cit.*

[3] The various types of status and status-conceptions which may become associated with identical positions are well illustrated by E. C. Hughes, 'Dilemmas and Contradictions of Status', *American Journal of Sociology*, March 1945, pp. 353–359; see also M. Sherif and H. Cantril, *The Psychology of Ego Involvements*, *op. cit.*, pp. 140 ff.

A *conscious class*, on the other hand, is constituted by the tendency of its members to act collectively in accordance with a conscious evaluation of their class position in relation to all other strata of society.

Class position, class, and conscious class constitute three levels of differentiation. Their personnel need not, and usually do not, coincide. Class parties, unions, and pressure groups are often manifestations of the third phase—the conscious class.

Before entering into an analysis of the intelligentsia let us make a few retrospective comments.

A. We do not maintain that human behaviour is solely guided by economic interests, but we do submit that the structure of actions so motivated provides us with a useful model for sociological analysis; a fact well demonstrated by Max Weber.[1] Although traditional conduct in itself is the opposite of rational behaviour, it often preserves a previous core of rationality. Tradition may stem from past interests as much as from magic.

B. Quite often the layman may not identify the play of rational interests in irrationally motivated actions. The observance of religious precepts, in itself non-rational, often serves rational ends. Max Weber's familiar analysis of Puritan asceticism furnishes a good illustration. The primary motivation of this asceticism was unquestionably religious, yet it corresponded to a rational attitude towards economic values, demanded by an evolving commercial capitalism. In the long run man cannot act in complete disregard of his location and undo the social conditions of his existence; what matters, therefore, is what he does and not what he thinks he does. Actions may consistently attain a certain end without being motivated by it. Quite often an infinite series of minor, though unconscious, adaptations will ultimately redirect an originally dysfunctional type of behaviour into rational channels.

C. Practically everybody has ambivalent motivations and more than one social habitat. Class position, therefore, is one of several locations and one of several motivations for action. This is particularly true of the intellectual, chiefly because of his greater involvement in inter-class communication. His

[1] Max Weber, *Wirtschaft und Gesellschaft*, Tübingen, 1922, chap. II: 'The Concept of Social Behaviour.'

political choices depend not only on his class position but on the understandings with others outside his class.

D. These considerations must remain meaningless as long as one adheres to the dogmatic conception of class as the Marxist theory presents it. From this viewpoint we cannot deal adequately with the intelligentsia as a social phenomenon. Contrary to its positivistic intention, the Marxist philosophy follows the medieval type of conceptual realism whose ontology by-passes the individual. This is a Hegelian trait of Marxism. It conceives class in the nature of a macro-anthropos and the individual merely as the tool of a collective leviathan. Marx' *class* appears to be as independent of the perceptions and reactions of the individual as the medieval universals. Once classes are so conceptualized they can easily be turned into verbalistic pigeonholes, and every individual is said to belong to one or another. Although the doctrine is not taught in this fashion, such a conclusion is hardly avoidable for those who think in the alternative of class or non-class. From here one cannot come to terms with such an elusive and ambivalent phenomenon as the intelligentsia except to declare the distinctive nuances which delineate this group as irrelevant and to proceed to identify it with one or another class, or to diagnose it as the tail of one or another kite.

The analysis of this stratum gives us an opportunity to uncover the fallacy of such an approach. Class as distinguished from class position cannot be thought of independently of the actions of individuals, but only as a group which homogeneously reacts to an identical economic position. Only his class motivations make an individual a member of a class. Once this is clear we are able to attach some significance to the varieties of motivations for political choices. Some persons are swayed by only one preponderant motivation, while others are subject to conflicting inducements. This is true not only of intellectuals, but of anybody who belongs to a well-entrenched occupation to which outsiders have no easy access.

We understand ambivalent situations only if we abandon the Hegelian realism which gives the Marxist concept of class its ironclad character and which makes the Marxist view impervious to a concrete psychology. We have to base the concept of class on actions and on individual preferences to be able to appreciate alternative situations, and to take cognizance of the fact that a class does not completely absorb and explain all actions of the concrete person. If, in spite of all this, we do not completely adopt the procedure of the sociological nominalists who attribute reality solely to the perceptions and acts of the individual, it is because they are prone to overlook collective situations in which individuals live and act, and the relative independence and dynamics of group structures. That the individual is the primary seat of reality is of course an assumption which seems inescapable to us, but it must not blind us to the objective conditions which confront the individual at every turn. These conditions channel and motivate his behaviour whether he is aware of them or not. The extreme consequence of the nominalistic view is an unstructured world, a social vacuum which makes the actions of the concrete person just as incomprehensible as a doctrinaire realism.

The procedure for which we plead is based on the following considerations. We contend with the realists that the behaviour of the individual cannot be adequately understood apart from his social relations. But we reject the 'realistic' practice of allocating—for political or religious reasons—priority to one particular grouping such as the class, race, church, or nation, and we oppose the interpretation of all other social aggregations as derivatives of the one 'real' grouping. We accept the aim of the nominalists to comprehend the behaviour and motivations of the person, but we oppose their tendency to construe the individual as a socially detached and residual entity. We believe that the individual as such can be understood only through his participation in a multitude of groupings some of which are coordinated while others overlap or even conflict. What makes a single being sociologically relevant is not his comparative detachment from society, but his multiple involvement. The process of individuation takes place in the very process in which the person becomes identified with overlapping and conflicting groups.

It is in this sense that subsequently we shall concern ourselves with multiple affiliations and ambivalent motivations, particularly as they are present in the situation of the intelligentsia.

4. TYPES OF INTELLIGENTSIA

We turn now from preliminaries to the factors which permit us to speak of the intelligentsia as a single social type. From what sources does the ambivalence of these individuals stem and whence do they derive their particular motivation over and above their class positions?

The one common attribute of intellectuals is their differential exposure to culture. This exposure, however, can mean a good many things, and most misunderstandings are due to the varying interpretations of 'being cultured'.[1] Let us differentiate.

1. The first type is implied in the distinction between *manual* and *intellectual* performances. Such a polarization is not altogether meaningless. It does point to distinct media and tools of vocational performances without reference to social rank. While in earlier times such a juxtaposition always connoted some social evaluation, a differentiation of rank for instance, the democratized work order of modern society has indeed freed the distinction between the two types of performances of their earlier value connotations.[2] In a society of occupational specialization the particular nature of work becomes increasingly an attribute of the vocation and less and less a symbol of status. To realize the modern trend one merely has to think of the old Roman differentiation between *opera servilia* and *artes liberales*. The former designated varied types of physical performances which did not befit free men, except military service, gymnastics, and contests, while the *artes liberales* already contain something of the later rating of the free professions.

2. A second stage in the evaluation of intellectual occupations

[1] The discussion of the subject must remain sterile so long as everybody has a different group of intellectuals in mind. My presentation of the subject in *Ideology and Utopia* suffered from my failure to distinguish the particular type which I called the 'socially unattached intelligentsia' from others. The misunderstandings to which this omission has given rise make it mandatory to elaborate the concept of intelligentsia with some care and precision.

[2] Compare the subsequent essay of this volume, on 'Democratization', and E. Zilsel, *Die Entstehung des Geniebegriffes*, Tübingen, 1926.

deeply involves social status: the earlier contrast between physical and mental performances gives way to the new differentiation between the *free professions* and the *trades*. The former designates a preoccupation with the arts, the sciences, and religion for their own sake and without remuneration. The freedom from pecuniary considerations is an important feature of the prestige which attaches to these occupations. Their pursuit for their own sake is possible only to gentlemen of independent means. A free profession in this sense entails not only a non-manual performance but a source of prestige and a particular vocational ethos, namely the disinterested devotion to a calling. Its high moral esteem, however, often veils the fact that the prestige does not accrue from the disinterested performance as such, but from the social position which makes it possible. This is well illustrated by the ancient custom that the physician who was trained in the Hippocratic tradition could only concern himself with diagnostics and prognoses, and was expected to leave surgery, therapy, and nursing aid to hired helpers. The same differentiation between the free professions and the paid vocations forms the background of the practice, prior to the rise of modern bureaucracy, of placing public affairs in the hands of honorary officials—unpaid squires (as in England) or independent patricians.

3. This gentlemanly rating of intellectual occupations is still present in a third distinction, namely between the *educated* (Gebildeten) and the *uneducated*. This differentiation still has much meaning in the small towns of several countries of South America and Europe, particularly Germany. These designations do not refer merely to the professions, academic training, or feudal ranks which no longer exist.[1] The term 'educated' in this particular sense includes such respectable folk as the doctor, lawyer, teacher, minister, merchant, and manufacturer, in short, personages who are accustomed to gather around the favoured tavern table and to meet at each other's homes. Three interchangeable principles of selection are here at work, namely *cultivation*, *rank*, and *income*. A substantial income may compensate for some lack of culture and *vice versa*. The resulting selection does not lack a certain measure of homogeneity. It is

[1] Compare for the following Mennicke—von der Gablentz, *Deutsche Berufskunde*, Leipzig, 1930, particularly p. 33.

based largely on similar social etiquette, a similar style of living, and a common sense of decorum. This social symbiosis produces a homogeneous culture, to wit a conventionalized form of selective social refinement.

4. This conventional hallmark of the 'educated' has been steadily losing currency ever since the rise of the absolute state and its trained bureaucracy. The bureaucratic hierarchy creates its own criteria of distinction by a new system of *certifications* for civil service careers.[1] On this new basis the educated have become identified as the possessors of diplomas and career monopolies. The former distinction of respectability gives way to the differentiation between those with and those without academic training[2], and in Germany to the further gradation of diplomas obtained after the 6th, 7th, and 8th high school grades.

[1] Weinstock is undoubtedly right in saying that there is nothing wrong with the rational selection of officials. It became an absurdity only when this machinery of selection was used as the basis for the abridged one year army service which the German Defence Act of 1876 made possible. This provision changed an educational selection into a social. Compare H. Weinstock, 'Das Berechtigungselend', in *Die Erziehung*, 1929, vol. IV.

[2] The Prussian system of certifications seems to have originated with Frederick William I. Examinations were first required of army judges, then after the Ordinance of 1713 of deputy judges also. From 1737 all judges of both higher and lower courts, including those of the peers' benches, were expected to meet prescribed standards of training and pass examinations. Strangely, the administrative colleges remained an exception; in these positions apparently practical experience was preferred to 'lawyers' tricks'. The next in order were the ministers. It is plain that the system of examinations was designed as a safeguard against nepotism, for it was ruled at the same time that no son should succeed his father in office. One must remember though that the promotion of an *esprit de corps* in the civil service usually coincides with an encouragement of sons to choose the vocation of their fathers. Frederick the Great considered this the main stimulus for the rise of a capable corps of officials. Compare Lotz, *Geschichte des deutschen Beamtentums*, Berlin, 1914.

1788 forms the most important landmark in the history of the German system of certifications. In that year a Royal Prussian edict instituted the high school maturity examinations. This same edict also introduced the distinction between certified and uncertified high schools by having the entrance examination to universities administered in the high schools themselves, that is in those which were so certified. It is interesting to know that the admission of exceptional students to universities already began in this period; it was only recently that this provision was reintroduced in Germany. Compare *Lexikon der Pädagogik der Gegenwart*, vol. II, 1932, article 'Berechtigungswesen'.

The standardization of training in itself is inescapable in an industrial society. An honorary officialdom of genteel layfolk would not be adequate to the needs of contemporary society. Nor can one question the democratic character of a system which makes measurable training the basis of qualification for positions, for schooling is accessible to everyone, at least in principle. Nevertheless, this system creates a new type of differentiation, not only because of the pecuniary requirements for an advanced type of education.

Thus, the bureaucratic management of German society added a new criterion of intellectuality to the earlier conventionalized, genteel concepts of cultivation: the possession of *applicable knowledge*. The systematized examinations test how much of the readily channelled knowledge the candidate has been able to absorb and whether he has mastered certain prescribed and standardized methods. Now, a differentiated society does, of course, require a personnel trained in operationally defined and apportioned subjects. But it is not necessary to obscure those aspects of an accumulated culture which are not indispensable for selected careers. Culture became conventionalized as early as the 16th century. Franz Blei says of the Rococo period that it almost succeeded in substituting literature for poetry.[1] The bureaucratic influence has added momentum to this trend, particularly in higher education. We shall come back to this subject at the end of this essay.

We have described four distinct criteria of cultivation and education. They correspond to four social types well distinguished by their occupational characteristics, their conduct, and their social orientation. Although these types originated in different phases of history they still exist side by side in contemporary society. It would be amiss to think that they do not represent some genuine features of an intelligentsia, but it would be equally wrong to see in them the only possible variants.

With whatever class or rank persons so described identify themselves, they all show characteristic deviations in their conduct from their peers who do not share their intellectual preoccupations. This joint interest is an alternative source of motivation which deflects the behaviour of the

[1] Franz Blei, *Der Geist des Rokoko*, p. xi, München, 1923.

individual from that course which his class position foreshadows. The teacher who does not accept remuneration for certain services, repudiates in a way his class position as a white collar worker. Government employees often reject unionization for the sake of a prestige which is solely rooted in their shared vocational conceptions.[1] The ambivalence of the educated and his deviation from his class model may be explained by the fact that a distinct universe of discourse tends to create a consentient group with a special *esprit de corps*, and to increase the distance between those who communicate within the acquired universe of thought and those who do not.

We do not plan to dwell on the preceding vocational typology of intellectuals. It was designed as a point of departure. The types of intelligentsia with whom the subsequent portions of this essay will deal differ from those sketched above by virtue of their comparative lack of vocational distinctions and their peculiar motivations which we hope to trace. It may be that the discussion will at certain points overstep the boundaries of sociological analysis towards a philosophy of culture. Still it is a matter of some difference whether a philosophy is presented as a substitute for a sociological analysis or as its extension. We hope to follow the second procedure.

5. THE CONTEMPORARY INTELLECTUAL

In our quest for an appropriate concept of the intellectual we must begin with those situations which afford a first glimpse of the phenomenon. The expression 'educated' does give an intimation of the matter, over and beyond its previously analysed meaning. The term 'being educated' alludes to something of an involvement in a situation which concerns us all without noticeably affecting everyone. Every person's cognitive horizon covers at least the area within which he must act and acquire a body of operational knowledge. His grasp of the human world may well extend beyond this radius of action, but no vocation and no position in society requires an awareness of the concerns of all men. It is the educated who keep *en rapport* with the state of our affairs, and not only theirs, and it is

[1] E. Lederer and I. Marschak, 'Der neue Mittelstand', in *Grundriss der Sozialökonomik*, vol. IX-1, p. 121, Tübingen, 1926.

in this sense that they are involved in a situation which concerns us all.

Although the previously outlined types of the educated were not so defined, one cannot maintain that this involvement is possible without some socially provided access to knowledge, such as the types mentioned represent. It would be, of course, even more risky to take for granted that all those whose social position affords access to knowledge *eo ipso* have it. To be more specific, knowledge evolves in two distinct streams:

A. In the *continuum of everyday experience* (a category to which Dilthey, Scheler, Heidegger, each in his own way, paid considerable attention) in which the individual is forced to solve practical problems as they arise in his own life. He meets these problems with the aid of a body of knowledge which he acquires spontaneously, casually, or imitatively, but without conscious method. Information so accumulated is embodied in the skills of the artisan, life experience, and *savoir faire*.

B. A different type of learning originates in the *esoteric* stream of transmission which, in a certain state of social complexity, becomes the vehicle of 'education'. The esoteric world view is not a spontaneous acquisition, but the product of dedicated effort and cultivated tradition.[1]

In simple cultures these two types of knowledge often merge into one another. Thus, tribally monopolized crafts—in themselves a field of daily routine—quite often constitute a secret subject, while magic whose source and substance is esoteric usually enters into the daily round of private activities. Increasingly complex societies, however, tend to separate the daily from the esoteric realm of knowledge and, at the same time, increase the distance between the groups which are in charge of them.

The overt separation of these two realms begins with the emergence of the vocational shaman and, particularly, with the rise of a magicians' guild and the eventual caste of magicians.[2] Monopolistic churches likewise tend to establish compact and

[1] See Florian Znaniecki, *The Social Role of the Man of Knowledge*, 1940, pp. 93 ff., and J. D. Bernal, *The Social Function of Science*, London and New York, 1939, p. 15 f.

[2] For a synopsis compare Gunnar Landtman, *The Origin of the Inequality of the Social Classes*, London and Chicago, 1938, pp. 111–226.

well-distanced strata of priests, whether castes or ranks. The evolution of learning and education passes a landmark of incomparable significance when laymen break and usurp the priestly monopoly of public interpretation. Prior to this the laity engages only sporadically in the formulation of public views on matters which lie outside the realm of daily and private experience. In European history, the substance of education changed with the laicization of learning in the period of humanism and, even before, in the restricted culture of chivalry. The sociological aspects of this incipient secularism have not been sufficiently emphasized, and we cannot comprehend the host of subsequent changes without clearly recognizing their origin in a relatively simple social shift. The key to the new epoch of learning lies in the fact that *the educated no longer constitute a caste or a compact rank, but an open stratum* to which persons from an increasing variety of stations gain access. No longer can any unitary view of the world become regnant, and the authoritative habit of thinking in a closed scholastic system gives way to what we may call an *intellectual process.* This process is basically the polarization of several co-existing world views which reflect the social tensions of a complex civilization. The modern intellectual who has succeeded the scholastic does not intend to reconcile or to ignore the alternative views which are potential in the order of things around him, but he seeks out the tensions and participates in the polarities of his society. The changed mentality of the learned, the fragmented outlook of the contemporary intellectual are not the upshot of a growing scepticism, a declining faith or the lack of ability to create an integrated *Weltanschauung*, as some writers regretfully maintain. Quite the contrary, secularization and the multipolarity of views are the consequence of the fact that the group of the learned has lost its caste organization and its prerogative to formulate authoritative answers to the questions of the time.[1]

The crux and turning point in Western history is the gradual dissolution of the compact caste-like strata. The scholar was the first to be affected by this shift. The manner in which he conceptualizes experience reflects the structure of his stratum. The caste-secure scholastic built a stationary and compact

[1] See Znaniecki, *op. cit.*, p. 114.

edifice of concepts, in accordance with his stabilized existence. He raised only questions to which he already had answers. He expressed doubts in order to dispel them, and he did not sensitize himself to facts which would not confirm his convictions. The modern intellectual has a dynamic bent and is perennially prepared to revise his views and make a new beginning, for he has little behind him and everything before him. His sensitivity to alternate views and divergent interpretations of the same experience, however, is a potential source of his shortcoming—namely a false catholicity and the illusion of having grasped the point of view of others when he merely perceived their utterances. Still, one should not try, as has very often been done, to belittle the significance of this intellectual process by applying to it the yardstick of an older stationary social system. The yearning for the security which that stable order provided should not blind one to the achievements which its heir has made possible. Nor will that lost unity of outlook hold a spell over those who are aware of its social basis.

Empathy is another, significantly modern, capacity of the intellectual. Little has been said so far about the sociological origin of this trait, and yet it is not merely a psychological phenomenon. Nor is this faculty of 'seeing someone else's side' as self-explanatory and timeless as it may seem at first blush. This trait distinguishes the modern intellectual from the scholastic variety and also from the solitary sage. The latter may possess wisdom, but insight to the point of periodical self-suspension is not his hallmark. Sympathy and understanding are, of course, universal traits, but not the urge to penetrate unfamiliar or baffling points of view. The wisdom of the experienced but 'uneducated' person may relate itself to others in so far as they share his milieu, while 'true education' is a source of insightful transcendence of one's own milieu.

No invidious comparison is attempted; one need not deprecate the enduring gains which accrue from open-minded living and long experience. The unquestionable asset of this self-taught wisdom is its unerring focus on real problems. The person who has acquired his judgment through the direct apprenticeship of life is not easily lost in a maze of intellectual fancy. His pragmatic bent to apply to his thinking the daily test of relevance will save him from the temptation of the educated to stray into the realm of specious and unverifiable constructs. The danger of this realism, however, lies in the fact that it may be bypassed by an unnoticed shift, and that it may continue to hold on to the maxims of a hard-won experience long after the drift of events has eroded their basis. This is often the origin of a false traditionalism whose norms no longer fit the existing situation. The paradox which a precipitous change may occasion lies in the fact that the sober and sure-footed realist loses touch with reality and turns into a utopian —a utopian of the past, to use G. Salomon's expression.[1]

Such are the limitations of a life-centred wisdom. It is confined to the things which directly enter the life-situation of the individual, and its coverage cannot be expanded much beyond that without education. Education does not merely widen the range of things we know about, for so long as they do not affect our point of view we still see events with the eyes of the traditionalist who taught himself how to stand his ground and meet the problems of an unchanging world. Education teaches us to discover our own affairs in the affairs of distant peoples and to penetrate another point of view by redefining our own. Surely such a propensity is not without its dangers; we have pointed to them already. An all-pervasive empathy may become easily a non-committal, flighty, and frothy intellectualism. Its virtuoso may soon lose his sense of proportion and while exercising his empathy on things recondite he may fail to play his part nearer home. Dangers these are, and no venture is without them. But the gains of education such as the modern era has made possible are unmistakable. They lie in the expansion of the self through its participation in a multipolar culture. One individual may live more than his own life and think more than his own thoughts. He can rise above the fatalism and fanaticism of solitary existences, whether they include individuals, vocations, or nations. The price of this gain is the

[1] The rural type of traditionalism which grows out of daily experience is well illustrated by excellent material gathered in the United States. Compare J. M. Williams, *Our Rural Heritage*, New York, 1925; G. A. Lundquist, *What Farm Women are Thinking*, University of Minnesota, Agricultural Extension Div., Special Bulletin No. 71, 1923; H. Bernard, 'A Rural Theory', *American Journal of Sociology*, XXII, and J. W. Thomas and F. Znaniecki, *The Polish Peasant in Europe and America*, 2nd ed., New York, 1927, 2 vols.

willingness to hold the self in abeyance at times, to rethink his premises, and to place a question mark beside absolutes. One cannot appreciate the educated mind without seeing the positive in the searching acts of scepticism—scepticism understood not in the frozen form of a philosophical system, but as a state of fruitful uncertainty.

This sceptical trend which originated in 17th-century France has almost bypassed Germany. Perhaps Nietzsche was the only German of note who understood the vitality of French scepticism as it evolved in varying situations from Montaigne through Pascal, La Rochefoucauld, and Chamfort to Stendhal. No previous age had the conviction of our period, namely *that we have no truth.* All ages prior to our time had their truths, even the sceptics.[1]

This approach shows its fruitfulness particularly in the pedagogical situation. The counsellor who is not truly educated may pass on the experience which was accessible to him in his own walk of life. He may help us out of difficulties, but he cannot teach us to rise above them. One can only master a situation by *looking beyond it.* We can only comprehend a phenomenon if we identify its concrete range of variability. This is the type of counsel we can gain from a genuine sociological analysis. It can illuminate an apparent impasse by disclosing its contingent character and the alternatives which are open to us. This is, incidentally, also the nature of the aid which a fruitful type of psycho-analysis offers. There is something incomparably positive in this modern capacity to see the tentative side of every situation, to reject every manifestation of fatalism, to evade seemingly inescapable alternatives, and to look beyond and behind apparent fixities.

Let us pause again to acknowledge the dangers of the modern faculty to evade issues and to question one's own convictions. There can be no doubt about the debilitating consequences of a perennial self-doubt, a paralysis which those who must hold their own can ill afford. Nor can one question that the facility to escape harassments easily crystallizes an irresistant and unheroic type unsuited for independent action.

[1] F. Nietzsche, *Aus der Zeit der Morgenröte*, 1880–81; R. Saitschik, *Deutsche Skeptiker: Lichtenberg, Nietzche–Zur Psychologie des neueren Individualismus*, Berlin, 1906.

But will not heroism at times degenerate into an empty pathos, and are there no occasions which turn intrepidity and singleness of purpose into mere obstinacy?

It is perhaps clear now how the perennially shifting axis of modern thought reflects the rise of an unprivileged and polarized intelligentsia which injects into the public interpretation of affairs as many points of view as are inherent in its varied social background. Once the earlier *esprit de corps* of the intelligentsia is broken and its compact organization discarded, the tendency to question and seek rather than to affirm becomes its permanent trait. The multipolarity of this questioning process creates a uniquely modern propensity to reach behind and beyond appearances and to explode any fixed frame of reference which relies on ultimates. Closely linked with this predilection is the tendency to outrun the time, to take one's stance beyond and ahead of each situation, and to anticipate alternatives before they become acute. Finally, there is the contrast between the closed system, the scholastic *ordo*, and the modern chariness of the closed perspective. This is but another expression of the contrast between the cohesiveness and homogeneity of the scholastic literati and the loose aggregation and polarized state of the modern intelligentsia.

These are characteristics not of the mind as such, but of the mentality of an open and fluid stratum whose sociological analysis furnishes a key to modern thought.

6. THE HISTORICAL ROLES OF THE INTELLIGENTSIA

We have attempted to locate the social basis of modern mentality. It appears that what we called the intellectual process—the multipolarity of views—ultimately goes back to the loose aggregation of interacting intellectuals. This fact does not yet give us a full sociological account of the mentality of our age, but it outlines the basic situation from which a typology of the intelligentsia becomes possible.

The intelligentsia as a specialized group in general and the post-medieval intelligentsia in particular constitute a central subject of the sociology of the mind. In this essay we shall concentrate on the latter type since its historical position lends it a greater significance to us. The Marxist sociology conceives intellectual manifestations only in the broad setting of major class tensions. One cannot deny that this simplified view does contain a core of truth in so far as the overriding conflicts of society are of basic interest to the sociological study of the mind. This unsubtle procedure, however, merely affirms that there is a relationship between class tension and ideation, without much concern about the intervening links. True, the mediate character of the relationship is not overlooked, but no attempt has been made to articulate it. The intellectuals who produce ideas and ideologies form the most important of the connecting links between social dynamics and ideation. Although it would be indefensible to construe ideologies merely from the situation of their authors and to ignore the wider stage on which they perform, neither will the larger frame of social tension in itself explain how the spokesmen of certain views happen to make their choices and to join particular groups. To these facts we have to pay distinct attention. We shall attempt to show through a few illustrative examples where the major problems of the sociology of the intelligentsia lie and through what successive steps they may be approached.[1]

We may envisage the question in its proper perspective once we have disposed of the familiar category of the 'functionary'. In so far as the Marxist sociology concerns itself with intellectuals it is in their capacity as functionaries and satellites. (Note the limited area from which the blanket term 'functionary' is derived; it connotes something on the order of the union official). Now, this homespun brand of sociology is not completely pointless. No doubt, intellectuals often are and have been mere purveyors of ideologies to certain classes. This, however, is only one of a variety of functions of ideation, and unless one is prepared to consider all, the study of the intellectual indeed holds little promise.

Let us, at this point, envisage four of the guiding questions which are basic to the sociology of this subject; the first two relate to the intrinsic characteristics of the intelligentsia, the last two concern its relationship to the social process at large:

[1] The aim of this study is to provide a possible pattern for studies of concrete groups of intellectuals, present or historical. I have encouraged a few dissertations on the subject.

1 the social background of intellectuals;
2 their particular associations;
3 their upward and downward mobility;
4 their functions in the larger society.

(*a*) *The Social Background of Intellectuals*

The social background of intellectuals is significant to us in so far as it helps to illuminate the group impulses which intellectuals often express. The original milieu of an individual does not furnish us with the necessary data for a complete understanding of his mental development, but it does indicate some factors of his particular predisposition to meet and experience given situations. To account for the dominant patterns of ideation under historically known circumstances we need not only analyses of individual life histories, but statistical data concerning the social (class or vocational) background and position of representative intellectuals. A traditional intelligentsia may, however, retain its commanding position in spite of the continued entry of newcomers. This has been the case in politics which, in several instances, the nobility continued to control well after the rise of lower strata to public prominence. Another matter to be considered is how much weight an individual's earlier status carries after his entry into the ranks of the educated; furthermore, whether the ranking strata continue to retain their cohesiveness in their changed roles, and whether or to what extent individuals renounce their previous status before joining the intelligentsia. The numerical index of the social background of the educated is, of course, only one of the data of interest. Equally important is it to know what situations lend weight to persons of one or another social background. Finally, one must not overlook the fact that in certain instances intellectuals merge their previous identity in a new affiliation of their own.

(*b*) *The Affiliations of Intellectuals and Artists*

Between the compact, caste-like organization and the open and loose group, there are numerous intermediate types of aggregations in which intellectuals may range themselves.

Their mutual contacts are often informal, but the small, intimate group forms the most frequent pattern.[1] It has played an eminently catalytic role in the formation of common attitudes and thought currents.

The early medieval organizations of artists reflect the nature of their performances. They were carried out in the typical fashion of crafts. The work was centred around a common workshop, performed in teams, and in accordance with the intermittent nature of employment it necessitated frequent migrations. The cooperative character of the work process explains the fraternal organization of medieval artists, the earlier art forms, and the fact that individuation in this medium begins fairly late. One of the first groupings of medieval artists is the masonic fraternity—'Bauhütte'—in Germany. The 'Bauhütte', first mentioned in the twelfth century in southern France and Germany, was the toolshed, workshop, and meeting-place of stone-masons, builders and sculptors. Fairly soon the Bauhütte becomes a fraternity which upholds common standards of performance, exercises jurisdiction over its members, and safeguards the secrets of the craft. Itinerant painters came closer to the free-lance type of artist, although they often found permanent employment as court painters in the households of princes, as for example the van Eyck brothers who bore the title of 'valet de chambre'.

Poets likewise formed attachments of various types. In the genealogy of the antique poet we find the clairvoyant; the early Germanic poet is known under the name of 'scop'.[2] Originally he belongs to the princely retinue, carries arms, and is distinguished only by his vocal talent. Quite often, however, a physical disability or some other peculiarity places him in the

[1] Useful references to the subject may be found in the cited works of Dehio and Hausenstein. Compare also E. Kris and O. Kurz, *Die Legende vom Künstler*, Vienna, 1939, a publication which the authors designate as a preparatory study towards a sociology of the artist.

[2] The Anglo-Saxon scop is a freeman who performs in the princely hall. He usually belongs to his liege lord's retinue, but quite often he carries on a wayfaring life, visits alien courts, and becomes a confidant of a prince. His art is considered more than a casual trade. His hosts reward his songs with golden rings, and he prefers to visit those who understand his songs and lavish gifts on him. At the same time he may own inherited land. The sources do not make it quite clear whether he rendered armed services.

position of a relative outsider.[1] Such a position is conducive to reflectivity or to an oppositional bent. This seems an early trait of the poet, for he is distanced within his rank before he becomes detached from it.

Besides the early poet we find itinerant minstrels and showmen who follow the tradition and role of the antique mime. They are complete outsiders, are in no way linked to the retinue of nobles, and do not belong to the honourable vocations, but are classed together with the rogues and harlots. These people possess from the beginning a separate organization and group solidarity, while the poets who share the status and rank of their noble peers acquire considerably later a distinct consciousness of their own.

Quite peculiar is the position of the troubadours and minnesingers. They are not outside the feudal hierarchy, although not a few of them are poor or impoverished knights in a marginal situation. The source of their nobility is of importance, for some owe it to birth while others descend from the so-called *ministeriales*. Schulte, whose studies are most pertinent to the subject, observes that these poets are usually grouped according to status. Thus the Heidelberg song script includes in its list of singers first the emperor, then the princes, counts, barons, ministeriales, and the squires; the last group comprises the urban aristocracy, the clergy, the scholars, the show people, and the burghers. Such is the hierarchy of the thirteenth century.[2] The fact worth noting here is that while the poet is well identified by rank and status, refinement and cultivation begins to become a levelling agent to the extent that princes and other notables already take pride in counting themselves with the *trouvères*.[3] Knights of modest circumstances, on the other hand, find a certain social compensation in the attribute of a poet, so much so that cultivation is already a factor of social advancement. That the poetical form depends on the status of the poet is well illustrated by the fact that Walther

[1] Paula Kronheimer, 'Grenzglieder des Standes', *Kölner Vierteljahrshefte*, Vol. 6, No. 3, 1927.

[2] A. Schulte, 'Standesverhältnisse der Minnesinger', *Zeitschrift für deutsches Altertum und deutsche Literatur*, vol. 39, pp. 185–251, 1895.

[3] F. C. Diez, *Die Poesie der Troubaduren*, Leipzig, 1883, and *Leben und Werke der Troubaduren*, 1883.

von der Vogelweide, a knight of marginal standing who drifts far in the direction of the wayfaring players, is the first to introduce their gnomic poem into courtly poetry. The linkage between art form and social rank is still direct and clear, and it is only in later periods that the social significance of form is no longer comprehensible without the detour of sociological analysis.[1] We may trace the changing literary style from its early periods to the zenith of courtly lyric poetry to a gradual shift in the social position of the author. Schulte notices that the earlier style is characteristic of the ranking landed nobility, while the later climactic period becomes the era of the poets of lesser nobility and ministerial ranks; in brief, the predominant influence passes from a stationary stratum on to relatively mobile groups. Schulte observes of the early period:

'Except for wars, the nobility stayed close to its soil; the baron lived on his land, and the ministerial ranks attended to their service. That is why the poets of the first period are much more sedentary than those of the climactic age. The record mentions only of H. von Veldecke, a baron, that he travelled. The court of Cleve was the first which we know to have sheltered a wandering noble singer. How different is all this later! We know of Reimar, Walther, Wolfram, Nithart, Zweter, and Tannhäuser that they lived and composed verse at the courts of rulers other than their native lords. Was it an impetuous urge to wander which carried vassals far away from their fief or was it destitution that made a poet of the vagrant knight?'[2]

We see here both forms of social mobility at work, to use Sorokin's categories: the stimulus and stir of vertical mobility and the horizontal expansion of the seen and experienced world. Those knights who still have standing among their peers and yet are not secure enough to be immune to new experience —these are the wayfarers and adventurers who open up new perspectives within the feudal hierarchy. Travel is a source of new experience only for those whose social position itself is un-

[1] Compare K. Y. Holzknecht, *Literary Patronage in the Middle Ages*, 1923, and Y. C. Mendenhall, *Aureate Terms; A Study in the Literary Diction of the Fifteenth Century*, 1919. One is reminded of the low esteem of the fine arts and particularly of the plastic arts in the antique world, because of the slave status of their practitioners. Comp. Zilsel, *op. cit.*, p. 112.

[2] Schulte, *op. cit.*, p. 247.

frozen. The nobleman who journeys abroad for his pleasure without the necessity to establish himself at every turn experiences new people and customs only as variations of familiar sights. Only the traveller who steps out of his social milieu and abandons his station to find a new one discovers alternatives and acquires a new horizon. This is how the relatively unattached and itinerant knights become spokesmen of a reflective and multi-dimensional view of life. The fact that they were not complete outsiders, but still had a feudal standing and spoke the language of their peers, assured them of a hearing and influence in medieval society.[1]

We have pointed already to the social differentiation of the minnesingers. The contemporary distinction between major and minor minnesongs has reference to that very differentiation. The ranking nobles cultivated the 'high minnesongs' (*hohe Minne*) while Walther and his peers of the lesser nobility not only adopted popular forms but also dared to vindicate love to maidens of the people. This marks a new attitude rather than a changed conduct, for we need not assume that love-making to girls of common birth is original with Walther. Thus noblemen of lesser rank acclimatize a more natural but already spiritualized form of attachment as the counterpart of the conventional love in the courtly strata of society. This is one of those instances in which the distinct standards of judgment of two different strata merge in the conceptual framework of a mobilized group which participates in both strata and shares their attitudes. Distinct codes in themselves do not clash as long as the strata which practise them do not merge. Conflict situations arise only when mobile buffer groups which retreat from above or rise from below become attached to both and adopt their values. It is in these marginal situations which provide access to formerly discrete worlds that a genuine intelligentsia originates.

Reference has been made to the *clergy*, the dominant group of literati of the middle ages, its compact organization, and its particular type of learning. Now we shall have to direct our attention to the intrinsic structure of the clergy, particularly as it reflects the diverse background of its members. A closed group quite naturally seeks to develop a unified *esprit de corps*

[1] Schulte, *op. cit.*, p. 249.

and to neutralize the effects of the diverse social orientations which its members carry with them. The later bureaucracy shows the same tendency. None the less, a *secondary differentiation* within, as we shall call it, may reflect something of the original diversity without. It is important, therefore, to take stock of the social composition of a closely-knit intelligentsia. In this undertaking we are able to draw on the important work of Schulte in the first place and on the studies of Stutz, Kothe, and others, all of which are helpfully summarized by Werminghoff,[1] who is our primary source in the following presentation.

The early Church stood on Christ's teaching of religious equality, and did not recognize secular gradations in Christendom. The practice of this original doctrine of restive lower classes underwent modifications as the Church became established in highly differentiated societies, particularly in Germanic areas. The Church itself introduced a gradation into the ranks of the clergy by the creation of secular and monastic orders. This distinction grew sharper as it became associated with a feudal type of differentiation. In summing up the social history of the Church hierarchy, Werminghoff remarks:

'The clergy always and from the beginning opened its ranks to freemen, and among them to those who were closest to the nobles of free birth. Later the lower nobility also found access to chapters, monasteries and cloisters; eventually they were followed by burghers. Since the eleventh century the German clergy presents a picture of diversity.'[2]

Kothe arrives at similar conclusions in his study of the clerics in Strasbourg in the fourteenth century.

Every society seeks to preserve its scheme of organization not only through its laws and institutions but by an appropriate allocation of command positions. If that is true of a democratic society, it is more so of a feudal order in which the nobility controls both secular and ecclesiastical key positions. The latter became institutionalized since the bishoprics and archbishoprics became the prerogatives of free-born noblemen. The

[1] Albert Werminghoff, 'Ständische Probleme in der Geschichte der deutschen Kirche des Mittelalters', in *Zeitschrift der Savigny-Stiftung für Reichsgeschichte*, Kanonische Abt., Vol. XXXII, Weimar, 1911.

[2] Werminghoff, *op. cit.*

monasteries of the feudal nobility received the sons and daughters of princes and counts, but closed their doors to persons of ministerial rank, to feudatory knights, and to the sons of the patriciate. This development began as early as the Merowingian Empire. These reservations might have stabilized the hold of certain families over the ecclesiastical hierarchy were it not for the institution of celibacy. Actually the predominance of the feudal classes in the Church was already declining in the fifteenth century; about 1427 the feudal monasteries relinquished their closed-door policy and after 1516 they admitted commoners.

Werminghoff's table, reprinted below, furnishes a good illustration of the foregoing.

OCCUPANCY OF BISHOPRICS

After W. Pelster and J. Simon, cf. Schulte, p. 67 and 349. The Church province of Cologne with Lüttich, Utrecht, Münster, Osnabrück and Münden; the Church province of Mainz without Prag and Olmütz, with Worms, Speyer, Strasbourg, Chur, Augsburg, Eichstädt, Würzburg, Bamberg, Halberstadt, Hildesheim, Paderborn, Verden. (Other Church provinces in German territories: Trier, Hamburg-Bremen, Magdeburg, Salzburg.)

'th Century	9	10	11	12	13	14	15	Total
Barons	.44	51	68	107	126	128	77	601
Presumptive free nobles	18	17	49	30	2	—	—	116
Ministeriales	—	—	2	2	31	47	44	126
Dependents	2	—	3	—	—	—	—	5
Burghers	—	—	—	—	2	17	3	22
Foreigners	—	—	1	—	—	3	1	5
Unknown	42	39	31	22	8	7	3	152
	106	107	154	161	169	202	128	1,027

Literature:

Aloys Schulte, *Der Adel und die deutsche Kirche im Mittelalter*, Kirchenrechtliche Abhandlungen, Heft 63-64. Stuttgart, 1910.

Albert Werminghoff, 'Ständische Probleme in der Geschichte der deutschen Kirche des Mittelalters', in *Zeitschrift der Savigny-Stiftung für Reichsgeschichte, op. cit.*

The table describes two significant trends: the gradual democratization of the Church hierarchy and, more important, the rise of the ministeriales whose social ascent outrivals any other medieval class. They are of dependent origin, but as servants of sovereigns they hold positions of influence and power. In the eleventh century they become an estate of their own, serve in the army, and are used as officials, minters, and money-changers. Their ambivalent status as dependents and yet wielders of power gradually changes as free-born nobles also join their ranks. Eventually they, too, find the doors to church offices ajar. Werminghoff emphasizes the interesting fact that the Roman hierarchy soon pursued the policy, also adopted by the later absolute monarchy, of neutralizing the local vantage ground of noble clans by the use of commoners. Still, the feudal preponderance in the hierarchy, which began to decline in the eleventh century, came to an end only in the nineteenth century when the Church opened its doors to all classes.

Although the clergy was not entirely free from a secondary differentiation of the feudal type, the Church was able to create a well-amalgamated and disciplined intelligentsia. Its place in the social order was clearly defined, and all clericals, regardless of their social background, were distinguished by *privilegia competentiae*, *immunitatis*, *canonis et fori*. Celibacy precluded hereditary tenure of offices, as it also helped to create a unified frame of mind in the *clerus*, and it prevented that measure of social ambivalence which found its way into the hierarchy from disrupting the unity of the Church.

The next phase in the formation of a literary intelligentsia is marked by two groups: the *humanists* and the *mastersingers*.

The symbiotic relationship of the *humanists* to the prevailing society was of two types: they either lived as protégés of patrons or they found employment in universities or chancelleries. In either case their existence was that of favourites depending on the whims of their patrons to which the clergy of the Church was comparatively immune.[1] The humanists find some com-

[1] From 1500 the universities were the scene of a clash of two generations of humanists. The older generation was of a patrician type; we find among them Semlinger, Pirckheimer, Erasmus, and Reuchlin. The younger humanists, the 'poets', were chiefly vagrant bachelors, veritable mercenaries who aimed their praise or invectives according to the opportunities for patronage. The latter type was, according to Joachimsen, predominant in Germany, although their lyric poetry did not gain a foothold in respectable society.

Employment in the chancelleries offered a somewhat larger measure of

pensation for their lack of security in fellowships of their own maintained through correspondence and visits. This private interchange takes the place of the international channels of communication which the Church used to provide for its scholars. The fellowships of the humanists served both as clearing-houses of learning and as agencies for the allocation of prestige positions. It was these channels which gradually solidified an erstwhile fluid public opinion, to use Tönnies' expression. For opinion does not crystallize in the public as such or in literary groups, but in an existing network of concrete associations. Their growth gains momentum at the same rate at which the formal channels of opinion—guilds, city parliaments, feudal assemblies—decline.[1] The intimate circles of the humanists bear the mark of a vocational and literary necessity and quite often they look more like diminutive organizations for ulterior purposes than deeply-felt friendships, the mask of which they sometimes assume.[2] These elastic and informal groupings do not check, and often encourage, certain traits for which the humanists were known, such as extravagance, public self-dramatization, and extremes of subservience to a patron.

The *mastersong* is a democratic manifestation cultivated by

independence. They were originally the domain of learned priests. During the sixteenth century the growth of Roman law enhances the influence of jurists in the chancelleries. There they soon develop the familiar traits of specialists who seek to make themselves indispensable, obscure the nature of their functions, and acquire the conceit typical of the exclusive possessors of a skill. The bureaucratic machinery lends itself to such a concealment by the use of an esoteric lingo and the adoption of complicated procedures which make the context of things incomprehensible to the uninitiated. Compare the good observations of von Steinhausen, *Geschichte der deutschen Kultur*.

[1] I have occasioned a study of opinion formation in a small and old German city. The interviews already effected indicate that an organized 'public' still survives in a traditional type of community, while it has vanished in Berlin. Once an author establishes himself in a cohesive community, he may count on its continuing support, while in a completely open and fluid milieu the public forms and responds from case to case, and it continues to remain open to the rise of new meteors, without attention to previous favourites. The rise of organized publics such as the community playhouses and the political theatre represents a countervailing trend.

[2] Albert Salomon, *Der Freundschaftskult des Humanismus*, unpubl., doctoral dissert., Heidelberg, 1921.

the common man who does not abandon his station but rather carries its meaning into his art. In a sense, the mastersingers form an élite, not only by virtue of their 'mastery' of certain forms[1] but on account of their deliberate closure.[2] Here again language offers a clue. The colloquial language is deliberately avoided and penalties are fixed for 'anything not composed or sung in high German such as is used by Dr. Martin Luther in his Bible translation or by the chancelleries of the princes and lords.'[3] The rejection of false opinions, superstitions, unchristian and unbefitting expressions, and the use of Latin words 'contra grammaticae leges' reveals the humble origin of this intelligentsia and its deference to the humanists. One can sense a certain lack of self-assurance in the devotion to rules, the fear of improvisations, and the loud counting of syllables in performances—a lapse which was held against the singer.[4]

We see in this self-imposed discipline of the common man a counterpart to the licentiousness of a labile intelligentsia which tends to place novelty and the *imprévu* above the safety of established usage. As a safeguard against improvisations, the mastersingers sought to bar the public just as the guilds shielded their crafts from free competition. Although the contests were held in public the circulation of mastersongs in print was not permitted.

There are various intermediate types between this lower-middle-class intelligentsia and the free intellectuals of the liberal bourgeoisie of a more recent period. We shall turn to the various forms of amalgamation in which these new groups emerge.

After the decline of the urban middle classes the princely courts became the centres of a revived feudalism and the seats of a new intelligentsia formed by the nobility with or without

1 Mastersingers were the itinerant or burgher composers of gnomic verse from the thirteenth century. They were distinguished from laymen who had no training in the song. Cf. Stammler, *Reallexikon der deutschen Literaturgeschichte*, *op. cit.*, art. 'Meistersang'.

2 There were 250 mastersingers in Nürnberg in 1540; the names of 262 were known in Augsburg between 1535 and 1644.

3 C. May, *Der Meistersang*, Leipzig, 1901.

4 The situation changed after 1500 when Hans Fols, a father, succeeds, after heated debates, in making new 'tunes' acceptable.

the rising bureaucracy, as the case might be. Humanism in the meantime grew increasingly courtly and conventional. Officials, clergymen, scholars, and nobles who had lost their military functions after the disuse of mercenary armies, all became favourites and dependents of princes. The aristocracy, except for the landed nobles,[1] constituted now a 'clerisy' of the court, the centre of all aspirations and opposition. The previous line of demarcation between society and the urban élite no longer existed; on the contrary, urbanity without rank and status was now of little consequence.

Intellectuals have been outsiders only since the middle-class revolutions. Sophistication prior to the advent of the bourgeoisie is an adjunct of status and breeding, non-existent outside titled society. The man of the world who embodies the ideal of the time represents everything worthwhile, and the ideal is modelled not only after the poet, artist, and scholar, but also after the official and, last but not least, the politician. One of the familiar incarnations of this paradigm is the travelling cavalier whose business ranges from politics to knavery, who is well versed in the affairs of the world, gallant and otherwise, and always the impeccable gentleman. Neither the countryside nor the shattered culture of the middle classes can match the creativity and magnetism of the princely centres. No wonder, since they are the vital foci of a new social organization and a new political system carefully balanced by the prince. Alternatively he raises commoners to prominence and noble rank or compensates dispossessed or politically outmanoeuvred noblemen by army appointments denied to commoners. The court of Louis XIV set an example which the German princes well heeded.

A different type of intelligentsia of some importance arose after the Renaissance in a growing number of restricted and semi-formal societies. The Florentine Academia della Crusca set the original pattern to be followed by a number of 'language societies' in Italy, Switzerland, Holland, and Germany. These

[1] Max Weber pointed to the prominent role of the English landed nobility and the titled classes of independent income who together formed the gentry in the history of English learning and cultivation. Cf. his *Politik als Beruf*, p. 21, translated as Ch. iv. of H. H. Gerth and C. W. Mills, From Max Weber: *Essays in Sociology*, London and New York, 1946.

societies comprised varied ranks of the aristocracy as well as scholars and educated commoners, and a princely patron.[1] Poets were well regarded, but much of the poetry circulated amounted to little more than rhymed sycophancy.

Even though commoners played a subordinate role in these language societies, it would be a mistake not to see in them the growth of a broad and inclusive social orientation which transcends the feudal horizon towards an early form of national consensus. Prince Louis, the patron of the best known of these language societies, the 'fruchtbringende Gesellschaft' of Köthen, declined the suggestion to convert the fraternity into an exclusive order of knights, on the ground that the society 'is solely concerned with the German language and the good virtues rather than with knightly conduct. . . .'[2] Quite striking is the emphasis in a society composed largely of noblemen on the cultivation of such middle-class virtues as sincerity, mutual confidence, equality, simplicity, 'natural' conduct, continence, truthfulness, objectivity, and tolerance.[3] When addressing each other, members used assumed names rather than titles. Publications appeared anonymously under the name of the society or the pseudonym of the author in order to direct attention to the subject rather than the person or his rank. The allegorical dialogues seem ponderous and mannered, but they plainly show the evolving mould into which an impetuous and untrained mentality was being cast. Harsdörffer's *Conversations for Women* well illustrates the effort to create a convention of civil discourse for people still deeply immersed in the ruggedness of provincial society.[4] Today the published tracts of these societies and the records of their Socratic colloquies strike us as stilted

[1] Ernest Manheim, *Die Träger der Öffentlichen Meinung: Studien zur Soziologie der Öffentlichkeit*, Leipzig, 1933, p. 81. The German 'Fruchtbringende Gesellschaft' (Fruit-Bearing Society) comprised up to 1662 one king, three prince-electors, 49 dukes, four margraves, 10 landgraves, 8 counts palatine, 19 princes, 60 counts, 35 barons, and 600 noblemen, scholars, and 'untitled notables'. The membership included officials, jurists, and army officers, but of the 800 members only two were clergymen.

[2] *Der fruchtbringenden Gesellschaft Namen, Vorhaben, Gemählde und Wörter*, Frankfurt a.M., 1646, cited in Ernest Manheim, *op. cit.*, p. 82.

[3] E. Manheim, *op. cit.*, p. 81–4.

[4] Cf. Joseph Nadler, *Literaturgeschichte der deutschen Stämme und Landschaften*, vol. II, p. 180 f., 1929.

and priggish, but we should not underestimate the social function of these ceremonial exercises. They inculcated a democratic etiquette in a sharply divided parochial society. They cultivated the vernacular of the middle classes, and they taught indifference to person and birth in matters of common concern. Most important, they established channels of inter-class communication and assembled local élites who learned how to use them.

Much as these language societies provide the nursery schools for the later literary spokesmen of the middle classes, they become the objects of criticism and derision as soon as an emancipated and self-assured middle-class intelligentsia begins to raise its voice in public. The rejection of artificiality and mannerism is basically a protest of the fledgling against continued parental tutelage. Boileau's opening salvoes against the Baroque reverberate throughout central and northern Europe, wherever self-aware middle classes seek a non-political medium to voice their aspirations. His expressions furnish the common literary denominator for such oppositional leanings: 'Aimez la raison'. 'le faux est toujours fade, ennuyeux, languissant'. 'Rien n'est beau que le vrai; c'est elle seule qu'on admire et qu' on aime.'[1] Present-day aversion to overcultivation and high-browism is still motivated by the same social leanings which Boileau expressed.

The opposition to the courtly Baroque, however, did not come only from outside. The court itself became the seat of a newly amalgamated intelligentsia which, without a principled opposition to the throne, loosened the atmospheric hold of the court over the educated public. It is the *salons*, the later by-products of court life, whose varied gatherings provide the transition from the courtly type of cultivation to a middle-class urbanity.

The salons as such are not a creation of the modern era. In a sense, one may speak of the salons of antiquity, if the Lyceum, the group around Aspasia, can be so regarded as Feuillet de Conches regards it.[2] We may add the feudal gatherings at the courts of Provence, the courts of the Italian renaissance

[1] Cf. W. Stammler, *Reallexikon der deutschen Literaturgescgichte*, Berlin, 1925–31, p. 123.

[2] F. S. Feuillet de Conches, *Les salons de conversation au XIIIe siècle*, 1883.

(Beatrice d' Este, Isabella of Mantua, and Lorenzo il Magnifico) and the society of women of the world (Vittoria Collonna, Marguerite de Navarre), not to mention the various English literary societies.[1] But the classical salon originates at the French court.

The court punctilio and the public formality of the reception hall almost naturally create a desire for intimate gatherings 'behind the scene'. They provide an outlet for gossip, intrigue, resentment, and the varied impulses which the ettiquette of the court inhibits. The Marquise de Rambouillet initiated the vogue when she partitioned her reception hall into small chambers and alcoves so as to limit each gathering to eighteen persons. The major architecture gave way to the atmospheric decoration of the smaller chambers, one of which was the famed Chambre bleu d'Artenice.[2]

Tinker's interesting study on the literary role of the salons lists six major characteristics. We have just mentioned the first—the *intimate locale*. The second is the *stimulating influence of the hostess*, who encourages talent, regardless of birth, and sets a high standard for the party. The primacy of intellectual distinction is well illustrated by the recognition Voiture, the son of a wine merchant, gained in the circle of the Marquise de Rambouillet. This open attitude is particularly characteristic of the salons of the third estate, such as that of the often mentioned Mme. de Geoffrins, the daughter of a 'valet de chambre'. The secondary role of wealth in these middle-class salons became well understood; a Mme. du Deffandud is said to have lacked the means to entertain her guests for dinner. Tinker's third characteristic of the salon is the literary, philosophical, or critical *conversation* usually held as a sequel to plays, sermons, or the reading of poems and essays. These were the occasions which gave rise to the impromptu critique, the short form, the *bon mot*, and the epigram.

Platonic love constitutes a fourth trait. Its focus is, of course,

[1] For the English salons compare Chauncey B. Tinker, *The Salon and English Literature; Chapters on the Interrelations of Literature and Society in the Age of Johnson*, New York, 1915, pp. 22–29. See also 'The Warwickshire Coterie', *Cambridge History of English Literature*, Vol. X, 1914, pp. 307 ff. and Valerian Thornius, *Salons*, New York, 1929.

[2] Tinker, *op. cit.*, p. 24.

the hostess, whose catalytic role is decisive for the conversation. Her social type is a far cry from the matron of the patriarchal family and the reticent housewives of puritan strata. The erotically charged atmosphere is symptomatic not only of the salon, but of the literature and art of the time. The fifth characteristic is the *preeminent role of women*, particularly the hostess.[1] She is, with one exception, a mature woman and considered the shining star of the salon, without becoming a learned lady.

The sixth and most important characteristic of the salon, mentioned by Tinker, is its timely role as a *mediator between life and literature*. This is significant in a period in which the princely patronage is on the wane while the democratic public is not yet formed. The salon fills the gap and becomes the heir to the earlier protective and promotional functions of the court. The salon offers authors and artists commissions, stimulation, and access to a selected public. Thus, the salons serve as a breeding-ground of literary demand, and as a clearing-house and market for the products of free-lance writers. In turn the writers who can no longer count on a continuing patronage are given opportunities to establish contacts with publishers, the agents of the emerging anonymous public, and to familiarize themselves with the fluctuating demand. This changed situation gives the author a new conception of himself: he faces his present employer, the public, as a social equal and he disdains permanent dependence on any single employer, so much so that d'Alembert could proclaim: 'les seuls grands seigneurs dont un homme de lettres doive désirer le commerce sont ceux qu'il peut traiter et regarder en toute sûreté, comme ses égaux, comme ses amis.'[2] A hostess of means provides funds, private pensions, and shelter, and she pays the printer's bill without humbling the writer or encroaching on his independence.

This exceptional era of the salons marks a turning-point in the development of the public from the feudal to the democratic type. The salons retained their social and literary functions

[1] Valerian Thornius calls the Rococo salon a 'woman's kingdom'. (*op. cit.*, p. 122.)

[2] d'Alembert, *Essais sur la société des gens de lettres*. Beljame characterizes the vicious circle of the poet who depends on the court as follows: 'c'est un cercle vicieux: plus ils ont besoin de la cour, plus ils s'abaissent, et plus ils s'abaissent, moins la cour fait pour eux.' (*Le public et les hommes de lettres au XVIII siècle*, 1881, p. 223.)

only as long as the public remained a tangible entity of manageable proportions. In a mass democracy the locus of selection gradually shifts from the small gathering to the anonymous public. The salons, moreover, mark the habitat of those poets and artists who have emancipated themselves from the upper classes and do not ally themselves with the lower strata, but endeavour to lead a free and unattached existence. For a time the salons are able to prevent the social disintegration of the creative intelligentsia, but as an emerging mass society gradually swallows up these literary enclaves, the intellectuals begin to drift apart. More and more they lose their previous contacts with society so that by the nineteenth century they exist for the most part in a state of social isolation. It is this marginal existence in a mass society which gives rise to new forms of amalgamation: the bohemian coteries and, more important, the *coffee-houses.*

The coffee-houses originated in the Near East, whence they reached the West via Constantinople, Vienna, and such port cities as Hamburg and Marseilles.[1] In London the coffee-house made its first appearance in 1652; the first Paris coffee-house was opened near the Stock Exchange in 1671. Its rapid spread in England gives us an intimation of its new and timely functions: the coffee-houses became the first centres of opinion in a partially democratized society.[2] Newspapers were still in their infancy. Periodicals resembling newspapers were circulated after 1662, but they were censored and the reading habit was not yet established. The coffee-house, on the other hand, presented a place for free expression, where pamphlets were read and speeches given.[3] The political

[1] For the following cf. H. Westerfrölke, *Englische Kaffeehäuser im Zeitalter Boydens und Addisons.* Jenaer Germanistische Forschungen, No 5.

[2] Cf. for the following Beljame, *op. cit.*, p. 172 ff.

[3] Addison in the *Spectator* (No. 403) describes humorously the goings-on in London coffee-houses: 'I know the faces of all the principal politicians with the bills of mortality; and every Coffee-house has some particular statesman belonging to it, who is the mouth of the street where he lives. I always take care to place myself near him, in order to know his judgment on the present posture of affairs. . . . I first of all called in at St. James, where I found the whole outward room in a buzz of politics; the speculations were but very indifferent towards the door, but grew finer as you advanced to the upper end of the room, and were so much improved by a knot of theorists . . . that I there heard the whole Spanish monarchy disposed of,

potential of the coffee-shop was evident in the French Revolution.[1]

The influence of the coffee-house on political opinion became so marked that in 1675 an ordinance was passed to put an end to them. The institution, however, was already too firmly entrenched and the ordinance had to be withdrawn. The subsequent development of the cafés took a characteristically English course—they transformed themselves into political *clubs*.[2] Instead of following up their development, let us dwell on the coffee-house as a new centre of group amalgamation.

Obviously these meeting-places owed their significance to the democratization of society and its élites. While the salons themselves exerted a democratizing influence on a semi-feudal society within the confines of small groups, the coffee-houses were almost entirely unrestricted. And while entry to the salon depended on introduction and social acceptability, the coffee-house societies became ultimately accessible to anybody who shared their views. Not the common style of living and not common friends, but like opinion constituted now the basis of amalgamation. The metropolis, which tends to detach the individual from his original milieu, makes such a new anonymous type of integration possible. The difference between the modern, open association and its early forerunner, the Greco-Roman sodality which joined persons regardless of kinship, illuminates the vast historical span that lies between them.

and all the line of Bourbons provided for in less than a quarter of an hour.' Quoted by John Timbs, *Club Life of London*, vol. II, London, 1866, pp. 39 f.

1 Cf. H. Cunow, *Politische Kaffeehäuser*, 1925, and Harold Routh's article on 'Steele and Addison' in the *Cambridge History of English Literature*, vol. IX, New York and Cambridge, 1913. See also N. G. Aldis, 'Book Production and Distribution, 1625–1800', p. 368, *Cambridge History of English Literature*, vol. XI, New York and Cambridge, 1914.

2 The clubs retained much of the character of the coffee-houses. First of all, they mostly centred around shared opinions. One club united in defence of a translation of Homer; another in defence of the Hanoverian succession; a third in defence of the ancients against the moderns. Since every man tended . . . to seek his own kind, the societies of gentlemen took on a factional character, whether their interests were literary, political, economic, or philosophical.' (Robert Allen, *The Clubs of Augustan London*, Cambridge, Mass., 1933, p. 34.) Second, the political clubs in particular 'were frequented by men of all ranks and professions, each group having a character and purpose of its own.' (*ibid.*, p. 34 f.)

The modern association which comes of age in the English and French coffee-house overrides rank and family ties; it is a product of a liberalized mass society in which the detached individual and his opinion form the bases of political alignments. In a sense the coffee-house coteries of the late eighteenth and early nineteenth century constituted the freest association of Western history; at no time was opinion as fluid and socially independent as in that period. In this regard the rise of a mass society with its more rigid divisions and alignments of views constitutes a regression. More of that later.

The individual, of course, was not entirely free even in the heydays of liberal society; in retrospect one can always trace the social sources of opinion. No society has set its members completely free, nor have ideas ever been conceived in a social vacuum. Indeed, the decay of the older, feudal type of stratification is accompanied by the growth of new class divisions.

To return from this digression on the coffee-house to the role of the salons. They were agents of selection as long as they were able to function as social 'elevators' and exert a controlling influence over the key organizations of learning and opinion-making. The salon of the Comtesse de Louynes was the last to have a voice in the Paris Academy elections (an influence which assured the election of the younger Dumas, Sardou, Flaubert, Gautier, Mistral, and Anatole France).[1] Moreover, the salons slowed the growth of political and literary élites and prevented an over-supply of intellectuals. The purely democratic method of selection inevitably produces an overflow in societies in which the writer, artist, and scholar enjoy a privileged status, as they do in Germany and the Latin countries. The salons not only functioned as organs of selection, but they sublimated the process of social ascendency and through their symbiotic character assimilated social outsiders and groomed promising talents for leadership. Of course, the salon proved to be a two-way channel to society—to the invited literati as well as to the hostess. The Jewish salons of Berlin owed their existence not only to the fact, mentioned by Mary Hargrave, that the Jews found compensation for their political disabilities in the cultivation of their homes,[2] but also to the fact that the

[1] A. Meyer, *Forty Years of Parisian Society*, 1912.

[2] Mary Hargrave, *Some German Women and their Salons*, London, 1912, p. 55.

drawing-room parties of women such as Henriette Hertz and Rachel Lewin served as windows to a larger and more varied world.

The conversations in the salon reflected its transitional setting as meeting-ground of an urbanized aristocracy and of mobile urban sophisticates. By contrast, the festive gatherings of the guilds were the affairs of only one class. The singfests or tavern-room banquets were occasions for merry-making with a prescribed agenda; they were framed by the common outlook and conventions of a homogeneous and cohesive stratum of burghers. The salon, on the other hand, commingled individuals of varied stations, loyalties, and views. The aristocracy still constituted a centre of gravity, but the intellectual climate and the character of the conversation formed a miniature replica of a competitive and mobile society in which status was no longer inherited but achieved and precariously held from one occasion to the next. The colloquy was an opportunity for conquest; the wit and flashes of originality opened careers, and the ability to triumph in the space of a few minutes was the key to success. But no triumph is lasting unless it is instantly converted into an appointment or a publisher's commission.

The salon exemplifies another trait of the modern association—its limited claim on the individual. Otto von Gierke has pointed to the inclusive character of the medieval corporations and the gilds. Their composite functions absorbed the entire person and a whole gamut of his interests—religious, legal, economic, and convivial. By contrast, the modern association affects the individual tangentially, involves only limited concerns, leaves him relatively free, and keeps his situation undefined. The same individual occurs in many intersecting groupings, and it is this multiple affiliation which produces the differentiated personality of the early nineteenth century.[1] He has avenues of escape, for he can withdraw from one group to another and his stakes in any one are limited. The salon is one of the first to set a pattern for behaviour in a fluid and impromptu situation: where nothing is prescribed the premium is on responsiveness and nimble wit, and where the

[1] G. Simmel, *Soziologie*, Leipzig, 1908, Chap. X, esp. pp. 710 ff. and 763 ff.

issues are limited one can meet them without gritting one's teeth.

It is no accident that the conservative clubs of early nineteenth-century Germany are still reminiscent of the medieval gild or the punctilio of court assemblies. I refer to such clubs as the 'Christlich deutsche Tischgesellschaft' and the 'Tunnel an der Spree'.[1] We find none of the informality of English political clubs; the tone of the meetings seems ponderous, the sessions have scheduled speakers, and records are kept of the stories told.[2] Although we find in these clubs some features of the salon, notably the amalgamation of junkers, government officials, and romantic liberals, the fluidity and informality of their English counterpart is missing and the climate of the German conservative clubs of the time does not yet reflect the social forms of a competitive society.

In sum, the special moulds of intellectual amalgamation furnish a significant basis for the understanding of the roles which the educated strata of a society play and, from case to case, they even throw light on the prevalent style of expression and the mentality which the more articulate elements of society evolve.[3]

(*c*) *The Intelligentsia and the Classes*

The foregoing discussion might create a biased impression of the intelligentsia as a self-begotten and self-perpetuating

[1] Karl Mannheim, 'Conservative Thought', *Essays on Sociology and Social Psychology*, ed. Paul Kecskemeti, London and New York, 1953.

[2] Some of the stories, notably those of Heinrich von Kleist, were promptly printed by the *Berliner Abendblatt*. Cf. R. Steig, *Kleist's Berliner Kämpfe*, 1901.

[3] We refer in this connection to Harold Routh's remarks in the *Cambridge History of English Literature* on the English writer. Routh traces his characteristic facility in writing clearly without becoming scholastic and circumlocutional to the influence of the early eighteenth century coffee-house. This is, we are told, the nursery of middle-class culture. Previously even pamphleteers used a bookish and scholastic style, for they were conversant only with printed matter. The coffee-house, on the other hand, centres around the conversation. 'The man whose mind is trained by the interchange of ideas is more adaptable and adroit than the book learner.' The coffee-houses were unwitting promotors of a new humanism and only these centres could put a writer 'in touch with the thoughts and sentiments of his time'.

group, for so far we have not considered its dependence on the larger society. This relationship is our present subject.

In a sense, intellectuals are renegades who have abandoned their parental stratum. This fact makes it imperative that we take stock of the circumstances of this detachment and the subsequent relationship of the apostate to his former class. New social opportunities accrue to an intelligentsia whenever a dominant stratum proves unable to discharge newly-emerging functions of leadership. These are the occasions for the selective rise of intermediate classes, and it was these situations in which the ministeriales advanced to prominence and elements of the middle classes moved into the scholarly professions.[1]

(*i*) *Types of an Ascending Intelligentsia*

I am inclined to distinguish between individual ascendency into an open group and advancement into a closed stratum. Both movements are accompanied by particular experiences which tend to solidify into distinct social attitudes.

Individuals who move up singly into an open and generally accessible stratum tend to evolve an individualistic and heroic philosophy of success.[2] Their attitude is likely to be activistic and optimistic. The individuals of the liberal bourgeoisie, for example, moved into positions which an expanding capitalism made available. Their rise constitutes the most spectacular example of upward mobility on a mass scale. Success came to the enterprising individual in much the same way as it came to the condottieri, the merchants, and the bankers of the Italian Renaissance. The entrepreneur could assume in good faith that almost anyone with energy and sagacity would ultimately make his way. Each person owes his success to himself, perhaps to his good fortunes, but not to the particular nature

[1] For the scholarly occupations compare F. v. Bezold, *Staat und Gesellschaft des Reformationszeitalters*, in *Kultur der Gegenwert*, ed. von Hinneberg, Part II, Div. 15/1. '. . . the overwhelming majority of scholars and artists came from middle-class or peasant families; the new culture was of urban origin, but it was only in the sixteenth century that its basically aristocratic character found an overt expression . . . in a group which became estranged from the ways of the people.' (p. 102).

[2] See Robert Merton, 'Social Structure and Anomie', *Social Theory and Social Structure*, Glencoe, Illinois, 1949, p. 131.

of circumstances. Indeed, how can anyone share the credit for his success with a particularly-structured society unless he can compare it with another? The individual, therefore, is quite naturally inclined to hypostatize his life history as the cosmic conditions of existence. He generalizes from the fact that he found the circumstances he knows responsive to his ambitions. He takes a hospitable attitude towards the class from which he has risen and maintains a help-yourself type of philosophy concerning society in general.

Movements into a closely knit rank with an established *esprit de corps* stimulated a different attitude. Individuals who rapidly rise into an exclusive group are inclined to acquire a new identification, to adopt the conventions of that group, and to accept the social hierarchy into which they have risen.[1] The rise of scholars in the bureaucratic state, occasioned by the growing need for government officials, particularly jurists, is a case in point. The rapid advancement of scholars constituted an exception in a rigidly-graded, caste-like society which offered little scope for notable careers, save the journeymen who would become master craftsmen and some hucksters who ended up as merchants.[2] The newly-risen scholars proved themselves able spokesmen of the existing feudal hierarchy in which they laid claim to a special nobility, the *nobilitas literaria*, as an equivalent of the *nobilitas generis*. Such a demand was outlined by M. Stephani, a jurist of Greifswald, in his *Tractatus de Nobilitate*, in 1617. At the tables of commoners the *doctores* should be seated as noblemen; in court their voice was to carry more weight than that of commoners: if, for example, a doctor and a commoner were both under suspicion of murder, the felony was to be attributed to the commoner, and so forth. The effect of these exertions, made in a voluminous literature on the *nobilitas literaria*,[3] was indeed a progressive upgrading of intellectuals.

A second consequence of upward movements of this type is the radical dissociation from the parent stratum. Again, the

[1] E. Lederer, 'Die Klassenschichtung, ihr soziologischer Ort und ihre Wandlungen,' *Archiv für Sozialwissenschaft*, Vol. 65, 1931, p. 539 ff.

[2] Cf. Truntz, 'Der deutsche Späthumanismus um 1600 als Standeskultur,' *Zeitschrift für Geschichte der Erziehung und des Unterrichts*, 1931.

[3] For further details cf. Truntz, *op. cit.*, p. 48.

ministeriales furnish a good illustration. Their intellectual productivity during the later period of the minnesong is an upshot of their deliberate assimilation of courtly culture. Another symptom of this retroverted disengagement is the inclination towards increasingly elaborate conventions. Such a tendency usually marks the point of social saturation. An advancing group begins to ritualize its achieved status when it has reached its apex and exhausted its opportunities. In their ascending phase the ministeriales attained status through service, particularly on horseback. Throughout most of the middle ages the qualification for mounted service ranked above noble birth. The equestrian sword was a badge of distinction, even in the hands of kings.[1] But in its stabilized period the ministerial nobility conventionalized its rank and made birth rather than service the hallmark of nobility.

(*ii*) *Types of Intelligentsia Formed of Displaced and Blocked Persons*

We now turn to those classes and particularly those intellectuals whose social expectations are thwarted. In reference to these E. Lederer speaks of tendencies towards isolation and self-glorification. A stratum which is abruptly thrown back upon its original position does not emulate the upper classes but assumes a defiant attitude and develops contravening models of thought and behaviour.[2] The situation itself makes such attitudes probable; to what extent they become acute depends on secondary factors, as for example the capacity to articulate and to evolve a counter ideology. Where the conditions for the crystallization of an articulate opposition do not exist, resentment becomes covert and its expression confined to the individual or his immediate primary group. Such a submerged animosity remains futile and socially unproductive. Where, however, circumstances provide an outlet for the collective expression of discontent, resentment becomes a

[1] Karl Weinhold, *Die deutschen Frauen in Mittelalter*, Vol. 1, p. 232, Third Ed., 1897.

[2] 'The effect of blocked mobility on the inner world of the individual can be observed in many situations, among a variety of people. Frustrated workers who find opportunity unavailable often cut down on work output. . . . Others may take a more positive stand, join a union and become union leaders who use the union hierarchy to satisfy their aspirations.' (W. Lloyd Warner, *American Life: Dream and Reality*, Chicago, 1953, p. 119.)

constructive stimulus and creates a climate for social criticism which in the long run a dynamic society needs.

This is the situation which advances social self-awareness and favours the rise of an intelligentsia. True, such strata may also emerge from a state of satiety, as often happens with the second generation of a newly-established stratum. R. Hamann has attempted to trace the culture of the early Renaissance back to the role of a second generation.[1] Cosimo de Medici, for example, was 'the business man who found his true medium in the bank, conscientiously attended to the affairs of state, and firmly believed in the inseparability of his and his country's interests. He lived simply and austerely . . . while Lorenzo the Magnificent neglected business, brought his private estate to the verge of bankruptcy, and made physical and spiritual pleasure his guiding principle.'[2] Inherited wealth, however, is not the most common source of a preoccupation with culture; far more frequent is the stimulus of an arrested personal advancement. Quite typical is the situation of the outdistanced strata of the upper classes, as Lederer pointed out and as the example of the minnesingers has shown. These thwarted individuals tend to veer away from the complacent outlook of their peers and to become articulate critics of their society.

Dissenting lower classes gravitate in the same direction. In the first phase of their conscious self-assertion lower classes react to the conventions of upper classes with the adoption of customs of their own and the creation of an utopia which poses both a counter-image of the existing order and a critique of its ideologies. It is only after a longer period of consolidation that the impulse to dissent matures into a rational critique of society and a realistic opposition.[3] Such utopias and counter-images are the creations of individuals and not of restive but inarticulate masses, although thwarted intellectuals may become their allies and spokesmen. It is their articulation of discontent and their deliberate counter-symbols which crystallize mass consensus and action. The originators of a class-consciousness

[1] R. Hamann, *Die Frührenaissance der italienischen Malerei*. Die Kunst in Bildern, Jena 1909, p. 23 ff. A. v. Martin, *Die Soziologie der Renaissance*, Stuttgart, 1932 and "Kultursoziologie der Renaissance." in *Handwörterbuch der Soziologie*, ed. A. Vierkandt, 1931. [2] Hamann, *op. cit.*, p. 3.

[3] For a discussion of this subject compare the chapter on 'The Utopian Mentality' in my *Ideology and Utopia*, London and New York, 1936.

rarely belong to the stratum whose self-awareness they awaken. It is this vicarious participation in a class situation which gives the intellectual a secondary footing in society. He can precipitate the responses of masses only by immersing himself in their situation and thus transcending his own position. He, the isolated individual, acquires in this process a collective orientation through extended contacts with a class to which he does not belong. In fact, he must follow in order to lead.

Dispossessed members of an upper class present a different type of career. They are mostly the products of displacement by intruders from below. Sometimes the partial displacement of an upper class is the result of its inability to bear the economic burden of prescribed class conventions. Nonconformity to costly usage often blocks the avenue to a customary type of advancement. Quite typical, for instance, is the perplexity of the sons of an upper class who are unable to finance a long waiting period which normally leads to privileged positions. These situations give rise to a distinct type of intelligentsia. (Needless to say we are dealing, as sociology in general does, with typical probabilities and not with fixed and predetermined life histories of individuals.)

Let us now sketch out the typical courses open to an intelligentsia which evolves in the uprooting process.

First phase. The above-mentioned pecuniary inability to sustain conventional habits is a typical source of frustration. We usually take our established customs and expectations for granted without much thought of their particular economic prerequisites so long as they are assured. We become conscious of our habits and dispositions when an economic change forces us to modify and adapt them to a new situation. Women, for instance, who are accustomed to a sheltered existence usually develop a marked sensitivity and a particular capacity for sympathy which they must discard when suddenly a lowered economic ceiling forces them to face the hardships of a keener struggle. The immediate reaction to such a change is usually a vague sense of discomfort. But when the discrepancy between a changed situation and an acquired disposition which has lost its earlier function continues, a stock-taking reflectivity ensues. Its trend will depend on whether it takes place in uprooted persons or in those whose rise was halted midway. The reflectivity of individuals who become intellectualized in the uprooting process marks the *second phase* and takes the following course.

The experience of change is accompanied by a continued identification with the previous situation. When this experience becomes generalized, we arrive at the philosophy of the 'good old times'; the ideology of traditionalism. Individuals who have not acquired the capacity for articulation will spontaneously idealize the past as the focus of their nostalgic dreams. Intellectuals in the same situation will adopt the current imagery of their time and accordingly elaborate a mythology of the archaic age, or a philosophy of history which glorifies the Middle Ages as a theory of slow, organic change; these are the ideologies which the romantic intelligentsia of Germany embraced in partial response to the revolutionary jeopardy of the landed nobility. The conceptual form varies from time to time, but the trend toward the traditional or romantic interpretation of change is recurrent wherever an intelligentsia forms from the uprooted elements of a class.

The *third phase* completes the process and makes the rejection of an altered situation final. This is often the upshot of a precipitous change which does not permit a gradual re-adaptation and which irrefutably thwarts the wish for better times. Now the traditional attitude becomes collective and reactive against the changed social order or its advocates. As every movement has a nucleus and a periphery, so the nucleus of a reaction consists of persons who cannot reconcile themselves to existing circumstances. One can diagnose among them three distinct types:

1 members of an older generation whose position does not permit a readjustment;
2 members of declining vocations; and
3 former recipients of independent income whose previous situation inhibits an understanding of change.

The *inability* to accept new facts creates its own ideology, as most social situations do, and it soon becomes a concerted *unwillingness*. These are the sources from which reaction derives its core troops. The intransigence and determination of such residual strata can at times sway wavering masses.

The *fourth phase* is reached by persons of a similar background but of a subsequent generation who are able to reconcile themselves to an altered state of affairs. Usually a reaction does not outlast one generation, and its disintegration begins with individuals who have not lost freedom of choice. Their detachment from their own stratum is usually accompanied by the typical symptoms of dissociation: an inner-directed critique and scepticism towards the older exponents of their group. These individuals pass through two stages of doubt. First they discount the creed and promises of the revolutionaries, but eventually they also lose faith in their own pre-revolutionary ideals. This is the sceptical state of a reactionary ideology and it marks the social genesis of scepticism.

Digression on the Social Roots of Scepticism

Pareto and his followers have offered a modern example of scepticism which bears some features of the double disillusionment just described. The offspring of Genoese patricians, engineer, one-time industrial executive, and later professor, Pareto had the sober and unsentimental attitude towards ideologies in general and toward democracy, liberalism, and socialism in particular, which is characteristic of the politically alert members of his class. But he was not committed to the creed of his own stratum. He saw in history a more or less stationary process in which élites continue to displace one another and masses are periodically set in motion according to certain laws of psychology. The essence of history is the struggle of the élites.

It is impossible to find a single formula for the various types of scepticism. Certainly not all types have social roots. Some varieties are based on purely individual experience which does not form groups, while others may be attributed to a temperamental predisposition. Whatever its basis, scepticism becomes a genuine and consistent response when it is sustained by typical social constellations. To study these is of great importance, for they invariably form landmarks of social change.

Generally speaking, *scepticism emerges from the eclipse of a group-centred world view.* Inasmuch as the assurance of a *Weltanschauung* depends on the security of its proponents, the individual begins to doubt the established creed of his group when his footing in it becomes insecure or when its cohesiveness is on the decline. Contemporary observations coincide in this regard with the lessons of history. Heberle, a student of social mobility in America, observes: 'Although breaches of law occur and the mores will be violated in a stable society, nobody questions their validity; only a mobile society kindles doubt and critique.'[1]

Let us return once more to the minnesingers for an illustration of a simple type of scepticism in a declining society. It was the alarming 'Zwivel', the doubt of the twelfth and thirteenth centuries, with which Wolfram von Eschenbach was contending. While the more firmly moored Wolfram sought to conquer and subdue his doubts, the urbanized Gottfried von Strassburg openly scoffed at ecclesiastical affairs. Whether the perplexity of a waning faith is resolved through an escape to tradition or shrugged off with cynical irony, it is the recurrent problem of an intelligentsia in a situation of social decline. When we contrast the first phase of the minnesong espoused by an upper nobility of the soil with the later period which flourished under the auspices of vagrant and marginal individuals, we realize that the uprooting process which sets intellectuals adrift passed through the same phases then as it does today.

The reader may wonder whether we do not unnecessarily confound doubts of the religious type with the shaken loyalty to a social system. On what thought level doubt is experienced and what its concrete object is depends on the conceptual edifice which a society builds around its mores. Scepticism cannot take the form of a sociological critique in a culture which is not socially reflective. The doubt of the uprooted individual takes the form in which a shaken system is ordinarily interpreted to him: the religious poet becomes an agnostic, the politically-conscious patriot turns into a cosmopolitan, and the metaphysician ends up a relativist. Of particular sociological interest, however, is the progress from the simple disbelief, which doubts one or another tenet, toward a radical scepticism or, as I would call it, a *double scepticism*. This arises when two different horizons impinge on the same person and when opposite creeds of equal vehemence lay claim to him. Such a

[1] R. Heberle, *Über die Mobilität der Bevölkerung in den Vereinigten Staaten*. Jena, 1929.

double view of things is often the result of a spatial coincidence of consecutive beliefs. By that I mean a situation in which an older group continues to advocate an earlier tenet at the same time that a rising group advances a new one. The individual who has lost his security in either group finds himself in the cross-fire of opposite contentions. He then discovers the perplexing fact that the same things have different appearances. This puzzlement marks the origin of a *genuine epistemology*, which is more than a mere elaboration and justification of a preconceived view. For epistemology is an expression of a shaken faith not only in one particular truth, but in truth as such and in the human capacity to know.

It is no accident, therefore, that a genuine epistemology made its appearance twice in Western history. The first time it originated with the Sophists and Socrates, the second time with Descartes. What else were the Sophists but urban intellectuals who experienced the impact of two concomitant ways of life: the older, feudal-mythological and the urban artisans' with their inquisitiveness about the making of things? Some moralists are inclined to see in the Sophists' flippant play with alternative solutions nothing but cynical tomfoolery. For a world in which everything used to have but one meaning it was a shocking experience indeed to discover the multiple criteria of truth. Socrates himself was a Sophist who toyed with ambiguities and contradictions before reaching conclusive solutions. As the Sophists conceptualized the conflict of two worlds, so did Descartes derive his theory of knowledge from the clash of modern science with declining scholasticism whose methodology he could not quite relinquish. Yet the scepticism which Descartes generalized to an epistemology became an impetus of modern inquiry.

As epistemology was born of a twilight situation of radical scepticism, so did psychology emerge from an ethical pluralism. Psychology becomes possible when the focus of attention shifts from the ethical norms of behaviour to the actual individual. But the individual remains a mere construct of the universalists until he is discovered in a situation which permits choices and escapes. Once the alternatives of man widen beyond the polarity of sin and salvation his conduct can become the subject of a typology for which the universalists had not even a nomenclature. It is the ethical disorientation and the Montaignean agnosticism which permitted the rise of an unparalleled curiosity about the empirical variance of human responses. Montaigne's tongue-in-cheek treatment of trivial incidents and momentous historical events on the same plane betrays an iconoclastic disregard for rank differences in human affairs and the future scientist's curiosity about the *omnia ubique*. Montaigne, like the Sophists, took delight in playing with appearances, as Rabelais relished laughing the ruffian's laughter. What stirred Montaigne was the mutability of man and his circumstances. 'The feelings for good and evil depend on the opinion we form about them. But the difference of opinions clearly shows that they come only conditionally to us.'[1] The conditioning agent which Montaigne had in mind was nothing else than the variable human psyche.

Scepticism enters its *fifth phase* when it proceeds beyond the stage of disorientation towards what I propose to call a second faith. Of course, not all individuals of a reactionary intelligentsia reach this phase. A few are favoured by social circumstances which permit scepticism as a permanent way of life, as was possible to Montaigne. But sooner or later most displaced intellectuals seek a way out of a state of suspense and back to an affirmative and categorical faith. A creed so embraced, however, lacks the artless and virgin simplicity of beliefs with which rising classes assert themselves. The second faith marks the rally of uprooted individuals who cannot endure isolation and are forced to find reaffiliation with an unshaken stratum.

One of the disciples of Pareto, the radical agnostic in Lausanne, was Mussolini, the emigrant and sceptic intellectual who had seen through the mechanics of history and found nothing to believe in. Such intellectuals do not put their trust in the apocalyptic hopes of primitive strata facing extinction. Futile as these hopes may be, they spring irrepressibly from a common impulse of despondency, while the second faith of intellectuals bears the features of a contrived mythology. This is particularly so when historical myths are devised in an age of positivistic and critical historiography. It is often forgotten that reassuring faith grows out of a self-confident group or an

[1] *Montaigne's Gesammelte Schriften*, edited by Joachim Bode, München-Berlin, 1915, Vol. 2, p. 144.

emergent social order and not from a deliberate compact of wavering individuals.[1]

As we attempted to locate the social genesis of scepticism, so we must now ask what the seat of affirmative beliefs is. Here again one should remember that although the predisposition towards categorical beliefs may be individually acquired, it is particular constellations which attract individuals so inclined, and present continuing impulses for the formation of apodictic convictions.

(a) The primary situation which encourages apodictic attitudes is that of the spokesmen of a homogeneous group. We speak more often than we realize not in our own name but for certain groups. We do so mostly without an explicit mandate and without knowing for whom we speak. By the same token a conflict which uniformly affects a whole group occasions more clear-cut and firm views than issues which divide it.

(b) The *second* component of an affirmative position lies in in the bi-polarity of a social situation. A group which seeks to assert itself against a single opponent evolves a more clear-cut conception of itself than a middle group which faces opposition on either side. The middle position is typically more tentative and less articulate than either extreme in a conflict of two. Witness the familiar dilemma of the liberal between the tradionalist and the radical.

The *third* opportunity for a categorical point of view is that of the intransigent outsider and critic who does not participate in a going concern and therefore need not compromise or make qualifications.

The characteristics of an intelligentsia which originates in the uprooting process become clearer when they are compared with those intellectuals whose rise is blocked. The latter usually adopt the prospective utopia of an ascending class rather than the romantic ideals of a retreating stratum. When they arrive at an impasse and enter the sceptical phase, their disillusionment does not become radical and complete, and they do not reach the point of double scepticism. They do not completely renounce their initial faith in 'progress'—the genuine disbelievers in progress usually come from classes which have

[1] Compare Ernst Bertram, *Nietzsche, Versuch einer Mythologie*, 1918, and E. H. Kantorowicz, *Friedrich der Zweite*, 1927.

grown accustomed to their past attainments and take success for granted. Advancing intellectuals of recent times incline toward a sociological orientation, chiefly because their success *increasingly* depends on familiarity with complex conditions. The 'elevators' of contemporary society, to use Sorokin's expression, are far from the simple channels through which the eighteenth century bureaucratic State or the medieval Church selected and trained their officials. By contrast, the literati of the upper classes are inclined to take their position for granted; since they have not experienced the making of a career in its small detail and lack the familiarity with the intricate mechanism which produces an average success, they are prone to rely on summary and sweeping conceptions. This is how occasionally we come to attribute an unanalyzed phase of the social process to the royalists or the republicans, to faith or agnosticism, and to heroes or human failings. Another manifestation of such aloofness is the retreat to internals—an occasional escape of persons who do not hope to master their circumstances. This tendency is reminiscent of magic which is 'internally' applied to things which are beyond external control.

A sober appraisal of social forces is, however, natural to those individuals of the upper classes whose managerial functions keep them in daily touch with the workings of a complex society. The executive of industrial, political, or military organizations is in a position to acquire the habit of seeing developments in their multiple relationships. His approach tends to be pragmatic and, although he is likely to be concerned with the immediate impact of events, his situation sensitizes him to involved relationships.

We have seen that the performance of an intelligentsia and its type of ideation depend on the circumstances under which it becomes reflective and articulate. Whether it is a displaced or a rising group or a stratum blocked in its upward movement, it tends to crystallize the dominant conventions of its society. Their nature varies from one culture to another, depending on the avenues through which an intelligentsia comes to assume key functions in a society. The variations may range from the gymnastic and poetical virtuosos of Greece through the literati of India, Judea, and Islam to the chivalrous, bureaucratic, and technical élites of the West. Once the intelligentsia assumes its place, it sets the pattern of cultivation for the dominant élite and through it for the larger society. In this sense we accept Lederer's summary formulation: 'When this stratum is in the lead of an ascending class, its conventions will permeate that class and set the standards for the socially desirable measure of cultivation. When the dynamic process, the searching inquiry, becomes conventionalized, some of its products are transformed into a static tradition.' And he adds: 'The convention of cultivation does not permanently set the norms of a class. The convention may vanish with the rise of another stratum whose interests and way of life offer no scope for it.'[1]

(*d*) *The Social Habitat of Intellectuals*

The last observation already touches on our present subject: the role of the educated in the larger society. Although the greater part of our contemporary intelligentsia constitutes an open and loose aggregation, it does enter, from time to time, into symbiotic relations to one or another class, and it frequently forms special groupings of its own. We have dealt previously with some examples of these amalgamations. Now we turn to what I propose to call the social habitat of intellectuals. We distinguish the following three types: the *local*, the *institutional* (or organizational), and the *detached habitat.*

The stage for the *local habitat* is set in small and middle-sized communities. Their culture owes its persuasiveness and durability to its firm roots in the continuing concerns and understandings of the neighbourhood. The older generations play their part in the survival of these local traditions. We find the sustaining groups usually attached to the local bodies of self-government and held together through friendship, patronage, and conviviality. At times the local élite may become a centre of regional culture of major proportions, a subject for which the reader is referred to Nadler's work.[2] The unconscious products of local

[1] E. Lederer, 'Die Klassenschichtung, ihr soziologischer Ort und ihre Wandlungen,' *Archiv für Sozialwissenschaft und Sozialpolitik*, 1931, Vol. 65, p. 579 ff.

[2] J. Nadler, *op. cit.* Good observations on the local intelligentsia may be found in J. Burkhardt, *The Civilization of the Renaissance in Italy*, London, 1944.

contacts, such primary culture grew in late medieval and modern painting and the various regional styles such as evolved in the Flemish, Cologne, and Burgundian schools. Quite naturally the intellectual climate of a city or region depends on the relationships of the local and the foreign élites.[1] It has been variously pointed out that learning and literature in patrician Nuremberg differed perceptibly from those in gild-dominated Augsburg. The humanism of Nuremberg was the culture of immigrants and perhaps of the younger generation of patricians—the older generation held aloof from the humanists. Men of the stature of Hans Sachs, Dürer, and Vischer were immigrants. In democratic Augsburg, on the other hand, where the gilds sat in the city council from 1368, the mayor, physicians, priests, and monks were the devotees of humanism. It is interesting to note that in Augsburg the educated physicians took the place of the thwarted poets, and it was there that the direct transition from the mastersingers to the humanists was easily made. The local setting of Augsburg culture makes it possible to interpret its literary life, including the finer details of style, in the light of the social alignments of the town.

The literati of *instituti ns* present a different type. Medieval Christian culture derived its international character not from medieval society but from the ubiquitous organization of the Church and the identity of its doctrine. The cathedrals were similar not in the same sense as that in which the tenements of industrial cities resemble one another. In the manufacturing centres it is similar needs and conditions which call for similar solutions, and even the urban masses are perceptibly losing more and more of their local and national peculiarities, while the international style of the cathedrals was due to the migration of stone-masons and architects and the far-flung network

[1] Holzknecht remarks of the relationship of the local and mobile intelligentsia of Greece: '. . . with Ibycus, Simonides, and Bacchylides, poets cease to be local poets, serving one state or deity, and offer their services to whoever seeks them. So likewise, for the first time Simonides (early fifth century B.C.) introduced the practice of selling songs of praise for money, a practice which was apparently shocking to the Greek taste, and at the same time poets became the friends and counsellors of princes. Petrarch did not occupy a more important place among the princes of medieval Italy than did Simonides in Greece . . .', K. J. Holzknecht, *Literary Patronage in the Middle Ages*, p. 7.

of the Church. This network and the identical doctrine constitute the social habitat of the clerics, and not their places of residence or social background. More generally, it is the social habitat of the intellectual, rather than his class or residence, which offers a clue to his ideation, although in the Church the latter components asserted themselves on an increasing scale and eventually disrupted the unitary outlook of the clergy.

Stable and well-entrenched political parties create their own intelligentsia. But there is today a substantial number of politically affiliated writers and professional persons who do not belong to the core organizations of parties. Their history goes back to the 18th-century political clubs of London.[1] We should distinguish these from the political functionaries proper—persons who are salaried and disciplined by political organizations. They resemble the institutional types of intelligentsia of earlier periods. The humanists of a past period form another example of an affiliated body of literati, namely those who performed in close attachment to a feudal stratum. Although they never evolved a well-knit organization of their own, comparable to the Church, their social dependence placed them in a position resembling that of an organizational intelligentsia. The standardization of learning made a certain internal homogeneity among the humanists possible.

The *detached* intellectual constitutes the third category. A large number of educated persons in our age have at least a passing acquaintance with this station in life. There are still many of them whose outlook is characteristically detached. They may have their political preferences, but they are not committed to any party or denomination. This detachment, however, is not absolute. One need only think of the majority of journalists who are bound by both the obvious and intangible commitments of the press. And yet, their political choices and

[1] 'During the reign of Queen Anne the writer without independent means almost necessarily allied himself with a political party. His bread was not buttered on the side of non-partisanship. His livelihood came most often from positions in the gift of Whig or Tory leaders. Before he was considered worthy of patronage he had to make a reputation for himself by producing some work of genuine literary merit, for which he was generally paid little. When his mark was made, he had often to defend his party with his pen in order to ensure the assistance which would allow him the leisure to compose further masterpieces.' (Robert Allen, *op. cit.*, p. 230.)

social affiliations are not easy to predict, for they fluctuate to a degree which is characteristic of this stratum only. The dependence of the writer on his employer does not prevent him from being affected by social, political, or religious currents which take shape outside his employer's office, his community, or his country. The journalist, the writer, the radio commentator, and the leisure-time scholar do not depend for their opinion on face-to-face contacts only. Spatial barriers mean comparatively little to them, precisely because of the medium of their occupation.

One cannot, therefore, adequately understand the behaviour of this stratum by taking into account solely its social situation, its class interests, or its habitats. Nor is it sufficient to consider the social movements or the intellectual currents in which individuals participate. Even the professional utterances of these individuals will not help materially to predict their responses. The very fact that they continue to face open alternatives, that they are in a position to make up their minds in a variety of ways, is likely to stultify any simplified approach to the role of this stratum. In Germany the same intelligentsia which echoed the ideas of the French revolution became soon the banner-bearer of romanticism and the restoration. The Italian intellectuals who supported the political left after the first World War helped to shape Fascism shortly after.

An understanding of this stratum will, unlike the analysis of a clear-cut class, require that we consider a large complexity of factors which bear on the situation of intellectuals. Of those, the most important are: the social background of the individual; the particular phase of his career curve—whether he is on the upgrade, at a plateau, or on the downgrade; whether he moves up individually or as a member of a group; whether he is blocked in his advancement or thrown back on his initial situation; the phase of a social movement in which he participates—the initial, middle, or the terminal shape; the position of his generation in relation to other generations; his social habitat; and, finally, the type of aggregation in which he performs. If complete determinism is impractical in any area of sociology, it is even more so in the approach to a group of individuals whose primary trait is that they are set adrift and therefore capable of vicarious participation in a great variety of social movements. Yet, even though we cannot effectively predict the behaviour of intellectuals, we are in a position to understand why a certain thought current emerges in a certain situation, what its future course is likely to be under circumstances already foreshadowed, and how individuals of known social characteristics may be expected to make their choices in given alternatives. In sum, the attempt at a prognosis from a well-circumscribed situation is not altogether futile.

7. THE NATURAL HISTORY OF THE INTELLECTUAL

The foregoing analyses have paid little attention to the traits of the intellectual as such. We are thinking particularly of his aloofness and inclination to withdraw from the practical concerns of society. One must trace this psychology with its assets and liabilities to the position which the intellectual occupies in the division of labour.

It has been often held against the intellectual that he is remote from life. While this is largely true, we must remember that a complex division of labour creates a general state of aloofness from which hardly anyone can escape. In a highly-differentiated society the overall scheme of things becomes increasingly obscure to most individuals. This holds true for the man who wields a drill press as much as for the official or the farmer. The horizon of the executive and the diplomat may include a larger part of the social apparatus, but they, too, lose touch with the masses and they, too, see only fragments of the whole. The question, therefore, is not what occupations afford a complete view of reality, but what segments of society are within the purview of given stations in life. In this regard the intellectual has a certain advantage. Not only is his potential compass wider, but his very aloofness helps him to escape the optical limitations of particular occupations and interests. He does not run the risk of the practitioner who is prone to conceive the world in the image of his vocation or his particular social contacts. The preoccupations of the intellectual sensitize him to stereotypes which conceal rather than expose existing problems, and he can withdraw from commitments which impose blinkers on him.

Still there can be no doubt about the morbid aspects of a

permanent state of disengagement. The person who must face the daily consequences of his actions cannot but acquire pragmatic habits and a critical view within the radius of his vocational practice. The intellectual lacks some of these restraints. He meets no checks when he dwells in the long-range perspective of things or on a level of abstraction on which one faces no consequences. Ideas which cannot misfire easily become ends in themselves and a source of solitary intoxication. The thinker whom events cannot refute is prone to forget the principal purpose of thought: to know and to foresee in order to act. Free and unimpeded ideation at times invites illusions of grandeur, for the mere ability to communicate ideas about vexatious questions seducingly resembles their mastery. Ordinarily the private conjurings of secluded individuals cause no ripples, but in crises an intellectual ecstasy may fall on fertile soil. Masses who grope for security occasionally follow a shaman whose utterances suggest omnipotence. This is the point at which the expectancy of an insecure mass and the ecstasy of the solitary intellectual can make contact.

The intellectual's proneness to lose touch with reality has something to do with his tendency to stay in his study and to meet only individuals of his kind.[1] Of no small importance, however, is the secure and financially independent existence which a large part of the literati used to have. The obvious assets of a leisure-class existence are balanced by its temptations, and practically all intellectual leisure classes face the same dilemma. Surely, a certain spare time is a necessary basis of cultivation, and the precondition of attention to affairs which do not wholly concern the daily satisfaction of wants. But a leisure-class existence is in itself a source of estrangement from reality, for it conceals the frictions and tensions of life and invites a sublimated and internalized perception of things. It remains a problem of our culture how to allocate to its intelligentsia the indispensable leisure in a form which will minimize aloofness and the temptation to escape into a realm of illusions.

Another trait of the educated person results from his book learning. It is in itself a source of remoteness and of specific

[1] Benjamin Disraeli's father offers a good example of the English variety of such a detached existence. Cf. André Maurois, *Disraeli; a Picture of the Victorian Age*, London, 1937.

delusions to which reference has been made earlier. We tried to show how the impression of an immanent evolution of ideas arises from the fact that the scholar encounters them in the library and not in their real setting. While books expose the student to situations to which he has no direct access, they also create a false sense of participation—the illusion of having shared the lives of peoples without knowing of their toils and stresses.

A third temptation of the intellectual is to retreat into his privacy. He is not the only one so inclined, but the leaning may impair his performance more radically than anybody else's. This characteristically modern inclination may be described as a tendency to withdraw certain concerns from public exposure. Park and Burgess refer to the phenomenon as a withdrawal or exclusion from communication.[1] The village affords little privacy. Geiger seems right in maintaining that the contemporary village still does not recognize a clearly demarcated area of intimacy or at least does not admit the polarity of the public and the intimate concerns to the extent the city does.[2] Domestic affairs are still open to public scrutiny, and it is the function of village gossip to realize the communal claim on the individual. The disappearance of this all-inclusive domain of the public in the city may be traced back to three factors. The urban dwelling creates isolation in proportion to its size. Not unimportant is the disappearance of the neighbourhood organization. Finally, the city occasions fewer common concerns which require the voluntary cooperation of each individual. The complex division of labour, including the expansion of public services, relieves the person of many civic functions which he must perform in the village, so that the interdependence of city dwellers loses its direct and manifest character. They can, therefore, retreat into the privacy of their apartments and withhold certain affairs from public judgment. We can appreciate the differentiating effect of urban isolation when we consider the degree to which people become assimilated to one another in the rural neighbourhood which makes continuous and unrestricted contacts inescapable.

[1] R. E. Park and E. W. Burgess, *Introduction to the Science of Sociology*, Chicago, 1928, p. 228 ff.

[2] T. Geiger, 'Formen der Vereinsamung,' *Kölner Vierteljahrshefte*, Vol. X, No. 3, 1919.

Modern privacy creates an aspect of the ego in which the individual is and wants to be different from anybody else. Originally an opportunity of certain élites, this privacy and individuation has become not merely a by-product of urban existence but an ambition and pride of contemporary man. It was the separation of the urban household from the workshop and office which first sharpened the division between the private and the public realm. The work pattern of the public official marks another stage in the sharpening of that distinction. His official behaviour during his work hours is fully exposed to the public, while after office hours he is free to withdraw into his privacy. The intellectual, on the other hand, tends to claim privacy for nearly everything he does, and where he succeeds the urban process of individuation reaches its apex.

The exemption from involuntary social contacts produces a tendency towards *introversion*. It opens up a new and second dimension of experiences in contrast to the overt and social. This product of intellectual isolation, hazardous as it may be in its extremes, has provided the model for a comparatively modern use of spare time. That leisure-time interests have taken a characteristic direction towards the 'deepening' of experience is due to the paradigm set by urban intellectuals. Were it not for their example, all spare-time interests of our time might take an 'outer' course, since a mass society tends to favour such leisure-time activities as sports, contests, public debates, and public performances.

The introversion of the intellectual is a fertile ground for the growth of a fourth trait: *schizothymia*. Its main characteristic lies in a critical tension between the person's inner and his outer world, which in extreme cases may impair his capacity to maintain normal social contacts. Wherever a stratum of literati has emerged, as Max Weber pointed out, it has shown an inclination towards private intellectual ecstasies, as contrasted with the communal rapture of peasants. This is still true today. The philosophy of contemporary 'existentialism' is basically a product of this process of withdrawal and estrangement from the public realm of reality. Some intellectuals hold out in this withdrawn role; others pass that stage. But there are some who do not overcome the pull toward isolation and yet cannot endure it. They are the persons who plunge into political activities with a solicitude which can be understood only in the light of that unresolved tension.

We have just touched on the life-history of the intellectual. It seems evident that his career partly depends on his temperamental reaction to the social distance which this particular way of life tends to impose on him. Following up this train of thought we may distinguish between three types of life history. The first is that of a *vocational* intelligentsia: persons belong to this stratum by virtue of a life-long career. France and the French revolution are unthinkable without them. The second is the *leisure-time* intellectual whose principal occupation which supports him is unrelated to his spare-time pursuits, although the latter may have a compensatory character. This type of intelligentsia gains importance with the decline of the independent leisure classes from which the literati of the first type used to recruit themselves. Bureaucratic cultures, such as the Chinese and the Prussian, are usually moulded by their leisure-time literati. The current bureaucratization of employment contributes to this trend by providing employment security and old-age pensions for increasing masses of workers. The total gain in leisure time creates a growing interest in pursuits of both the creative and the receptive type. (One basis of the differences between French and German culture is the predominance of the literati in the former and the official in the latter.)

The third type of intellectual preoccupation is incidental to a *passing phase* of life. Adolescents and early adults, particularly students, quite often experience an involvement in questions far beyond their career interests, but shed these leanings as they pass the period of storm and stress and settle down to a vocation. The German youth movement in itself was such an episode. Youth movements have often served as a cultural ferment, particularly in Germany (the 'Sturm und Drang' and 'Young Germany'); but they are far from being universal manifestations. The sudden recession of the youthful concern with the major questions of the time is perhaps characteristic of societies which block the social contacts of the young adult as soon as he begins his career. But whether the impulse passes or not, adolescence as such presents the most powerful impetus toward an intellectual agitation. It is an age of uncertainty and doubt in which one's questions outrun the scope of one's inherited answers.[1] I propose to call this urge to reach beyond the radius of one's action and immediate situation the *transcending impulse*. It is basic to every intellectual process.

The impulse flares up for the first time when the adolescent discovers the cultural heritage of his society and its ideological polarities. The realization that his immediate milieu is not 'the' world at large and that there is more than one way of life occasions the first distance experience and the first urge to transcend his environment. As he gains distance from the primary group the world no longer seems the same. When this adolescent urge to reach out is not thwarted it marks the beginning of a genuine process of education. But when adverse circumstances defeat the transcending urge, the adolescent abandons the distance he gained from his primary environment and ceases to question the horizon within which he has grown up. Lisbeth Franzen-Hellersberg's study of the early life-history of a working girl offers an insight into the maturation of underprivileged strata. The study well demonstrates how the lack of leisure destroys the usual channels of adolescent sublimation and, we may add, blocks the impulse to reach beyond the primary situation.[2] Available experience with boarding students in adult education homes (*Volkshochschulheim*) shows that the late exposure of mature persons to a broader type of education precipitates a belated adolescence with its characteristic crisis symptoms. Suddenly adult persons act like children in puberty; they pass through the experience of doubt and a newly-gained distance, with a tumult and vehemence which is characteristic only of adolescents of the well-to-do classes.

The symptoms of maturation are of particular significance to us, for this process marks the most universal genesis of intellectual sensitivity. The phases of this process give us an insight into the elusive subject of intellectual responsiveness more

[1] See Kurt Lewin's excellent observations on the subject in 'Field Theory and Experiment in Social Psychology: Concepts and Methods,' *American Journal of Sociology*, May 1939, pp. 874–884.

[2] Lisbeth Franzen-Hellersberg, *Die Jugendliche Arbeiterin*, *Tübingen*, 1932. Valuable material is contained in A. Aichhorn, *Wayward Youth*, London, 1936.

adequately than any historical analysis. Dissociation from one's previous reality and the seeking of distance from the primary environment are the principal impulses, as we have seen. It is with a sense of liberation that the adolescent discovers alternative interpretations and new values. Self-assertion and defiance accompany this experience. The second phase takes the opposite direction: it reveals uncertainty and the tendency to drift from one viewpoint to another. Although the manifestations of this second stage are fairly uniform, the resolution of the suspense varies. Some cannot bear to live in a state of multiple possibilities and grope for a firm footing. This in itself can take on different forms, which correspond to the various types of modern intellectual. One type seeks to establish an identity, by adopting a radical solution, mostly of a political kind. An overpowering wish to attain distance from the home, the primary environment, often leads to an oppositional course: those who grew up in a rigorously traditional home may develop revolutionary leanings, while those who depart from a liberal milieu will choose a conservative course. The development, however, may become more complex and lead through a phase of oppositional radicalism eventually back to the original point of departure, to a return to the family or the church. These are typically intellectual metamorphoses, for they are actuated by doubt and the transcending impulse. Intellectual fanaticism is not the product of a tacitly accepted heritage, but the expression of an anxiety to end the wear and tear of a state of suspense by the adoption of a categorical creed.

There is, however, another type of solution. Some find it possible to endure and even to relish an open horizon, a state of suspense without final certainty, and a continuing exposure to the alternatives which are inherent in a culture. This suspense, too, is a feasible course. With some it is an episode of youth, while others adopt it as a way of life.

Without attempting a detailed analysis, let us summarily indicate the various paths which intellectuals of the last type, mostly sceptics, usually choose. Some persons evolve an æsthetic view of life and become virtuosi of empathy, the capacity to live the roles and thoughts of others. They are the connoisseurs, the specialists in refined pleasures, the humanists. Others stabilize the impulse to transcend and to doubt into a routine of by-passing ultimates. They become the perennial ironists and sarcasts, the acrobats of *esprit*, and the professional critics of smugness and the Philistine (Heine, Börne, and the oppositional intellectuals of the 1830s). Finally there are those who preserve the productive core of their scepticism. As steadfast seekers of truth they expose hypocrisy and self-deception. Their radical disillusionment is like leaven in the bread, although they do not provide the dough.

8. THE CONTEMPORARY SITUATION OF THE INTELLIGENTSIA

The present study has attempted to trace the social roots of this ambivalent stratum and to understand not only its psychology but its social functions. This proved to be also a sociological approach to the history of the mind. Concrete samples offered illustrations of the procedure here advanced.

At the conclusion it is hard to escape the question of what the foreseeable role of intellectuals in our society may possibly be and what the future has in store for the intellectual process as we know it. The two questions are practically identical. Although the decline of a relatively free intelligentsia does not necessarily spell the end of thought and inquiry, the comparative and critical approach which an atmosphere of multi-polar viewpoints stimulates may come to an end. We must, therefore, examine the survival chances of the groups on whose shoulders the free intellective process has rested. It may well be that this process as we understood it is ephemeral and confined to a few brief historical interludes. One of these falls in the period of the free city states of Greece, perhaps a short phase of Roman history marks another, and the period since the Renaissance—by no means in its entirety—constitutes the third of these episodes.

We have grown accustomed to equate this particular type of intellectual process with the mind as such. Yet, when we consider the vast periods and spaces in which an institutional type of thought prevailed—medieval Europe is only one instance—we can hardly escape the conclusion that the intellectual process here described is but an aspect of liberalism broadly understood. The abdication of liberalism has all but ended the era of critical evaluation, and one must be blind not to see the dwindling force of its protagonists. Let us not fall under the illusion that free thought and inquiry have a long and impressive history. Nor was the intellectual output of the liberal era overwhelmingly liberal. In a larger sense the intellectual process was the byproduct of historical decomposition. Liberalism and free ideation are but an episode between periods of institutional culture. Can they be more than a transition? A measure of critical thought could co-exist with the Church when it passed its zenith. The succeeding major structures—the absolute State, mass democracy, and, of course, the Soviet Revolution—not only gravitate towards collectivism of one or another type and towards dogmas, but they are better equipped to control thought than the Church was.

We who possibly live at the terminus of a period cannot ignore these facts if we wish to keep our bearings.

Education is one of the major areas in which the spirit of inquiry is on the decline. The bureaucratic trend in education is inevitable, and it may be shortsighted to resist it. Increasing specialization calls for a growing army of experts, and the large-scale organization of government, private enterprise, labour unions, and parties make uniform standards of training necessary. We have referred already to the Prussian system of certifications and its original aim of training career officials who could replace the dignitaries of a semi-feudal administration. It all boils down to the simple principle that the rational recruitment of skilled personnel for large-scale operations requires consistent training and selection. But unnecessary is the over-emphasis on the manipulative aspects of knowledge and the zeal with which institutions have come to train graduates for certification in the mastery of prescribed subjects in the prescribed interpretation. The retailing of knowledge in standard packages paralyses the impulse to question and to inquire. Knowledge acquired without the searching effort becomes quickly obsolescent, and a civil service or a profession which depends on a personnel whose critical impulse is be numbed becomes rapidly inert and incapable of remaining attuned to changing circumstances. It should be possible to train and select officials who will not lose their initiative and capacity to invent once they are vested with the security of their office. A civil service which does not train an intelligentsia of its own, defeats itself in the long run.[1]

We see a proliferation of this system of training to meet certification requirements in technological institutes, schools of business administration, and teachers' colleges. Their graduates are absorbed by the State, the expanding professions, and the rapidly growing private bureaucracies.[2] Now, there is nothing wrong with the increasing scale of industry, commerce, medical and public services. It is because of their growth that such essentials as food, shelter, health services, and transport have become more broadly and more adequately available. Nor is the mass education which they require anything to regret. Moreover, the influx of new strata into the professions and the administrative hierarchies can be a source of new impulses and fruitful criticism. These are badly needed in any large-scale organization which all too soon acquires a vested interest in its own inert conventions. Traditionally established strata are inclined to take the customary shape of things for granted; it is the rising individual who is in a favourable position to take a fresh look at the newly-gained ground. But these assets of the upgrading process are potential and not automatic. Large and well-entrenched organizations are usually able to assimilate and indoctrinate the newcomer and paralyse his will to dissent and innovate. It is in this sense that the large-scale organization is a factor of intellectual desiccation.[3]

Bureaucracies narrow the field of free inquiry in another sense. Political parties, industrial organizations, and labour unions have adopted the practice of maintaining a professional staff of public interpreters—public relations experts, as they are called in the United States. They fight the battles of their corporate employers for favourable public opinion and earn their bread as purveyors of tailored ideologies through the mass media—press, radio, television, and film. These promoters are usually trained intellectuals, equipped with the tools of

[1] Compare Karl Mannheim, *Die Gegenwartsaufgaben der Soziologie*, Tübingen, 1932.

[2] See Abraham Flexner's acid comments on the narrowly conceived vocationalism of a number of American Universities, in *Universities*, New York, 1930, p. 208.

[3] See R. Merton, 'Social Structure and Anomie,' *op. cit.*, pp. 170 ff.

free inquiry, who discharge their duties as experts of directed thinking, as specialists in arriving at fixed conclusions from variable premises. We have here a vigorous trend towards a new type of scholasticism. The Marxist wing of the labour movement reached the dogmatic stage some time ago and was the first to establish a new pattern of thinking in a closed system. It is true that the diverse ideologies do not form a consolidated body of doctrine and that their competitive setting tends to limit their hold on public opinion. But the growth of bureaucracies and their increasing centralization progressively cause the range of free inquiry to shrink outside the various technical fields.

The area of independent inquiry is, however, narrowed, not only by the inroads of directed thinking. Free inquiry is also losing its social basis through the decline of the independent middle classes from which, particularly in Germany, an older type of the relatively unattached intelligentsia used to recruit itself. No other stratum or alternative plan has arisen to assure the continued existence of independent and uncommitted critics. The outsiders of the late Middle Ages who kept the stimulus of free inquiry alive could take refuge in the many niches and crevices which a loosely-organized society left open. The existence of the outsider in a highly-institutionalized society, such as ours is, is more precarious and more trying.

Much of this is inevitable and even desirable. But we must take account of the trend if we are to deal with it. Social determinists may wonder whether intellectuals who customarily reflect the current can also influence it. After all, is the intellectual not a mere crest of the wave? Can one expect the weather-cock to control the wind? The extreme determinist who interprets the sociological point of view as a systematized interest in mass behaviour overlooks the fact that every major phase of social change constitutes a choice between alternatives. Society outlines the alternatives, but minorities can play their part in the making of choices. Whether the intellectuals are such a minority depends partly on them. True, as a group they do not control power and resources. They do not even join the same parties, and we find them in opposite pressure groups and in conflicting classes, but they do leave their stamp on the public interpretation of affairs, and at times they have played a part in the making of choices when choices existed.

What then can the intellectual do? First of all let him take stock of his limitations and potentialities. His stratum is not above parties and special interests, nor can any political programme or economic promise weld it into an action group. The only concern which this stratum has in common is the intellectual process: the continuing endeavour to take stock, to diagnose and prognosticate, to discover choices when they arise, and to understand and locate the various points of view rather than to reject or assimilate them. Intellectuals have often attempted to champion special ideologies with the self-abandon of persons who seek to attain an identity they do not possess. They have tried to submerge in the working-class movement or to become musketeers of free enterprise, only to discover that they have thereby lost more than they hoped to win. The apparent lack of social identity is a unique opportunity for the intellectual. Let him join parties, but with the point of view which is particularly his, and without the surrender of that mobility and independence which constitute his assets. His affiliations must not become a source of self-abnegation, but added occasions for critical analysis. Bureaucratic machines are well able to create the like-mindedness and conformity they need, but to survive in the long run they also must use critical judgment which the controlled mind does not produce. Democracies sometimes falter for lack of conformity, while dictatorships usually fail in the end for want of independent scrutiny. A free society cannot default on both scores with impunity.

A stratum does not have to become a party or a pressure group to be conscious and to attain its ends. Women and youth arrived at their position in society by pressing home their claims individually, in small groups, and in whatever situations they found themselves. A group such as the intelligentsia abdicates only when it surrenders its self-awareness and its capacity to perform in its own peculiar way. It cannot form a special group ideology of its own. It must remain as critical of itself as of all other groups. After all, though, the intellectual process is in all its phases the product of concrete situations, let us also remember that the product is more than the situation.

PART THREE

THE DEMOCRATIZATION OF CULTURE[1]

I. SOME PROBLEMS OF POLITICAL DEMOCRACY AT THE STAGE OF ITS FULL DEVELOPMENT

1. A democratizing trend is our predestined fate, not only in politics, but also in intellectual and cultural life as a whole. Whether we like it or not, the trend is irreversible, and hence it is the supreme duty of the political thinker to explore its potentialities and implications. Only in this way will it be possible to influence the trend of democratization in a desirable sense.

The assertion that the dominant trend of our age is toward an ever fuller development of democratic patterns of thought and behaviour may sound paradoxical in view of the frequency with which dictatorships nowadays are superseding democracy.[2] These dictatorships, however, constitute no proof that political reality is becoming less and less democratic in its essence. Dictatorships can arise only in democracies; they are

[1] Translator's Note: The original title of this essay, 'Demokratisierung des Geistes', cannot be rendered exactly in English. While 'culture' has a wider meaning than 'Geist', the term 'mind' which might be used instead of 'culture' would be too narrow. The essay analyzes the historical process of 'democratization' as it manifests itself in characteristic changes in various cultural fields, particularly philosophy, art, and religion. The process itself is conceived as a social process at bottom, rather than as a self-contained process taking place in the realm of thought or mind. Hence, the expression 'democratization of culture' seems more appropriate to designate it than the alternative expression 'democratization of mind'.

The German text has been rendered in free translation, clarifying obscurities and omitting redundant passages but closely reproducing the meaning intended by the author. The omission of longer redundant or incompletely developed passages is marked by dots.

[2] Translator's note: This paper was written in 1933.

made possible by the greater fluidity introduced into political life by democracy. Dictatorship is not the antithesis of democracy; it represents one of the possible ways in which a democratic society may try to solve its problems.

A plebiscitarian dictatorship may be characterized as the self-neutralization of political democracy. As political democracy becomes broader and new groups enter the political arena, their impetuous activity may lead to crises and stalemate situations in which the political decision mechanisms of the society become paralysed. The political process may then be short-circuited so as to enter a dictatorial phase. This is a danger that threatens precisely those societies in which political democracy suddenly reaches its full development.

At the early stages of democratization, the political decision process was controlled by more or less homogeneous economic and intellectual élites. Since suffrage was not yet universal, the masses could not influence governmental policies. Those who actually wielded political power knew from long familiarity with governmental problems what was actually feasible; they did not embark upon utopian schemes. But when suffrage becomes universal, groups not yet familiar with political reality suddenly become charged with a political function. This leads to a characteristic discrepancy: strata and groups whose political thinking is reality-oriented have to cooperate with, or contend with, people experiencing their first contact with politics—people whose thinking is still at a utopian stage. The bourgeois élite, too, had passed through that stage, but that was about a century ago; in our age, when full democratization sets in, groups are yoked together in the political process whose outlook is not 'contemporaneous'. This must lead to disturbances.

Democratization, then, means a loss of homogeneity in the governing élite. Modern democracy often breaks down because it is burdened with far more complex decision problems than those facing early democratic (or pre-democratic) societies with their more homogeneous ruling groups. Today we can see the full extent of these problems; precisely because democracy has been realized in our age, for us it is not merely an ideal but a reality which has its bright and dark sides. We can no longer view democracy as the sum-total of ideal aspirations contrasting with an imperfect reality. The adequate attitude towards democracy is no longer one that equates it with every perfection that free-floating fantasy can conceive of. Rather, the required attitude is one of sober stock-taking, involving an awareness of the possible defects of democracy as a prerequisite for correcting them.

2. It is one of the characteristics of our age that believers in the ideal of democracy tend to be repelled and disappointed by its actuality. They discover to their dismay that in a political democracy the majority need not be 'progressive' in its attitudes and aspirations. While the democratization of political life at first actually favours 'left-wing' tendencies, it may happen that 'conservative' or 'reactionary' currents get the upper hand as a result of the free play of political forces.

Before democracy was achieved and tested in its actual functioning, it was customary to expect that it would necessarily usher in the rule of Reason or at least tend to confer political power upon people whom one considered 'rational'. When these prophecies were first made, they were not unrealistic. At that time, the distribution of social and political forces was such that irrationalism and conservatism went hand in hand with the rejection of political democracy, while pro-democratic attitudes were associated with belief in the rule of Reason. This distribution of roles had persisted for a number of generations. Eventually, however, it became evident that besides the 'democracy of Reason' there was also a 'democracy of Impulse', to use Scheler's terminology (in German: 'Vernunftdemokratie' versus 'Stimmungsdemokratie'). Democracy, as we now see, is not necessarily a vehicle of rationalizing tendencies in the society—on the contrary, it may well act as an organ of the uninhibited expression of momentary emotional impulses.

Likewise, democracy at one time was viewed as an instrument guaranteeing international harmony. We now see that the opposite tendency, too, is inherent in democracy: national self-assertion and aggressiveness may thrive precisely in a democratic soil. A similar ambivalence is apparent in the relation between democracy and individualism. On the one hand, democracy fosters the freedom and development of the individual personality; it stimulates individual autonomy by giving each person a share in political responsibility. On the other hand, however, democracy also develops powerful social mechanisms inducing the individual to give up his autonomy. When strata not yet ripe for political responsibility are suddenly admitted to a share in power, they are more likely to make use of mechanisms of this sort than to stimulate individual freedom. Democracy officially emancipates the individual; actually, however, the latter tends to abdicate the right to follow his own conscience and to seek refuge in the anonymity of the mass.

3. We may say in sum that democracies as a rule are not destroyed by non-democratic enemies; they collapse as a result of the working of the innumerable self-neutralizing factors that develop within the democratic system.[1] Besides these organic, structural dangers, we may also mention a more peripheral factor, that is, the dysfunctioning of particular democratic institutions. Thus, C. Schmitt correctly emphasized a weakness of parliamentary democracy, consisting in the fact that parliaments sometimes are unable to reach decisions by which an emergency situation can be mastered.

II. THE PROBLEM OF DEMOCRATIZATION AS A GENERAL CULTURAL PHENOMENON

A. THE THREE FUNDAMENTAL PRINCIPLES OF DEMOCRACY

1. What we have said up to now about certain fateful problems arising in the course of the democratization of political life will serve to prepare us for an inquiry of wider scope in which our subject will no longer be political democracy in a narrow sense but the democratization of Western culture as a whole. We have discussed the problem of democratic politics, because we wanted to show in a familiar context how certain powerful, inescapable trends associated with democracy can be accounted for in sociological terms. But is it not possible to attempt a similar sociological analysis of fields other than that of politics? In its non-political aspects, too, our culture is passing through a radical transformation process. In trying to understand this

[1] We do not deny that anti-democratic forces may contribute to the downfall of democracies. Groups participating in the political process in a democracy may be wholly anti-democratic in their orientation.

process, we may take the clue provided by the sociological analysis of the democratization of politics, and formulate our question as follows: *How does the shape, the physiognomy of a culture change when the strata actively participating in cultural life, either as creators or as recipients, become broader and more inclusive?*

2. Before we try to answer this question, we have to meet a possible objection. Is it at all justified to speak of a 'democratizing' tendency beyond the sphere of politics proper? In a society whose tradition is essentially idealistic in the German sense, this objection will carry much weight, for such societies are wont to look upon their culture as divided into separate, watertight compartments whose self-contained autonomy must never be questioned. To a German idealist, the suggestion that a mundane thing like political democracy might represent a tendency also operating in the sacrosanct realms of art or philosophical thought will sound like blasphemy. But what if it could be shown that political democracy is merely one manifestation of a pervasive cultural principle? This is in fact the thesis we propose to defend.

That there are certain essential differences between the artistic or intellectual products of aristocratic and democratic cultures was noticed by Nietzsche; he made many penetrating observations along these lines, even though his comments show a pronounced élitist bias and a strong resentment of democracy. Nietzsche's romantic disciples as a rule do not go beyond trivialities—democracy levels everything, it ushers in the dominance of mediocrity and the mass, and so on. Such judgments may have their partial justification, but they do not go beneath the surface. The real task, in fact, is to push through to the fundamental, structural differences between aristocratic and democratic cultures. This is a problem in comparative sociology.[1]

3. Our next task, then, is to indicate the nature of democracy as a structural, sociological phenomenon, one that can be

[1] We recall the distinction made in the first essay of this volume between general and historical sociology. We shall treat the problem of democracy as a formal, structural phenomenon, rather than as a historical one. That is: we shall not inquire into the conditions of the genesis of certain historically existing democracies like the Greek *polis* or the late medieval commune; we shall try to identify the essential traits that distinguish each and every democracy from a non-democratic ordering of society.

studied in the narrow sphere of politics as well as in the broad context of the cultural process as a whole.

To start with political democracy: its basic, formative principle is obviously that all governmental power emanates from the people. Every individual is called upon to contribute his share to the determination of governmental policies. This implies a basic attitude which reaches beyond politics proper and shapes all cultural manifestations of societies of the democratic type. Political democracy, in fact, postulates the sharing of governmental power by all because it is convinced of the essential equality of all men, and rejects all vertical division of society into higher and lower orders. This belief in the *essential equality of all human beings* is the first fundamental principle of democracy.

This principle of the essential equality of all men and the actual behaviour patterns reflecting it in society have two roots: an ideological and a sociological one. Ideologically, the belief in the essential equality of all men derives from the Christian conception of the brotherhood of all men as children of God. Without this conception, our society could never have developed a political order granting equal status to all. On the other hand, however, this teaching could not have informed social reality if it had not been for certain favourable shifts in the social and political structure of Western societies. The pressure of broad middle and lower strata gaining an increasing share in social and political influence was needed to transform the Christian principle of the equality of all human beings into an institutional and political reality. The idea as such had existed before, but it had little political relevance as long as it was understood only in relation to religious experience and found no application to things of the world. The equal treatment of all individuals as a basic feature of modern society was imposed by the growing power wielded by lower social strata.

The principle of the essential equality of all human beings as such does not imply a mechanical levelling, as hasty critics of democracy are prone to assume. The point is not that all men are equal as to their qualities, merits, and endowment, but that all embody the *same ontological principle of human-ness.* The democratic principle does not deny that under conditions of fair competition some individuals will turn out to be superior to others; it merely demands that the competition be fair, i.e. that some people be not given a higher initial status than others (e.g. in the shape of hereditary privilege).

4. This takes us to the second fundamental principle of democracy: the recognition of the *autonomy of the individual*, of the vital selfhood (*Eigenlebendigkeit*) vested in each and every person as the atom of society. In pre-democratic societies, social coordination was based upon the fact that most individuals were denied an autonomous life of their own. The social will was not shaped by impulses contributed by the many; it was determined from above, either by an absolute monarch and his staff of bureaucrats, or by powerful feudal coteries. Democracy, however, is essentially predicated upon the mobilization of all individuals as vital centres, not as a mere ideological or abstract principle, but as a living reality. We see in this the creative, vitalizing function of democracy and, at the same time, the potential danger inherent in it; for the life of a democratic society always skirts chaos owing to the free scope it gives to the vital energies of all individuals. . . .

The process of the release of individually centred vital energies has an interesting counterpart in the history of ideas. The modern concept of the 'organism' could be developed only at a time when society itself was transformed into a system in which the individual particles, though interdependent, also had their own, self-centred life. As the philosopher Erich Kaufmann has shown, the term 'organism' came to be used first in a political and social rather than biological context.[1] In this as in other cases, concrete social experience has furnished those categories which could then be used for the analysis of natural phenomena.

Kaufmann has traced the specifically modern concept of 'organism' to Kant. The term itself had already been used by earlier legal thinkers, but in a sense more akin to our own concept of 'mechanism': it denoted a system put together by a craftsman for some specific purpose, rather than a living being evolving spontaneously and seeking to maintain its internal balance. May we suggest that absolutist society in fact

[1] Cf. Erich Kaufmann, *Über den Begriff des Organismus in der Staatslehre des 19. Jahrhunderts*, Heidelberg, 1918.

corresponded to the paradigm of 'mechanism', and that society entered the stage of self-steering, 'organic' life only in the age of democracy? (It may be added that eighteenth-century Deism had also conceived of God as a craftsman who moved the universe 'from without'.)

In our age, the social process draws its energy from living cells rather than from passive, inert particles. This remains true even in the dictatorial degeneration of democracy. Modern post-democratic dictatorships essentially differ from earlier authoritarian regimes. For the latter, exacting obedience from the mass was no problem, since they could always rely on the docility of the common man. The former, however, must first mobilize mass forces in order to gain power, and then take drastic steps to counteract the potential adverse effects of the wide diffusion of vital energies throughout the society.[1]

5. All this indicates an inner contradiction inherent in the democratic organization of society. Democracy must mobilize the vital energies of every individual; but having done so, it must also find a way to dam up and in part neutralize these energies. Orderly social life would become impossible if every individual constantly made full use of his right to influence public decisions. This would spell the end of all social cohesion. Hence, all democratic societies need certain neutralizing devices involving undemocratic or anti-democratic potentiali-

[1] 'Docility' in aristocratic-authoritarian regimes and 'self-neutralization' in democracies correspond to two types of socially induced stupidity. The former consists in the mass of people being prevented from learning, from acquiring new knowledge. Aristocratic societies are set in their thought-ways; they do not advance towards new knowledge, much in the way in which old people refuse to learn. According to Lichtenberg, old people are immobile in their thinking, not because they are biologically unable to learn new things, but because their claim to authority would be weakened if they conceded that they are not omniscient. Aristocratic élites wielding traditional authority often refuse to admit new knowledge for similar reasons.

In democracies, on the other hand, we often observe failure to think and learn due to the fact that the people let some organization or machinery do their thinking for them. One may mention in this connection the tendency observed in American social science to develop new knowledge without 'thinking' about reality, relying solely upon routines of fact-finding, questionnaires, etc. Carl Becker related this to the 'talent for "organization", which is so characteristic of Americans' (cf. *The United States, Experiment in Democracy*, 1920, p. 180).

ties. These devices, however, are not imposed upon democratic society from without; they consist essentially in a *voluntary* renunciation by the mass of the full use of its energies.

This voluntary abandonment of the individual's autonomous aspirations may assume many forms. There is, for example, that susceptibility to propagandistic manipulation which we observe precisely in fully developed mass democracies. One may see in this and related phenomena signs of the degeneracy of democracy; when this trend goes to the limit, as it does in the cult of a 'leader', society ceases to be democratic altogether, since the institutions that enable the individuals to shape political decisions 'from below' are abolished. However, even a healthy democracy requires a certain self-limitation on the part of its individual members. Thus we see that *direct* democracy cannot exist in societies of large size. The governmental system of modern territorial states of democratic character is *representative* democracy. That is, the actual shaping of policy is in the hands of *élites*; but this does not mean to say that the society is not democratic. For it is sufficient for democracy that the individual citizens, though prevented from taking a direct part in government all the time, have at least the *possibility* of making their aspirations felt at certain intervals.

It is in politics as in culture at large: democracy does not imply that there are no élites—it rather implies a certain specific principle of élite formation. Pareto is right in stressing that political power is always exercised by minorities (élites), and we may also accept Robert Michels' law of the trend towards oligarchic rule in party organizations. Nevertheless, it would be wrong to over-estimate the stability of such élites in democratic societies, or their ability to wield power in arbitrary ways. In a democracy, the governed can always act to remove their leaders or to force them to take decisions in the interests of the many.

Democracy, then, has its own way of selecting and controlling its élites, and we can take this to be the *third* fundamental characteristic of democracy both in a narrow political and a broad cultural sense.

6. In the following parts of this paper, we shall discuss the way in which the cultural process as a whole is shaped and influenced by the three fundamental democratic principles we have

distinguished, that is (1) the *potential ontological equality of all individual members of society*, (2) the recognition of the *vital selfhood* of the components of society, and (3) the *existence of élites* in democratic society, together with *novel methods of élite selection*. We shall treat these points, not as ideal desiderata, but as features to be detected in actual social reality. In other words: we shall not attempt to prove that in all democracies, all individuals are actually treated on an equal footing, or that their autonomous vitality is always respected. Our point is, rather, that the actual social process in societies evolving towards democracy cannot be understood without assuming formative trends putting 'horizontal' equality in the place of 'vertical', hierarchical inequality, and so on. . . The scientific, sociological problem consists in seeing this process as a whole, a *Gestalt*, and also in validating this synoptic view by a detailed analysis of the myriad small changes entering into it. 'Morphology', distinguishing large *Gestalt*-like entities, as wholes, and 'analysis', dividing them into their smallest components, must go hand in hand.

B. THE PRINCIPLE OF THE ONTOLOGICAL EQUALITY OF ALL MEN

1. In pre-democratic society, all social authority is inextricably linked to the idea of the ontological superiority of the wielder of authority. No person, family, or institution can exert authority without being regarded as made of 'higher' stuff than the ordinary run of humanity. We may think in this connection of the magic origin of the institution of kingship.[1]

It will be seen that our methodological position is, so to speak, double-edged. Here as elsewhere, we reject the whole-

[1] Thomas and Znaniecki (*op. cit The Polish Peasant*, vol. I) have postulated a certain correlation between magic on the one hand, and authoritarian control on the other: magic practices essentially consist in issuing commands to nature. (Later addition.) This analogy, however, is of problematic value: magic is in all probability not of authoritarian origin. The magician usually seeks to restore a normal condition disturbed by extraordinary influences, e.g. he tries to produce normal rainfall after a period of drought. In other words, he enters upon the scene in emergencies for which the normal institutions of society are not sufficient. Magicians are also competent to deal with the uncontrolled region beyond the confines of the group, in trade or war with others. . . .

sale denial of the legitimacy of the morphological, 'Gestalt' approach in the cultural disciplines (cf. on this Karl Mannheim 'On the Interpretation of Weltanschauung', in *Essays on the Sociology of Knowledge*, London and New York, 1952, pp. 33 ff.). But, on the other hand, we also maintain that a purely morphological approach is not sufficient for the scientific treatment of any subject. A more 'microscopic', causal, functional, analytical approach is also necessary to supplement global, 'morphological' insights. The slogan that 'mechanistic' theories are appropriate in the natural sciences but are out of place in the cultural sciences misses the point. The radical application of 'mechanistic' causal analysis was successful in the natural sciences, not because inorganic nature alone is congenial to this approach, but because such analysis is essential to all scientific endeavour. We merely maintain that in the cultural sciences one must go beyond causal and functional analysis and combine it with a morphological approach.

We now take up the cultural implications of the three 'fundamental principles' of democracy one by one, beginning with the principle of 'equality'.

2. In the process of the democratization of politics, authority does not disappear, but it no longer involves a qualitative jump from the lower orders of mankind to an élite deemed higher in essence. At most, there is a quantitative, non-essential difference between the leaders and the led. The same transition from qualitative, essential distinctions to quantitative, non-essential ones, however, can also be observed in other fields than that of politics, and this change in the evaluation of human models is one of the chief characteristics of the process with which we are concerned, that is, the democratization of culture. In pre-democratic cultures, for example, talent or genius is considered as an irreducible datum—something like a magic charisma that sets off certain individuals from the ordinary run of mankind. Pre-democratic education works very largely with such concepts of human excellence. It considers the man of genius as he appears at the full height of his powers; his genius is an ultimate datum, unrelated to the facts and circumstances of life in terms of which the development and maturing of ordinary individuals may be understood. The authoritarian, pre-democratic mind shuns the idea of process and genesis in

favour of static, hierarchically ordered models of excellence. The democratic mind, on the other hand, stresses the plasticity of man.

When Goethe says, 'This is what thou art—thou canst not escape thyself,' he voices a pre-democratic sentiment. The typically democratic mood, however, is one in which we feel that 'everything could be different'. The democratic type of mind, then, is prone to explain phenomena in terms of contingency rather than essence. Now there is nothing in this style of thought (the one that prefers contingent to essential explanation) that is manifestly and explicitly related to the democratic attitude towards equality and authority. Yet, to the sociologist of culture, the two things are closely interrelated. Not that the democratic thinker necessarily denies human 'greatness'; he merely re-interprets it, seeing in it a manifestation of that human perfectibility which is the universal heritage of man. The 'great man' is great, not because he is different from others in his primordial substance, but because he has had greater and better opportunities to develop himself.[1]

3. It is interesting to see how the democratic attitude is penetrating into a field traditionally dominated by the authoritarian outlook, that of musical education. The essential difference between the musically gifted and ungifted has always been treated as a fundamental datum in the teaching of music. Recently, however, pedagogues like Jacobi have come to deny a fundamental distinction of this kind. According to this new doctrine, every child is potentially 'musical'; manifest differences in musical gifts are merely due to early experiences.[2]

Whether these theories are correct or not does not interest us here; we have mentioned them merely as examples of a 'democratic' approach towards education. According to this

[1] Landsberg makes a good distinction between two versions of the democratic doctrine of equality. The first version is that of Rousseau; it postulates equal perfection *innate* in every human being. The second is found in Locke and Helvetius; according to it, the equality of all men is based upon the fact that they have no *innate* properties whatsoever.

[2] A similar position is being taken in psycho-analytic circles towards the problem of intellectual gifts in general; a periodical for psycho-analytical pedagogy devoted in this sense a special issue to the problem of 'intellectual inhibitions'. (Cf. 'Intellektuelle Hemmungen', *Sonderheft der Zeitschrift für Psychoanalytische Pädagogik*, vol. 4, Nos. 11–12, 1930.)

approach, proficiency in music or other arts is not the appanage of exceptional individuals; the ability to acquire it is no less universal than the ability to learn to speak. Children become 'unmusical' because they have been discouraged from making music. They then do not develop beyond a primitive, infantile level of musicality. Similarly, if some people draw figures in a primitive, infantile fashion, it is because they have been discouraged from cultivating their artistic ability.

The point of these theories is that they do away with the idea of essential differences between human beings by tracing manifest differences to environmental factors. The underlying belief in the plasticity of man (pedagogical optimism) is a typical democratic trait. Pedagogical pessimism on the other hand is related to a pre-democratic, aristocratic outlook.[1]

4. We can observe the difference between pre-democratic and democratic patterns in the relationship between teachers and pupils in general. In pre-democratic school systems, the teacher is placed high above the pupils. The latter must look up to the former in every respect. In a democratic school system, however, the excellence of the teacher consists in meeting the pupils on their own level. Meeting half-way those who do not yet know is the modern pedagogic principle. This principle may be misunderstood and wrongly applied to the content of that which is to be taught. When this happens, vulgarization will be the result; anything that is not easily assimilated by the untutored mind will be put aside. The correct application of the principle, however, consists in a patient articulation of the material of study until the average intellect can grasp it. Moreover, the modern educator will always pay attention to the psyche and also to the social background of the pupil. Formerly, 'learning in school' involved in the main an obedient acceptance of things that were over the heads of

[1] In evaluating the merits of pedagogical optimism versus pedagogical pessimism, we may start from two different questions. On the one hand, we may ask whether the new pedagogical postulates are valid, i.e. whether some or many or all manifest differences in intellectual or artistic proficiency can be traced to environmental factors. On the other hand, we may also treat those postulates as heuristic principles suggesting that it is better to try to treat as many fields of endeavour as possible as open to improving influences than to recognize insuperable limits set by heredity. Is pessimism not a pretext for evading the challenge of educational problems?

the pupils. Later, perhaps, when they are fully educated and become worthy of what is being transmitted to them, they will grasp its full meaning. Modern education, however, shuns this awestruck approach. Instead, it starts from the postulate that anything that is transmitted in the process of teaching can be reduced to crystal-clear simplicity, with no 'higher' obscurities left to admire without comprehension. As we see, the democratic mind puts its trust *a priori* in that which is transparent and clear, whereas aristocratic cultures prize the recondite and the obscure, e.g. in the shape of the over-refinement and over-specialization of scholasticism. For the aristocratic mind, that which is culturally valuable must exist on a higher level, not accessible to the ordinary run of mankind. We can see, here as elsewhere, that people's attitudes towards cultural objects follow the paradigm of their basic social relationships. Where the political and social order basically rests upon the distinction between 'higher' and 'lower' human types, an analogous distinction is also made between 'higher' and 'lower' objects of knowledge or æsthetic enjoyment. . . . .

5. The dominant epistemologies of different ages show the same difference. When Descartes proclaims 'clear and distinct' ideas as necessary for true knowledge, or when Kant specifies 'necessity' and 'universal validity' as the essential characteristics of scientific judgments, they apply 'democratic' criteria to epistemology. These criteria imply that nothing can be accepted as true unless every human mind can grasp it. For the authoritarian, aristocratic mind, however, it is axiomatic that only sublime intellects and superior individuals can attain truth, or that God will reveal Himself only to chosen persons. Obviously, *this* concept of 'revealed truth' is inconsistent with democracy.[1] The democratic mind rejects all alleged knowledge that must be gained through special channels, open to a chosen few only. It accepts as truth only that which can be ascertained

[1] (Translator's Note: The author seems to have had in mind the Hebrew prophets as chosen mouthpieces of 'revealed' truth—a sociological type studied by Max Weber. In the theological doctrine of nearly all Christian churches and denominations, the revealed truth as held by the Church is addressed to all men and can be accepted by all. That this 'universal' truth is revealed first to chosen instruments is less important, in this theological context, than the expected universality of its acceptance. In Thomism, man is 'by his nature' destined for the acceptance of revealed truth.)

by everybody in ordinary experience, or that which can be cogently proved by steps that everybody can reproduce.

Clearly, this definition of truth is closely related to the fundamental democratic principle of the essential equality of all men. In addition to this, however, the modern concept of knowledge also reflects another aspect of democracy: its demand for unrestricted publicity. According to the dominant epistemology of the modern age, valid knowledge refers to the public world. Just as in politics, every individual has a claim to a share in control, in the field of knowledge every item must be subject to scrutiny by all individuals. Consequently, democratic cultures have a deep suspicion of all kinds of 'occult' knowledge cultivated in sects and secret coteries.

6. Unlimited accessibility and communicability, then, characterize the democratic ideal of knowledge. There are, however, limits to accessibility and communicability, even in democratic cultures. There is much knowledge that is accessible to, and communicable among, experts and connoisseurs only. And the case of the 'connoisseur' in the field of art is even more extreme than that of the scientific 'expert' and specialist. In order to be a connoisseur of art, one must be immersed in a historic tradition and cultivate a specialized taste. All this had a certain affinity to pre-democratic types of knowledge. The devotees of art form a closed community within society at large; their experiences are not generally communicable.

Scientific experts, too, develop a language of their own, incomprehensible to outsiders. But the scientific community is not as radically separated from society at large as is the community of æsthetic connoisseurs. Scientific thinking, in fact, is highly formalized and supremely objective; it leaves no room for subjective, purely private experiences. In principle, every scientific theory and finding could be grasped and reproduced by every normal individual. If the non-expert cannot follow the scientist, it is not because the latter's experiences are beyond the range of the former's receptivity, but because the layman rapidly loses his way in the intricacies resulting from the repetition and combination of basic mental operations that are simple in themselves. As against this, critics and historians of art derive their insights from a type of experience that cannot be shared by all men. Theories developed in these fields cannot be formalized and objectivized in such a way that every individual can reproduce them in his own mind. Connoisseurship (which is indispensable to the historian or art) is not teachable in the way in which natural science is teachable. The learning of formalized procedures of research does not suffice to make one a connoisseur. In order to become one, the student must come into contact with the works themselves, and be stimulated by them to the depths of his personality, emotionally, intellectually, and spiritually. Such experiences are not fully and readily communicable. They may even be confined within the limits of an epoch of art; connoisseurs of modern art may be insensitive to the specific values of Renaissance art, and *vice versa*.

7. We may say in this sense that certain types of knowledge are non-democratic in character, since they are accessible only to the élite of connoisseurship. Now it is interesting to observe what happens to these types of knowledge in a democratized culture. The first reaction will be to devalue them. Even though the connoisseur's judgments are undeniably 'empirical' in a certain sense, they do not represent 'exact' knowledge, since nothing is 'exact' unless it is fully communicable and demonstrable. (One may well doubt, by the way, that the current definition of exactness in terms of communicability and demonstrability is the only possible one.)

The second response of a democratic culture to this type of knowledge will occur within the disciplines in question themselves: they will try to satisfy the dominant, generally recognized criteria of exactness by adopting more 'objective' methods. For example, the attempt will be made to *articulate* the connoisseur's response to the work of art more and more, in the hope of obtaining a number of demonstrable, controllable observations instead of an unanalysed, global intuition.

This 'articulation' of a global intuition must be distinguished from 'analysis', even though these operations are often confused. When we 'analyse' a complex object, we are interested in discovering the simple, elementary parts of which it is composed. The object as a whole disappears in this process: it will no longer be recognizable from the elements brought to light by the analysis. 'Articulation', on the other hand, while it also seeks to discover simple components of a complex whole, never loses sight of the way in which the parts combine to make a whole. The complex object always remains in sight during the process. For example, I may point out the details of a façade one by one, calling attention to the various features of the windows, balconies, doors, etc. This is 'articulation', for the detailed observation of the parts merely serves to attain a fuller understanding of the whole.

Everyday, pre-scientific experience has always made use of the procedure of 'articulation', while the natural sciences, afraid of remaining on a 'pre-scientific' level, have abandoned 'articulation' and cultivated 'analysis' exclusively. Articulation, however, must be recognized as a legitimate method. There are certain cultural objects which we cannot study satisfactorily without learning to see how the whole emerges from the parts.

By refining and developing their methods of articulation, those cultural sciences which have to do with æsthetic and similar objects achieve a gain in communicability. They can in this way become more and more attuned to the democratizing trend of our culture, even though the communicability they can attain must remain limited.

8. In the foregoing discussion, we have stressed the contrast between analysis and articulation. From a sociological point of view, however, their parallelism is more important. The dominant impulse in both is to enhance the communicability of knowledge—and both achieve it through increasing abstraction, though in different ways.

There is an intrinsic correlation between the increasing abstractness of the symbols used in communication, and the democratic character of the culture. Élites which are not impelled to make their knowledge generally accessible will not engage in formalization, analysis, and articulation. They will content themselves, either with unanalysed intuition, or with sacred knowledge reserved for an élite and handed down among its members *en bloc*.

The urge towards abstraction and analysis is not imposed by the things themselves. Its origin is a social one; it arises from the size and structure of the group in which knowledge has to be shared. When knowledge must be communicated to many persons of different position and background, it must be couched in 'abstract' terms, for 'concrete' communications are intelligible only to those whose experiences and associations are very similar.[1]

9. We may conclude that a democratic society is more likely than an aristocratic one to discover 'abstract' relationships among things. At the same time, such a society will tend to bar qualitative elements from its experience and to minimize the value of qualitative knowledge.[2] This, to repeat, is an outgrowth of the trend towards greater communicability, which is in turn a manifestation of the democratic ontological principle of human equality.

C. THE AUTONOMY OF THE SOCIAL UNITS

1. We shall now try to show how the second formative principle of democracy, that of the vital autonomy or living selfhood of the individuals as social units, manifests itself in cultural domains usually seen as far removed from the political and social arena. We shall begin with modern epistemology; it seems, in fact, that the democratizing trend in culture finds its earliest fully conscious realization in epistemological reflexion.

We have already seen how 'ontological equality' as a fundamental democratic principle reflected itself, say, in the Kantian criterion of 'necessity' and 'universal validity' as defining genuine

[1] It would be an exaggeration to say that the size of the inter-communicating group and its heterogeneous composition in themselves are sufficient to explain the degree of abstraction of communications. The process of increasing abstraction has other aspects as well; the necessity of communicating with many heterogeneous elements is only its group origin.

On social mobility as a general source of abstractness in thinking and communication, see W. I. Thomas, *Source Book for Social Origins*, Boston, 1920, p. 169.

[2] How tendencies out of tune with the dominant social process can nevertheless maintain an underground existence is a complex problem that we cannot take up here. It may be mentioned, however, that certain forms of experience doomed by the dominant trend of culture, such as the aesthetic, qualitative experiences mentioned in the text, may save themselves by becoming objects of reflexion. While aesthetic creativity and receptivity are weaker in our time than in earlier ages, our historic sense and proficiency in articulation are greater. When there is a great deal of talk about 'Gestalt', quality, and concreteness, this does not mean that these things are experienced very strongly; they are objects of reflexion, which is a different thing altogether. . . .

knowledge. In addition to this, however, there is a doctrine which first appears in Western philosophy with Kant and separates post-Kantian from pre-Kantian thought; this is Kant's version of epistemological idealism. Its essence is the assertion of the original *spontaneity* and *creativity* of the epistemological subject and of the act of cognition. This is the philosophical formulation of our second fundamental principle of democracy.

In earlier philosophies, whether 'idealist' or 'realist', the knowing subject appears as essentially dependent on the object of cognition. The former merely reflects the latter; it does not create the object. In these philosophies, social experiences of dependence and hierarchy are drawn upon in order to characterize and account for the act of cognition. After all, epistemology can derive its basic concepts only from pre-theoretical, social experience.[1] In pre-democratic cultures, the average individual is debarred from conceiving the idea that he could gain knowledge, and criticize traditional beliefs, by a spontaneous use of his own mental energies. Even charismatic leaders of opinion such as prophets and the like do not, in such cultures, proclaim new truths in their own name; they either transmit messages directly inspired by God, or demand a return to the purity of an earlier, sacred tradition that is neglected or violated by a corrupt generation.

It is when society changes and new groups become politically active that more and more individuals are induced to interpret reality from their own personal viewpoint. During the Renaissance period, for example, certain individuals not exercising any traditional authority could rise to positions of political power as professional military leaders (condottieri) or as successful capitalistic entrepreneurs. Their experiences awakened in them feelings of self-asserting independence; the type of the 'heroic' individual was born, and this eventually opened up paths towards independent, not tradition-bound, modes of thinking. There was a long and arduous way, with many backslidings, from this to a general recognition of each individual's claim to autonomous thought and to a re-interpretation of human cognition as a creative rather than passive, receptive

[1] Cf. the paper on 'Structural Analysis of Epistemology' in Karl Mannheim, *Essays in Sociology and Social Psychology*, London and New York, 1953, pp. 15 ff.

activity. At long last, however, the process reached its culmination in the new epistemological idealism associated with Kant's name. In one of his essential activities, cognition, man developed a radically new image of himself.

The point we want to stress is that it was not the new philosophy which regenerated social reality. It was the other way round: society changed by making more and more individuals capable of exercising autonomy, and it was this process which made the new conception of knowledge as a spontaneous and creative act possible.

2. Kant's concept of natural law, which is derived from his idealistic principle of the creative role of consciousness, offers a striking parallel to the democratic idea of social law. In Kant's system, the 'lawful' regular character of the natural processes is guaranteed by the fact that the fundamental laws of the process are those of Reason itself. When the knowing subject discovers regularities in nature, he merely comes face to face with laws originating within his own reason. Likewise, the democratic citizen encounters in society no laws except those which he himself has enacted as legislator. In both cases, the law is seen to exist and to be binding because, rather than being imposed by an outside authority, it has been formulated by the same consciousness which must abide by it. It must be added, however, that in Kant's philosophy, consciousness as the source of the law is not the empirical consciousness of each and every individual. It is a more abstract consciousness-in-general ('*Bewusstsein überhaupt*') which is present in each individual as a creative faculty of knowing.

It goes without saying that this 'consciousness-in-general' implies the ontological equality of all men; it is a symbol of the identical 'human-ness' which makes man what he is. It is, however, characteristic of the Kantian, idealistic version of this egalitarian principle that 'consciousness-in-general' as the symbol of man's ontological essence is not conceived in empirical, psychological, or anthropological terms. It is, rather, seen as a Mind writ large, an impersonal force responsible for knowledge as such, of which the individual minds are merely the vehicles. All this has to do with the spiritualistic background of this type of idealism; it is unrelated to the specifically democratic character of Kantian thought with which we are here concerned. Yet, within that spiritualistic tradition, the concept of 'consciousness-in-general' represents a democratizing development. In the earlier spiritualistic tradition, the Spirit was essentially superhuman and supernatural. In Kant, it appears thoroughly humanized. It is, further, a 'democratic' feature of the Kantian consciousness-in-general that its authority and dignity rest precisely upon the fact that the experiential forms, categories and ideas involved in consciousness-in-general engender universally shareable and communicable knowledge. Kant's thought is focused upon the 'transcendental' (defined by him as that upon which the possibility of experience is grounded) rather than upon the 'transcendent' (that which lies beyond experience).

3. There is only one step from the Kantian consciousness-in-general to a characteristic feature of modern, democratic society: its faith in the all-healing virtue of free discussion. Carl Schmitt was not wrong in describing this faith as fundamental to modern parliamentary democracy.[1] He was also right in pointing out that people expected so much from discussion because they believed that articles of a universal 'Reason' were present in the mind of every individual and that therefore a wholly reasonable conclusion would necessarily emerge when individual minds were rubbed together.

Pre-democratic ages have had no use for discussion. They recognized, as ways to truth, only conversion or illumination. Those who refuse themselves to the true faith are simply lost; one cannot argue with them. Likewise, in early forensic practice, 'proof' based upon orderly deduction from general principles is unknown. Judgments are 'found', either by a kind of magic, formalistic ritual, or by intuition, by appeal to a sense of justice.[2]

[1] Cf. Carl Schmitt, *Die geistesgeschichtliche Lage des heutigen Parlamentarismus*, Munich, 1923.

[Translator's Note: It is noteworthy, however, that Schmitt, following Donoso Cortés, referred to this faith in discussion in order to heap scorn upon democracy. To these anti-democratic thinkers, "discussion" was the epitome of futility.]

[2] On this early forensic practice, see Justus Möser's paper (1770), 'How Our Ancestors Shortened Trials' (Möser, *Collected Works*, Berlin, 1842–43, Vol. 1), taken up by the leader of the 'historical school' of German jurisprudence. C. von Savigny, in the school's manifesto, 'Vom Beruf unserer

Genuine 'discussion' as a way of discovering truth is found first in a typically urban milieu, among the sophists of Greece and in Socrates. The essential preparatory stages were scepticism and systematic doubt. When nothing was taken for granted, one could try to find truth only by carefully defining terms and agreeing on rational methods of deduction. In such discussion, partners could be chosen at random (a good argument had to be convincing to anyone); thus, Socrates talked to anyone he met in the market-place and appealed to the spontaneous reasoning faculty present in him. This is how the first genuine discussions of which we have a record came about; their essential scheme has remained unchanged to our day.

The essential feature of genuine discussion is that no argument from authority and no dogmatic assertion based upon mere intuition is admitted. Truth can emerge only from radical doubt, as the residue which is left when anything that can be doubted has been eliminated. The final conclusion must not be held as a dogmatic belief in advance: the *possibility* of its falsehood must be admitted, if there is to be any genuine proof.

4. The type of argument we find in the writings of the Schoolmen is, therefore, no genuine discussion in our sense. The conclusion is given in advance; it is firmly held in an attitude of faith. If over and above the certainty of faith rational proof also is sought, this represents a concession to a mentality entirely different from that of the believer. Since the 'democratic' approach of antiquity still survived in the medieval world, demanding rational proof, the Schoolmen undertook to provide it, i.e. to prove that which is not provable. But the 'discussion' launched under such auspices was a sham. To the democratic mind, all initial positions have the same right to be considered; they are all on the same level. In the scholastic discussion, however, the initial admission of the possibility of adverse positions was nothing but make-believe. A real latitude existed, of course, regarding questions not decided by dogma; but on the important issues on which the dogmatic position of the Church was clearly defined, argument merely served to

Zeit für Gesetzgebung und Rechtswissenschaft' (1814). Cf. E. Rothacker, 'Savigny, Grimm, Ranke', in *Historische Zeitschrift*, Vol. 128 (1923), pp. 415–445.

justify an already existing belief, rather than to establish original truth.

We find such a 'scholastic' type of discussion, using rational argumentative steps to justify an independently held and dogmatically sacrosanct position, in historical situations in which the ferment of intellectual uncertainty and of a genuine search for an elusive truth still survives from earlier ages and must be silenced in the interests of conformity. We may call this the 'neutralized' type of discussion.

The sophists still lived in the element of genuine quandary and radical searching.[1] Socrates basically belonged to this type, even though his goal was to overcome uncertainty and to find final truth. In Plato, we already see the 'romantic' reaction to the rationalistic ferment of the age of the sophists—in the dialogues, the free-wheeling, unconstrained method of discussion is sometimes used to demonstrate definite theses, initially held to be certain.

5. A notable example of silencing genuine discussion by using its formal schema in order to justify a conclusion given in advance is provided by Hegelian dialectic. All the antithetical positions developed by the age of the Revolution and rationalism on the one hand, and that of the Restoration and romanticism on the other, whether in logic, or in politics, or in private experience—all these positions are represented in the theses and antitheses dialectically marshalled by Hegel. The discussion, however, is being steered towards a predetermined solution. In fact, it appeared, in Hegel's time, that a new stability, a new synthesis was emerging from the conflict of two worlds—that of feudalism and of the bourgeois. The new stability was to be based upon the consolidated position of the victorious bourgeoisie (one could not know, at the time, that this stability would soon be challenged by the new radicalism of proletarian revolutionary movements). This expectation, that of a world in which past conflicts are resolved in a higher harmony, provides the content of the Hegelian conclusions; in the dialectic, discussion 'neutralizes' itself.[2]

[1] Cf. the preceding chapter, 'The Problem of the Intelligentsia', in this volume.

[2] [Translator's Note: This is true of Marxist no less than of Hegelian dialectic.]

6. In genuine discussion, all participants are equally and jointly responsible for the conclusion reached. This equal distribution of *responsibility* is one of the characteristics of democratic society. It contrasts sharply with the pre-democratic order of things in which responsibility is concentrated in one point. In the old Chinese monarchy, for example, the Emperor had to be deposed if grave misfortune befell the people under his rule: this was a sign that the Emperor's life was not according to the Way (the 'tao'). In early society, responsibility is borne by charismatic personalities, prophets or saints. Later, traditionally entrenched power groups may act as guarantors of the 'correctness' of the social process. In the traditional system, the correctness and truth of the prevailing order seem to be guaranteed by the long duration of its existence. Romanticism also sees in mere 'growth' a criterion of value and rightness. It is common to all the e pre-democratic patterns of order that the source of social authority is not the autonomous life of the units of society but something outside and above it—either direct divine revelation or—at times when divinity can no longer be consulted directly—tradition, time, the imperceptible 'growth' of institutions.

Authoritarian ages do not recognize the joint responsibility of all. Something like joint responsibility does, however, exist in primitive democracy (i.e. in homogeneous primitive communities). This primitive, pre-individualistic democracy must, of course, be distinguished from modern, mature democracy in which all citizens share in responsibility as autonomous agents. It is true that in the primitive democracy, authority is not hierarchically graded; all are on the same level. But at the same time, the individual is wholly controlled by the group—he cannot act or think except according to the group's directives. . . . Durkheim speaks in this sense of a 'mechanical solidarity' as characteristic of primitive societies.[1]

In modern, mature democracy, solidarity is not automatic; it must be realized anew all the time through conflict and stress. Since all social units are fully autonomous agents they would

[1] Cf. Emile Durkheim, *De la division du travail social*, Paris, 1922, esp. chaps. II and III of Book I; also P. Fauconnet, *La Responsabilité, Etude de Sociologie*, Paris, 1920, and R. Hubert, *Manuel élémentaire de Sociologie*, Paris, 1925, pp. 301 ff.

prefer to go their own way. As long as acute massification does not set in, however, a middle road on which all can agree can always be found. Impulses coming from below find adjustment in compromise expressing the representative will of the moment. At this point, only norms endorsed by all are valid; they must be constantly scrutinized, revised and reasserted from below. In this way, responsibility becomes individualized; it is, as a rule, not only implicitly assumed but also consciously experienced as such.

7. We cannot say at present whether this individualized responsibility represents the final stage of democratic development. Right now we seem to have reached a turning-point. When the incomplete democracy in which economic and intellectual élite strata occupy the positions of control is suddenly transformed into full democracy, the tendency towards the full autonomy of all social units goes to the limit and at the same time massification results in the self-neutralization of democracy.

In the incomplete democracy, the enlightened self-interest of the leading groups is tempered by the voice of conscience. While this does not result in perfect social justice, it does have the result that the individual has well-defined rights which are generally respected. This balance between morality and self-interest, however, is overthrown when propagandistic dictatorial movements come to the fore. The individual then counts for nothing. Large groups make themselves homogeneous and clash with other groups equally moving under centralized command. All the gains made in the moral sphere, such as the refinement of conscience and the tempering of interest by rational, impartial morality, are lost. Only large collective welfare interests, statistically determined, can get a hearing, aided by the aggressive élan of competing leader cliques.

8. Such things as the making, enforcement, and administration of law undergo decisive changes under the impact of the self-neutralization of democracy. Under incomplete democracy, the trend was towards an ever-growing refinement of the ethic of intention ('Gesinnungsethik') according to which the individual must be judged according to the *intent* behind his actions rather than the *effect* produced by them. This had the result that nearly every action, when sufficiently analysed and understood,

had to be excused; in the end, hardly any lawbreaker could be punished, since psychology and sociology jointly demonstrated that he could not help acting as he did. At the dictatorial stage, however, subjective intentions become well-nigh irrelevant. Nothing counts except the objective outcome of the action to be judged. Did it, or did it not, interfere with the optimal functioning of the body social?

The law at this stage has little to do with justice as a moral category. The question before the legislator is how to frame commands which, given the probability distribution of the foreseeable responses of the individuals, will minimize the likelihood of anti-social behaviour. The law, coupled with propaganda, thus becomes an instrument of social manipulation. The judge, on the other hand, will have to determine the degree of liability to punishment, not in terms of subjective intent but in terms of the actual effect that an action had upon the integrity of the existing social order. We are, in this way, thrown back to the stage of the 'mechanical solidarity' of primitive democracy—the individual is nothing but a specimen of his group.

9. Will this be the eventual consummation of the development of democracy? Nobody can tell. The phenomena we just described may well present a transitional stage. That stage may be of long duration—it will last as long as massification prevails. It must be stressed, however, that 'massification' cannot be overcome by reducing the number of individuals actively participating in the political process. The solution, in other words, cannot be found in a return to the élitist pattern of pre-democratic societies or of incomplete democracy. Our culture can overcome massification only by getting away from the compulsion to integrate people in huge, homogeneous masses, in which their autonomous individuality is drowned.

The first step towards overcoming massification might consist in the creation of numerous small communities providing all their members with an opportunity to arrive at responsible, individual conclusions. In this way, the large numbers of people who participate in the political life of fully developed democracy could become rounded individuals, as were the responsible élite members at the stage of incomplete democracy. If these communities of autonomous individuals could achieve a balance among themselves, self-neutralization would gradually recede and disappear. We may look towards the emergence of such a higher type of fully democratized but no longer massified society as an ideal. In practice, however, we cannot expect such a process to unfold itself painlessly. Social learning is likely to be accomplished in painful convulsions, precisely at the stage of democracy when social energies are fully mobilized.

10. As we said in the opening section of this study, democratic society always lives under the shadow of possible disorder and chaos, since in principle all social units have a claim to assert themselves and there is no certainty that they will compromise their divergent interests and aspirations before their conflict becomes acute and violent. The democratized individual, too, is constantly aware of chaos lurking in the depths of his own personality. There is no pre-existent pattern of order guaranteed for ever in a democratic world; order and integration must always be created anew. This is essential to democracy as a way of life; it is therefore futile as well as thoughtless to condemn democracy in the name of the ideal of order. Order and fluidity, discipline and openness are antithetical human ideals which find their embodiment in different social systems of authoritarian and democratic character respectively. Neither type of society can be properly judged from a viewpoint firmly anchored in the other's basic ideals. Thus, an authoritarian thinker will be apt to be irritated by the lack of discipline and order in a democratic system and by the many abuses to which this gives rise. At the same time, however, such a critic will overlook the positive elements inherent in the very openness and formlessness of democracy.

Human existence may fall short of realizing its full potentialities if it is too systematically disciplined. If socially imposed taboos and inhibitions bar all access to the unconscious, mental and emotional life may be frozen in a rigid cast. The order thus achieved, however, will be superficial rather than real. For the forces of chaos and the impulses of the unconscious do not cease to exist when they are banished from consciousness and deprived of expression. Rigid authority, particularly in its dictatorial form, can hide them; beneath the surface, however, they will be active and may burst forth in a sudden explosion. In a democracy, potential crises announce themselves at an early stage; in this way, society is forewarned and the various social strata can immediately react to change in the pressures to which they are subjected. We may say in this sense that democracy is the most elastic (and hence adaptive) of all social systems. The impression of 'chaos' and disorder may even be wholly misleading: what appears as chaos may be, in reality, a quick, instantaneous adjustment to a series of changes. . . .

11. Full self-expression, with its positive and negative, adaptive and chaotic, potentialities, is not attained simultaneously by all social strata. It may be observed at the early stages of democratization that groups enjoying the privilege of security become fully 'mobilized' and autonomous in their thinking while the bulk of the population still persists in its tradition-bound attitudes and behaviour. Such differences in the degree of autonomy are apt to be transitory; it is a mistake to assume that they are necessary features of every social order (or, as Michels says, that all groups are necessarily and always governed by oligarchies). The long-range picture may be very different from the short-range one. In the short run, however, the differences may be very real.

We know that the thinkers of the Enlightenment felt that the common man was not yet ripe for their own rational way of thinking. Religion, they thought, was necessary to keep him within bounds. At a much later stage, when democracy degenerates into dictatorship, we see something similar. The élites at the top are purely power-minded, disillusioned, and cynical about all ideologies, including their own official one; at the same time, they see to it that the masses' faith in the official myth is kept unimpaired. The leaders' thinking is wholly reality-oriented and rational, except for the one irrationality of their lust for power; that of the masses is drugged and controlled by demagoguery.

12. Society can be governed for long stretches of time on the basis of an uneven distribution of autonomy and responsibility. Such regimes may even appear to have discovered the secret of stability, since they can manipulate their masses so well. And the masses will be quiet and contented, as long as a modicum of prosperity is maintained; what price they pay for this prosperity and order will not be immediately evident to them. The reckoning, howeve , will come eventually. It may come in

chaotic, irrational fashion; society may blindly stagger from one extreme to another, since the masses, unable to assign responsibilities correctly, act from mere emotional impulse. Scheler, as we noted above, expected this dominance of blind impulses to be the final stage of democratic development. It may, however, be something different—a stage in a painful learning process. For eventually, the masses which had been kept out of contact with reality will come face to face with it. They will learn to appraise policies in terms of what they do to their own interests. To be sure, an enormous price in suffering may have to be paid before the masses shed their illusions and become as enlightened, as reality-oriented, as the élites had been.

13. A more even distribution of clarity and enlightenment may also come about in a different fashion. Leading groups may discover that it is to their own interest to accelerate the process of enlightenment and learning, in view of the dangers inherent in the existence of large masses swayed by blind emotion. Educating the mass in reality-oriented ways of thinking, that is, a real democratization of the mind, is the paramount task at the stage of fully developed democracy. A certain gain in this direction could be achieved even if, at first, schools were established by the different parties to study social reality from their own partisan point of view. Teaching in such schools would be one-sided to begin with, but a less partisan approach would eventually impose itself. There are many reasons for this: the need to understand the opponent; the need to win over opponents and uncommitted groups; the need to form coalitions with others; and the need to find a common ground among major rivals who in a democracy must expect to alternate in the government and therefore must get away from the idea that once in power, they can and must make society over completely in their own image. Finally, as I said elsewhere,[1] the coexistence of rival schools of thought in itself tends to slough off whatever is extreme, one-sided and irrational in each of them.

Clearly, education in realism in this less painful fashion can be undertaken only in democracies whose functioning is not yet dominated by dictatorial and self-neutralizing forces.

[1] Cf. Karl Mannheim, 'Competition as a Cultural Phenomenon', in *Essays on the Sociology of Knowledge*, London and New York, 1952, pp. 191 ff.

D. DEMOCRATIC ÉLITES AND THEIR MODE OF SELECTION

1. Is it not a contradiction in terms to speak about 'élites' in a democratic society? Does democratization not do away with the distinction between 'élite' and 'mass' altogether? We need not deny that a trend towards levelling, towards the abolition of élite strata, is inherent in democracy. But it is one thing to say that a trend exists, and another to assume that it must go to the limit. In all democracies that we know, it is possible to distinguish leaders from led. Does this mean merely that the democracies that have come into being thus far have been imperfect or imperfectly democratic? Should we not say, rather, that there is a democratic optimum of the élite-mass relationship which falls far short of the complete disappearance of the élite? An optimum need not be a maximum; if democracy involves an anti-élitist trend, this need not go all the way to a utopian levelling of all distinction between leaders and led.

We assume that democracy is characterized, not by the absence of all élite strata, but rather by a new mode of élite selection and a new self-interpretation of the élite. In periods of rapid change, there must be small groups that explore new cultural possibilities, and perform experiments in living for others. In this fashion they create new types of experiences which may later become the general pattern. What changes most of all in the course of democratization is the distance between the élite and the rank-and-file. The democratic élite has a mass background; this is why it can mean something for the mass. Now it may happen that, after some time, this élite abdicates its role again. The mobilized mass will then recapture the experimenting élite, and will regress to a primitive level instead of forging ahead towards a richer life. If, on the other hand, the vanguard succeeds in transmitting its new insights, first to intermediate groups and ultimately to the mass itself, the democratization of culture will be a levelling-up process rather than a trend in the direction of equalitarian mediocrity.

2. One may study the genesis and the role of élites in democratic societies from various points of view; we shall mention five important areas of research in this field. Presumably, con-

siderable research effort will be devoted to these problems in the future. In the present paper, we shall content ourselves with more general considerations of an introductory kind, without trying to treat any of the problems fully.

The problems we propose to discuss are the following:

(a) The mode of selection by which élites are recruited from the mass.
(b) The inner structure of various élite groups, their mutual relationships, and their relation to society at large.
(c) Their self-interpretation and self-evaluation, and their assessment by outsiders.
(d) The social distance between élite and mass, understood primarily as the function of élite consciousness.
(e) The cultural ideals produced by various élite groups.

We shall discuss the first three points briefly, reserving the last two for a fuller treatment.

(*a*) *Élite Selection and Democracy*

1. Élite selection assumes many forms in different societies. There are numerous shadings from unrestricted competition to rigid monopoly, as exemplified by feudal or caste stratification.

In some societies, conditions are so fluid that any individual may attain any position. The basis of selection is broadcast in pioneering societies at the earliest stages of their development. Self-governing societies of farmers usually impose few restrictions on the choice of leaders.[1] The American colonies, New Zealand, Australia, South Africa, and to some extent Brazil offer examples of this. Expanding bureaucratic empires frequently use commoners of ability in preference to hereditary privileged classes (Russia, 7th-century China, Egypt, the Roman Empire under Justinian). Commercial aristocracies (England, the Italian Renaissance cities) have often absorbed selected commoners in their élite strata while maintaining rank distinctions. In other societies, certain conditions (such as economic or military pressure) have led to rigid caste stratification, barring practically all vertical mobility; examples of this may be found from early Indonesia and India to Ethiopia and the Sudanese empires.

[1] James J. Leyburn, *Frontier Folkways*, New Haven, 1935.

2. In modern society, élite selection takes three major forms: (i) bureaucratic advancement, (ii) unregulated competition, (iii) class pressures. People who rise into élite positions show marked differences, depending on which of these three mechanisms was operative in their ascent.

The bureaucratic type of élite selection favours methodical workers who have a flair for meeting every situation in terms of prescriptions previously laid down. Their perspective must be limited to rules and regulations; individuals who show free-ranging interests and propensities for improvisation are passed over in promotion.

As against the systematic and prearranged pattern of bureaucratic advancement, competition for leadership in political arenas such as nineteenth-century parliaments is unregulated. The essential thing for the seeker of political prominence in that milieu was not proficiency in some special field, but a generalized popular appeal and magnetism, compounded of oratorical ability, stamina, identification with collective causes, intellectual resourcefulness, and so on, down to such elusive but important things as erotic glamour.

With the rise of class parties in the 20th century, political success began to depend to a lesser extent on personal magnetism and more on party regularity. Not the personal endowment of the individual but the strength of the group which he represents is basic for advancement into political élite positions.

3. In so far as the difference between democratic and non-democratic élite selection is concerned, the most important thing is obviously the *breadth of the basis* of selection. A system is democratic only if élite recruitment is not limited to members of a closed group. But even where élite recruitment is democratic in this sense, élites different in their structure and self-interpretation may be formed, depending on certain aspects of the *mode* of their recruitment.

There is a characteristic difference in this respect between the mode of recruitment of liberal and labour leaders. The former rise in the political world individually, that is, the degree of influence and of political power that they achieve does not depend on the increase in power of any given social stratum. A labour politician, however, rises in the political world only if, and because, labour as an entire group rises. This difference in the origin of the élite position of the two types leads to characteristic differences in their mentality.

Before labour parties appeared on the European political scene, the rise of politicians to prominence and power was largely an individual affair. When a politician achieved fame and influence, he did not feel that he owed this to his being associated with a distinct stratum or interest group. Had he chosen to represent another interest group (e.g. protectionists instead of free-traders), he would have made his mark nevertheless; it all was a matter of his own superior gifts. Such personal histories tended to produce a 'heroic' posture and a general outlook according to which one's career depends on his own endowment rather than on the impersonal social configurations within which destiny has placed him. 'Life', according to this philosophy, gives the same opportunities to everyone; there are everywhere chances to be exploited.

Against such a background, rise into an élite position (not only in political careers but also in a competitive economy) appears like the fruit of personal achievement. Newcomers who enter the ranks of the élite by such a route tend to believe in the decisive role of the exceptional individual in human affairs. In drama, they look for strong-willed heroes; in history, for great personalities. Nor can we say that, as professed by this type, individualism is a mere ideology, unrelated to real life as he experiences it. This individualism is a straightforward enough distillation of a peculiar kind of life experience, even though it is wholly inadequate as a general theory. For a sociologist, it is easy enough to see the working of social configurations where the naive individualist perceives only personal merit and achievement.

This 'heroic' type of individualism is capable of great spiritual sublimation. In German idealism, the individualist outlook of the liberal bourgeoisie has achieved depth and moral dignity. Yet idealism and its successor, existentialism, also tend to isolate the individual from his fellows, and to make him blind to man's dependence on fellowship and communication. In their metaphysics, these types conceive of man as a non-intercommunicating monad. What one man can mean to another finds no recognition in this philosophy of the self-made man.

The typical outlook of labour politicians achieving élite positions is entirely different. It is not true, of course, that the group they represent rises together with them; on the contrary, they enter a higher social stratum when they become influential. Yet they cannot forget for a moment that their own rise in society has been indissolubly linked to their identification with a particular group interest and with the relative increase in that group's influence. Even when they leave their original social peers far behind and ascend to a lonely peak of eminence, they are not likely to generalize this experience in terms of a 'great man' theory of history. They are far likelier to hold that group forces and collective factors are behind the achievement of the individual. As we see, élites differing as to their mode of recruitment are apt for this very reason to adopt a different outlook towards 'life' and 'destiny'.

An analogous difference may be seen in the attitudes of these two types of élite member towards culture and civilization. In keeping with their 'heroic' and individualistic outlook, élite members who rise individually are likely to feel that the highest peaks, the great masterpieces are the essential content of culture. The works of supreme geniuses determine the value of a culture as a whole. Culture appears here, not as a continuous flow of cooperative achievement, but as a discontinuous series of sublime moments of creation. The average, the day-to-day effort of the many is devalued. This is, however, what élites recruited by a collective mechanism view as the essence of the cultural process. Their self-esteem is rooted in modesty. They like to contemplate the gradual accumulation of small gains, the confluence of many tiny streams into a mighty river. Continuity in space and time is what they value, and they emphasize transitions and differences in degree where the other type focuses upon qualitative, essential differences. In education, they hold the good average to be more important than the top achievement; in history, they maintain that the destiny of groups, and of mankind as a whole, depends more on the steady efforts of the anonymous mass than on the awe-inspiring flights of rare genius.[1] Needless to say that it is the outlook

[1] [Translator's Note: While such typical differences in outlook probably did exist in nineteenth- and twentieth-century Germany, nothing corresponding to them is likely to be demonstrable in modern American society. For

of the collectively recruited élite which corresponds to the 'democratizing' trend with which we are concerned in this paper.

(*b*) *Group Structure and Relation to Other Groups*

The inner organizational structure of élite groups and their relative position towards other groups also have important consequences for their interpretation of man and the world. For example, in the Middle Ages, the intellectual élite of university teachers was organized in corporations and thus had the same position within society at large as any other officially recognized autonomous occupational group. In the 19th century, on the other hand, the social position of a large sector of the intellectual élite was that of the bohemian, without corporate ties, without a well-defined place in society; the members of this group lived in a curious milieu in which self-styled or genuine men of genius were thrown together with black sheep from aristocratic or bourgeois families, déclassé drifters, prostitutes, matinée idols, and other fugitives from organized society. Even for young men who later were content to enter well-regulated bureaucratic or professional careers, it was customary to spend a few anarchic and unregulated years while they were students. All this exerted a considerable influence upon their thinking. Where intellectual élite groups exist outside normal society, the ideas produced by them are likely to have a 'romantic' tinge. Such intellectuals will cultivate a set of values far removed from the concerns of ordinary people. As artists, they will become aesthetes dedicated to the cult of *l'art pour l'art*; as thinkers, they will seek the abstruse and the esoteric. This is inevitable in a society which has no need for the services of the intellectual in pursuing its 'serious' business. But the scene may change. During periods of acute social conflict, political ringleaders may become acutely aware of the propagandist potential of art. They will then take the artist seriously and give him a 'responsible' job; the artist may respond by

one thing, America lacks a political élite group of labour background, since there is no labour party contending for governmental positions on the national scale. For another, the philosophy of the American self-made man involves no excessive admiration for political, artistic, scientific, or philosophical genius.]

becoming politicized and adopting the belief that only 'socially significant' art is good art.

We assume that 'democratization' involves a lessening of the distance between intellectual élite groups and the other sectors of society. As democratization progresses, the ties between intellectual strata and society at large are likely to become closer and more organic. This need not mean that art will become crudely propagandist, but only that it will have a more organic function in life than '*l'art pour l'art*' has had.

(*c*) *The Self-Evaluation of Aristocratic and Democratic Élites*

The problem of the self-evaluation of intellectual élite groups has been treated in detail elsewhere.[1] From the point of view of the 'democratization' of culture, the important thing is to see how the self-evaluation of cultural élite groups changes as the culture becomes more democratic.

Intellectual groups existing in an aristocratic environment are apt to see themselves as they appear to their social superiors. The self-esteem of the artist depends on his success in acquiring aristocratic patrons; that of the teacher, on the relative number of his aristocratic pupils. Gradually, however, these groups develop standards independent of the verdict of the socially dominant groups. How intellectual peers judge each other will be more important than how they are judged by outsiders. Finally, the standards in terms of which the cultural élite judges itself become less exclusive and narrow. Intellectual prowess which sets the élite apart from the uninitiated both in high and low social groups will no longer be treated as the supreme human value. The intellectual will no longer look down upon the manual worker, just as he is not looking up to the aristocrat. He will treat his speciality as being essentially on a par with other skills—possibly superior to others in quantitative terms as involving more knowledge and training, but not superior in an essential and qualitative terms, as the realization of a higher human type.

(*d*) *Social Distance and the Democratization of Culture*

1. The word 'distance' designates in ordinary usage spatial

[1] See the essay on 'The Problem of the Intelligentsia' in this volume.

distance between things.[1] In the present context, however, we shall apply the word (metaphorically) to social rather than spatial relationships, and we shall be interested not so much in static distances as in acts *creating* distance (as when a thing is moved *away from* another). Distance as a social phenomenon is *produced by* agents who are interested in maintaining social distance between themselves and others, precisely when they live closely together in a spatial sense.

Social 'distantiation' in this sense is akin to, but not identical with, 'alienation'. The latter consists in the cooling off of emotional relationships. When we become 'alienated' from someone, we undo ties of identification that formerly had bound us together. Similarly, we may become 'alienated' from places or groups in which we had once felt at home. But this is not what makes the essence of distantiation.

The element of spontaneous activity 'creating' a distance is well brought out in a visual example used by Bullough.[2] A ship is approaching port: the town can be seen quite distinctly. Then mist descends and the town again 'recedes into the distance'. This is 'distantiation', for the town remains spatially near; it becomes more distant only in a psychological sense. Of course, however, it is not the subject's social act which creates the distance; the subject merely registers greater distance because his sight is blurred by mist.

In the social field, 'distantiation' may well express itself, quite literally, in a movement away from the other, as when we keep ourselves at a distance from a threatening individual. Such behaviour is often found in animals.[3] In Révész' observations on monkeys, the first few times the animals were fed, each

[1] On the problem of social distance, cf. G. Simmel, *Soziologie*, Leipzig, 1908, pp. 321 ff. and 687 ff. R. E. Park, 'The Concept of Social Distance', *Journal of Applied Sociology*, vol. VIII, No. 6, E. S. Bogardus, 'Social Distance and Its Origin', *Journal of Applied Sociology*, 1925, W. C. Poole, Jnr., 'Distance in Sociology', *American Journal of Sociology*, Vol. XXXIII, 1927. R. E. Park and E. W. Burgess, *Introduction to the Science of Sociology*, London and Chicago, 1924, p. 440. L. von Wiese, *System der allgemeinen Soziologie*, 2nd ed., pp. 160 ff. A. Walther, 'Soziale Distanz', *Kölner Vierteljahrshefte für Sociologie*, 1931, pp. 263 ff.

[2] Cf. E. Bullough, 'Psychical Distance as a Factor in Art and an Aesthetic Principle', *British Journal of Psychology*, vol. V, 1912–13, pp. 87 ff.

[3] Cf. Géza Révész, 'Sozialpsychologische Beobachtungen an Affen', *Zeitschrift für Psychologie*, vol. 118, 1930. The author points out that there

monkey sought to fight off all others, but as soon as one animal established its superiority over all others, all except the weakest and hence privileged 'baby' kept a safe distance from the champion, particularly at feeding time. Dominance and fear imposed both spatial and social distance.[1]

We assume that social 'distantiation' first appears in the form of avoiding actions actually creating spatial distance. Later, social distantiation becomes more 'sublimated', no longer necessarily requiring *spatial* avoidance. Certain types of distance-creating behaviour, however, are still being characterized in everyday speech by means of spatial metaphors, as when we speak of somebody being kept 'at arm's length'. Such expressions have the connotation that a distance greater than normal, or than expected by the subject who is kept 'at arm's length', has been created. Within each social milieu there is a 'normal' distance which interacting individuals are supposed to observe. Deviations from the norm are noted as undue 'aloofness' or as uncalled-for 'forwardness'. Metaphors involving spatial distance are typically used to characterize such infringements of rules for social behaviour. The ritual of social intercourse changes when we pass from one degree of intimacy to another; when, in a situation calling for the observance of one ritual, a person incongruously applies another, our feeling is that he is 'too close' or 'too distant'. In the case of objects of everyday use or works of art, too, we may speak of the 'normal' distance at which they should be located.

Another important example of social distance is the vertical distance between hierarchical unequals: the distance created by power. This is reflected in an enormous number of behaviour patterns developed by hierarchically stratified societies. We may mention differences in dress from one caste or class to another, differential modes of address, ceremonials of deference, gestures of submission, and so on. In the sociology of culture, and in such a study as ours in particular, the problem of vertical

are 'fundamental social power relationships which come into being regardless of the intellectual level of the species in question' (p. 148).

[1] For similar observations, cf. S. Zuckerman, *The Social Life of Monkeys and Apes*, London and New York, 1932; C. R. Carpenter, 'Field Study in Siam of the Behaviour and Social Relations of the Gibbon', *Comparative Psychology Monographs*, vol. 16, No. 5, December, 1940.

distance and distantiation is, of course, paramount. It is important to see that vertical distantiation may concern, not only the mutual relationship of two groups, but also the relationship between a person or group and inanimate objects of cultural significance. There is, in other words, a difference of 'high' and 'low' among cultural products. This spatial metaphor is neatly illustrated by cases in which things of 'high' significance, like objects of worship, are placed so high that one has to look up to them. In speech also, there is a difference between 'high' and 'low'. Certain 'high' subjects demand a solemn vocabulary and cadenced delivery, while 'lower' topics can be treated in a less strait-laced fashion. In the erotic sphere, the difference between 'high' and 'low' is particularly conspicuous: idealizing 'love' comes into being through a 'distantiation' of sexuality, and the object of such love is put on a 'pedestal', just as the experience itself is of a 'higher' nature. . . .

Beyond 'social' distantiation, whether in the sense of vertical distantiation or degree of intimacy, one may discern a more fundamental type of distance between man and man that we may call 'existential' distance. This is the distance between the I and the other purely as a person, regardless of conventionalized social relationships. Sometimes the other himself, as a person, is extremely vivid for me in an upsurge of empathy; at other times, he recedes into an existential distance, he is not real and present to me as a person. A particular variant of existential distantiation is self-distantiation: the experience that I am a stranger to myself, or rather that I can be more or less close to myself. Like other forms of existential distantiation, self-distantiation cannot well be observed in isolation from its concrete, social, and historical context. There are cultural and social constellations which virtually impose self-distantiation; others make it possible to overcome self-distantiation, to recover oneself. During such epochs, many individuals seek to restore the integrity of their existence, to get closer to the real core of their being. . . .

The various types of 'distantiation' we have just distinguished are subject to change in the course of history, and it is the task of cultural sociology to ascertain the regularities involved in this process. Our own leading hypothesis is that the most fundamental, causally decisive type of distantiation is the social one. How the pattern of distantiation of cultural objects (see p. 207 above) changes will be determined by what happens in the sphere of power, that is, of vertical distantiation. In fact, the fundamental character of a culture as an aristocratic or democratic one depends primarily on its vertical distance patterns. Democratization means essentially a reduction of vertical distance, a de-distantiation.

2. Let us consider, for example, a pre-democratic (aristocratic or monocratic) culture. Its essential feature is the 'vertical distance' between the rulers and the ruled—and we mean this in the sense that innumerable psychic acts asserting and acknowledging that vertical distance are the chief mechanism through which the rulers wield power. Of course, the rulers control a great many material instruments that help them maintain their power (e.g., weapons and means of communication), but it is not these material things that endow them with power. It is, essentially, their subjects' propensity to look up to them, to consider them as higher beings.

Hierarchically organized groups within the larger society, such as armies and bureaucracies, may also be considered in this sense as products of acts of distantiation. The regular and reliable occurrence of these acts makes these organizations what they are. Vertical distance is the constitutive principle in which the very existence of such groups is grounded.

In the aristocratic society, the ruling strata 'create' a distance between themselves and the lower groups by meeting the members of the latter, so to speak, from a higher level. Every contact between 'high' and 'low' is made subject to a highly formalized ritual. Dominating the lower groups is not merely a matter of giving orders and enforcing obedience. It consists, to a very large extent, in the maintenance of a vertical distance which becomes an organic part of the thinking, not only of the rulers but also of the ruled. This psychic distantiation is just as much a part of the aristocratic hierarchical order as is the uneven distribution of advantages and risks.

Strict standards of conduct, prescribing a formal etiquette for every occasion, are a powerful instrument for maintaining distance. Aristocratic cultures frown upon spontaneous, impulsive behaviour which is deemed vulgar. They adopt such behavioural ideals as the Greek 'kalokagathia' or the medieval

German *mâze* (measure); we may also mention in this context the code of chivalrous conduct worked out by the Provençal nobility which became a universal norm. These examples show that aristocratic cultures tend to maximize distance not only in the vertical dimension, i.e., between 'high' and 'low' groups, but also among equals. The typically aristocratic attitude is 'distance' and formality even in the intimate circle.

Distantiation in the hierarchically organized society affects not only inter-personal relations but also attitudes towards cultural objects. Certain social norms and institutions are endowed with absolute authority—critical thoughts concerning them are tabooed. Aristocratic societies have their official philosophy which must on no account be questioned.

Aristocratic élites typically seek to create an 'élite culture' of their own. They see to it that certain essential features of their group culture, such as forms of social intercourse, pastimes, patterns of speech, but also various techniques and systems of knowledge, shall be unshareable by the many. (Intellectual élite groups of the aristocratic type, such as priestly castes, adopt in this vein sacred languages of their own such as Sanskrit or Latin.)

The adoption of the vernacular for literary or liturgical purposes is, considered from this angle, an important vehicle of the democratization of culture, and so is the irruption of 'lower' (technological and industrial) concerns into the sacred precincts of 'science'.

Aristocratic speech is typically formal, stereotyped, and stylized. Its horizon is severely limited: certain 'low' objects are excluded from it. Things which have the greatest urgency for strata struggling for bare existence, such as food and money, and the means of satisfying elementary needs in general, must not be mentioned. On the aristocratic level, one pretends not to notice such elementary concerns. This finickiness and delicacy becomes more extreme as an aristocratic group grows older, and comes to consist of members who have inherited (but not created) their privileged position. A 'first generation' of a ruling group which has a direct experience of risk and struggle in war or in finance does not yet possess this extreme delicacy. Its descendants, however, tend to look away from the 'facts of life' until they no longer live in the world of real things but in a second world of artificial symbols.[1] The 'cultivated' speech of these sheltered upper strata separates them from the common man; this is one of the most important social barriers between classes in stratified societies. Where 'high' and 'low' speech exist side by side, full intercommunication is no longer possible. To the common man, elegant speech appears unnatural and hypocritical; to the upper strata, popular speech is coarse, brutal, and degrading.

One of the symptoms of distantiation is the tendency of terms designating lower social groups to acquire a pejorative value connotation. A well-known example is the change in the meaning of the word 'villain' in English and 'vilain' in French. Originally, these words designated the 'villager'; in modern English, the word is a synonym of 'rogue', and in French, it means 'ugly'.[2] Words originally referring to élite strata tend to change their meaning in the opposite direction (cf. 'courteous').

We may see a further characteristic of aristocratic speech patterns in their tendency towards rigid regularity; they seek to exclude the 'chaotic' and irregular. Fulfilling the requirements of an aristocratic society, the French Academy in the 17th century undertook the standardization of the French language. The French linguist Brunot made a painstaking study comparing the *Dictionary* of the French Academy (1st ed., 1694) with a later, unofficial and 'democratic' document, the French *Encyclopedia*.[3] He found that the *Encyclopedia* used an infinitely richer vocabulary, since it treated in systematic fashion a large number of technological and industrial processes which the Dictionary had excluded from consideration. According to Brunot, the difference is not one of subject matter only; the entire use of the language is a different one, since the 'new' language is replete with metaphors and turns of phrase inspired by 'vulgar' concerns, while the 'old'

[1] On this difference between generations, cf. Richard Hamann, *Die Frührenaissance der italienischen Malerei*, Jena, 1909, pp. 2 ff.

[2] On the changed meaning of 'villain', see Carl Brinkmann, *Wirtschafts- und Sozialgeschichte*, Berlin and Munich, 1927, p. 40.

[3] Cf. Frédéric Brunot, *Histoire de la langue française des origines à 1900*, vol. VI, Paris, 1930.

one largely limited itself to courtly, refined phrases and metaphors.[1]

3. The study of certain changes in fashionable vocabulary enables us to follow the process of democratization of culture. It is a symptom of democratization that certain key terms antithetical to the static and hierarchical spirit of aristocratic culture become fashionable in times of transition. We have already referred to the changed meaning of the term 'organism' in a similar context. Brunot, in the work cited above, refers to the vogue enjoyed by the term 'fermentation' as one of the symptoms of the change in outlook described by him. Other words which (although coined earlier) come into general use during the 18th century include 'social' and 'civilisation': their new vogue reflects a general re-orientation of thinking, a branching out into new realms of experience. 'Progress', of course, is a key term summarizing one of the chief aspirations of the Enlightenment period.[2] Together with the related term 'evolution', it signalizes nothing less than the advent of a new ontology, of the rethinking of the sum and substance of human experience from a radically new viewpoint. The static ontology which equated 'real' being with what is unchanging and permanent is replaced by a dynamic one, intent upon seizing 'real' being precisely in whatever is going through a process of change.[3]

[1] [Translator's Note: It should be noted that the change in question was one of content and style, rather than of linguistic form. The Encyclopedists expressed their unorthodox views in an academically correct language. Throughout the literary and political upheavals of recent times, the standardization of the French Language, initiated before the foundation of the Academy but codified by the latter, has remained virtually unchallenged.]

[2] On the history of the idea of progress, cf. Jules Delvaille, 'Essai sur l'histoire de l'idée de progrès jusqu'à la fin du XVIIe siècle', Doctorate thesis, Paris, 1910; V. de P. M. Brunetière, 'La formation de l'idée de progrès au XVIIIe siècle', in *Études critiques sur l'histoire de la litterature française, 5me série*, Paris 1902–07, 6th ed., 1922 ; J. B. Bury, *The Idea of Progress*, London and New York, 1932.

[3] On these implications of 'progress' and 'evolution', cf. F. Brunot, *op. cit.*, pp. 107 ff.; John Dewey, 'Progress', in *International Journal of Ethics*, vol. 26, 1905; A. J. Todd, *Theories of Social Progress*, New York, 1918; W. R. Inge, 'The Idea of Progress', in *Outspoken Essays*, London and New York, 1922; W. H. Mallock, *Aristocracy and Evolution*, London and New York, 1898; W. F. Willcox, 'A Statistician's Idea of Progress', *International Journal of Ethics*, vol. 23, 1902.

It is one of the characteristics of this new ontology that it puts 'function' and 'process' in the place of 'Gestalt'. Conservative thought is 'morphological'. It explains the world in terms of unanalysed and unanalysable given wholes in their unique *Gestalt.* As against this, liberal and progressive thought is analytical; it decomposes the seemingly monolithic entities of the traditional world view into functional elements. The sociological explanation of this dichotomy is a complex and difficult matter, but one aspect of it at least may become clearer precisely through the use of our concept of distantiation. '*Gestalt*', in fact, is the product of a specific type of distantiation. A social entity like a group or an institution will appear to me as a static whole, a *Gestalt*, only if I am far enough removed from it, that is, from a distance. If I am a part of the group myself, I can see from within both its internal divisions and the mechanism that makes it run. For someone far removed from the governmental sphere—say, a provincial farmer—'the government' is a monolithic unit, something like a mythical figure or a person. The insider, however, has a very different picture of the whole thing—he sees intrigues, jockeying for position, competition—anything but monolithic unity. In short, the outsider must see things morphologically; the insider, analytically.

4. If we combine this conclusion with some of our earlier findings concerning different modes of élite selection, it will be seen immediately how democratization entails a shift from the morphological to the analytical outlook. In status-bound societies without vertical mobility, the morphological view is practically all-pervading. The mass of people is in the position of the outsider, contemplating from afar the central authorities like the Papacy or the Empire. These powers have their unique, *Gestalt*-like concreteness; the people experience them through the medium of their symbolism and their ritual. What actually goes on 'within' the precincts of power is shrouded in mystery. The secret was pierced for the first time in the West during the Renaissance period, when in the course of social changes new élites penetrated into the top region and came to see the actual process instead of the stereotyped symbol. We may mention Machiavelli as one of the first writers to analyse events in the highest strata of society in terms of a mundane power process,

stripped of their metaphysical aura of mystery. This disillusioned, realistic, analytical attitude towards 'high politics' eventually became quite universal in the 17th century. It came to be taken for granted that the substance of politics is a struggle for power in which everything is calculable and nothing is sacred.

The same sequence, running from the mystifying concealment of the realities of the power process to their disrespectful debunking, repeated itself in more recent times. During the age of absolutism, the disillusioned and analytical attitude towards the political facts of life was in no way prejudicial to authoritarian rule, because that attitude was largely confined to the wielders of power themselves. They could afford to look at their world without prettifying illusions, since their authority was unchallenged. The people did not participate in the political process and was not aware of its inner mechanism; again it perceived the central authorities as a towering *Gestalt*. When the process of democratization began, however, large groups of outsiders became interested in the governmental process and challenged the authority of the rulers. Public opinion demanded an accounting for the exercise of authority, and a wholly realistic account, admitting that all was merely a matter of power and nothing else, would have been quite unsatisfactory. It became necessary to idealize the process, and to provide ideological justifications of power. It was at that time that the theory of the state as a civilizing agency was developed.[1] This corresponded to the novel need felt by the bourgeois middle class and the professional bureaucracy to experience authority, not as naked power, but as an instrument of the universal good. Such ideologies of power, however, lost their suggestive force when very large numbers of people, formerly excluded from political influence and from higher education, penetrated into the sphere of government and of official culture. As they took cognizance of the inner workings of the system of which they previously had only seen the symbolic façade, their awe and respect were gone. Democratization,

[1] Cf. Friedrich Meinecke, *Die Idee der Staatsräson in der neueren Geschichte*, Munich, 1925 (English Translation, London and New Haven, 1956), p. 353; also Karl Mannheim, *Ideology and Utopia*, London and New York, 1936.

in fact, means disillusionment; it is often pointed out that democratic parliamentary regimes cannot command respect because the public is constantly aware of the non-edifying bickering among parties that makes up much of the parliamentary process. We may also mention in this context the 'iconoclastic' aspects of the sociology of knowledge. The latter, in fact, refuses to contemplate the representative works of a culture 'at a distance' and adopts an analytical attitude towards them, exploring the minute interrelationships among the myriad impulses impinging upon the cultural process. Thus, the advent of mass democracy puts 'analysis' in the place of 'Gestalt', just as the novel analytical methods discovered by Machiavelli's generation did. There is, however, a difference between the two epochs; during the Renaissance, only a few exceptional intellectuals practised the 'analytical' view, whereas in the age of modern mass democracy, this approach is universally shared. The secret of political analysis is no longer confined to 'manuals for the Prince' or to 'Political Testaments' for the use of the élite but becomes altogether public.

When this happens, the emphasis is placed in the beginning upon the ressentiment-laden 'unmasking' of the evil practices of power-holders. Such a response is understandable when people see for the first time the profane reality behind the sacred symbols that they had been led to adore from afar. The joy of debunking, however, is of short duration; in time, the realities of the power process come to be taken for granted. The dominant feeling then tends to be one of concern about this Leviathan, together with a sense of responsibility for taming him. In pre-democratic times, the masses, while reduced to a passive role, had also the advantage of not being burdened with responsibility for the shaping of their own destiny. The world was simple, traditional routine took care of most economic and social problems, and where decisions had to be made, these could be entrusted to a central élite. Democratization, on the other hand, seems to be associated with a growing complexity of the social and economic process, involving the necessity of making choices and of applying analysis instead of just trusting in the automatic working of tradition.

All this does not mean to say that the advent of the modern analytic approach is solely a matter for the broadening of the élite. In fact, it may happen that participation in the decision-making process becomes broader and more democratic without a noticeable advance in analytical thinking taking place. For the latter to come about, a certain maturity of critical intelligence is needed, an ability to overcome the suggestive power of symbols, resulting from 'distantiation'. But mere change in social location does not necessarily create this ability; the latter must have other sources as well. We may say, however, that greater proximity to the seat of power is *necessary* (without being sufficient) for the discovery of its inner mechanism.

5. A contrast similar to the one just discussed is that between 'genetic' and 'systematic' thinking. The modern, analytic mind prefers to use the 'genetic' approach, whereas authoritarian cultures recoil from it and seek a system of timeless truth, untouched by historical changes and vicissitudes. To the authoritarian mind, 'validity' must be independent of 'genesis'.[1]

This contrast again seems to be analysable in terms of 'distance'. Traditional authority, perpetuating itself through a series of generations, gradually pushes its origin back into a mythical distance. Such distant origins are incommensurable with anything that can be observed here and now; authority, then, comes to be experienced as timeless and existing by necessity. Traditionally sanctioned authority leaves no room for the idea that 'things could be otherwise'; its wielder acts as if he were just a timeless embodiment of superiority. When a new generation grows up in a traditionally governed society, it will tend to grant these claims of the authority-wielders, since its members cannot remember any time when things were different. Such generations, then, are not likely to think in 'genetic' or analytical terms. Sceptical, 'destructive', analytical thinking is likely to be found among the members of generations that had gone through radical changes in the realm of power.[2]

It is clear from the preceding discussion that the traditional way of thinking, while antithetical to the genetic method, does not ignore the problem of the origins; what it does is to place them at a mythical distance where they are no longer subject

[1] Cf. Karl Mannheim, *op. cit.*

[2] Cf. 'The Problem of Generations', in Karl Mannheim, *Essays on the Sociology of Knowledge*, London and New York, 1952, pp. 276 ff.

to realistic analysis. The origin of power is not laid bare but concealed in a sacred myth. A later variant of the conservative philosophy of history replaces the supra-rational myth by a rationalistic interpretation. History appears as meaningful, as the unfolding of a rational plan. Such interpretations serve as a justification of the prevailing authoritarian order. How power is generated—this question remains unexamined; it is banished from consciousness. A democratic society, however, cannot well ignore the problem of the genesis of power, since its mechanism involves precisely the generation of power in the course of the democratic process.

Nevertheless, this point is not valid without qualification. In democratic societies, too, the origin of power and authority is subject to a certain amount of distantiation, in keeping with our general point that democracy reduces vertical social distance without completely eliminating it. Distantiation does not disappear in democracy; it merely assumes a different form. Accordingly, democracy does not dissolve *every* problem of social authority into a problem of genesis. It uses genetic analysis to discredit pre-democratic authority, but its own basis of authority is also 'distantiated' in a certain way. How does this democratic distantiation differ from the traditional one? Primarily, one may suggest, through its *impersonal* character.

Traditional authority is centred in persons or families elevated above the rest of society and endowed with personal or hereditary charisma. The origin of this authority is often spelled out in myths: the Japanese Mikado as 'Son of Heaven', the high castes of India as 'Sons of the North'. Democratic authority, however, is not bound to any person as such. It is conferred only temporarily and conditionally upon certain individuals. But while the mythically sanctioned distantiation of persons is absent in democracy, the fundamental institutions do become 'distantiated'. They are elevated to symbolic dignity as myths. The electoral procedure or basic documents like the Constitution come to play such a mythical role.

Under certain conditions, individuals do achieve a heightened position in a democratic society as stars, idols, and popular heroes; but this is due to specific factors that need not detain us here. Myths that are organic to democracy grow up around collective concepts like Rousseau's 'volonté générale'. We look at this in an un-mythical, realistic way, as a certain mechanism of social integration; for Rousseau himself, however, the concept has a transcendent meaning.

6. We may mention, as a typically democratic instance of 'distantiation', the treatment of 'abstract' collective entities ('abstrakte Kollektiva' in L. von Wiese's terminology) as concrete, active subjects: the 'state', the 'party', the 'class', and so on. Similarly, processes are sometimes transformed into substances: 'socialism', 'romanticism' as substance-like entities. The treatment of business corporations as 'juristic persons' illustrates the same tendency. It is characteristic that conservative thinkers have vehemently opposed the 'distantiation' of such abstract and rational entities as 'the state' or 'law'. For these thinkers, a collective entity *could* be endowed with authority, but only if (like the Church) it presented itself in a rich garb of symbolism that put it above and beyond everyday reality. No authority could accrue to mere 'profane' instruments of social integration.[1] The modern mind, however, tends to isolate certain strands of social reality and endow them with a higher, metaphysical dignity (cf. the Marxist treatment of History as a dialectical drama enacted by antithetical social forces).

This combination of the analytical approach with distance-creating myth-making introduces a certain ambiguity into democratic thought. We find an integrally analytical, nominalist outlook in democratized groups only when they are in the opposition. And even this is not true of all of them. Liberals and anarchists lean towards integral nominalism, but the Marxists oppose their own brand of 'realism' (the term is used here, of course, in the sense of the medieval dichotomy of realism v. nominalism) to the conservative brand. All that we can say is that the analytic and nominalist approach is likely to come to the fore when the democratizing trend is dominant, so that eventually the democratic 'distantiation' of abstract entities, too, will be subjected to critique. But critical analysis cannot hope to eliminate *all* distantiation whatever.

[1] The clash between the conservative view and the modern 'distantiation' of rational, social instrumentalities is vividly illustrated in Hegel's polemic against the conservative von Haller, cf. *Philosophy of Law*, pars. 257–59.

In the above, we contrasted pre-democratic distantiation (putting persons or concrete groups upon an inaccessibly high pedestal) with democratic distantiation (personifying and hypostatizing abstract entities). The latter is, in fact, far more characteristic of our own age than the former. Nevertheless, it would be a mistake to see in Western history a unilinear progress from the 'pre-democratic' to the 'democratic'. What is 'later' is not necessarily more 'democratic'. Thus, we may already look upon the Middle Ages as driving underground the earlier, typically urban and rationalistic tradition of the Greek city states. As against this, the dominant culture of the Middle Ages stressed irrational, mystical, 'primitive' thought patterns, even though elements of the rationalistic tradition of antiquity were preserved precisely in learned clerical circles. Further, a genuine process of cultural democratization set in during the late Middle Ages when urban groups became culturally dominant in Europe. After this early upsurge of democratization, a retrograde tendency set in, and European society became 're-feudalized'. We shall now discuss these phenomena in some detail.

7. We shall turn first to the democratizing tendency as it manifested itself in the late Middle Ages. The underlying social change—i.e., the growing strength of urban groups—was accompanied by radical stylistic transformations in the realm of art, literature, and religion. To begin with art: contrasting with the highly stylized, unrealistic character of earlier medieval painting and sculpture, late medieval art about 1370 begins to be dominated by what might be called 'intimate realism' ('Nahrealismus'). The essence of this new style is that all things are represented as they appear in the context of man's everyday activities. In this we see a radically new attitude, a revolutionary self-assertion of man who discovers the dignity of his normal, ordinary activity. The phenomenon can best be characterized as one of *de-distantiation*. Sociologically, it is intimately connected with the rise of urban democracy in which the individual found an ever-widening scope for influencing political, economic, and cultural life. The distance separating the average individual from the central authorities became less; culture responded to this by boldly adopting the everyday perspective of the average individual as the one valid for art and religion.

The perspective of everyday life had, of course, existed before, but it could not be culturally representative; this became possible only when the changed social background resulted in a shift of the ontological accent towards what was experienced as 'real' in everyday life.

An analogous trend may be observed in church architecture. Early medieval churches show in their architecture maximal 'distance' between the faithful and the priest; the altar, scene of the central act of the Catholic cult, is placed at the end of parallel naves, symbolizing the 'infinite' distance between man and the object of his faith. Late medieval churches, however, have a more intimate character. They serve for private worship as well as for the exceptional solemnity of high mass.[1] The layman plays a more conspicuous and active role in the Church, and the interior of church building visibly reflects this: the lateral naves disappear, and the interior becomes an undivided hall.[2] The altar can be seen from every point. There is no longer one exclusive, privileged perspective pointing towards the altar; it may now be viewed from every direction. In this lack of a privileged axis of orientation we see an expression of a new attitude. It reflects, not chaos and disorder, but a novel desire for clarity which is characteristic of the new urban middle class. It must be possible to grasp the entire space from every point. This transparency of the surrounding space reflects a changed attitude of faith. The earlier sense of awe-inspiring, inscrutable mystery gives way to a sense of security and confidence. The 'distance' between the average individual and the central symbols and objects of faith diminishes. Religion becomes less anxiety-laden. We can observe a parallel change in medieval social relationships; while feudal authority is distant, mysterious, and anxiety-provoking, the social climate in the cities is characterized by far greater rationality and security. Social distance between the élite and the people again tends to become greater during the subsequent period. The culture of the Baroque age is far more aristocratic than that of the late medieval urban culture. But at any rate late

[1] Cf. Dehio, *Geschichte der deutschen Kunst*, Berlin-Leipzig, 1919, vol. II, p. 135.

[2] On this change, cf. Bechtel, *Wirtschaftsstil des späten Mittelalters*, Munich-Leipzig, 1930, pp. 59–66.

medieval church architecture with its development of the undivided hall shows a maximum of security within the community.

Did this change in church architecture precede or follow an analogous transformation of the social structure? The historian Bechtel, whom we have been following in our discussion of late medieval church architecture, comes to the conclusion that the change in architectural forms antedated the corresponding change in economic life.[1] The artist according to him creates new forms in his medium before society at large changes its character; economic changes are determined by changes in the realm of ideas, not *vice versa*. This conclusion, however, is open to doubt. To be sure, we see a fully developed economic system based upon new techniques and concepts only after the parallel transformation of art has run its full course. But this does not mean to say that the original impulse has come from art or from other purely spiritual or intellectual forces. In our view, the first impulse comes from social reality, from the changed relationships (particularly the changed 'distance') among social groups. These impulses produce their effects, so to speak, in microscopic fashion, long before large-scale cultural changes, either in art or in economic life, become visible. It may well be that artists appear in the van of social change, but if they are 'pioneering' in this fashion, this merely shows that they are quicker than others to react to social changes and to give them visible expression.

In the fourteenth century, religious life underwent a momentous transformation that reflected itself in a changed relationship between laity and clergy. In the early Middle Ages, the emphasis was placed upon the liturgy of the mass. In this, the community played a passive role, in keeping with the authoritarian, 'distantiated' role of the Church. In the late Middle Ages, however, the sermon begins to play a preponderant role. The Church speaks to the faithful as thinking individuals; their 'vital selfhood', to recall one of our categories of the process of democratization, must be appealed to. Preaching becomes a kind of agitation.[2] At the same time, confession also gains in importance: the priest enters into contact with the faithful as

[1] Cf. Bechtel, *op. cit.*, p. 244.

[2] Cf. Karl Lamprecht, *Deutsche Geschichte*, vol. XII, p. 40.

adviser on an intimate scale, and not only (or predominantly) in his liturgical role.

Another significant religious phenomenon of the same period is the growth of mysticism. The mystic seeks, and achieves, a more intimate union with God; here again, religious life shows a pattern of de-distantiation. What is most characteristic of the period in question is, however, that mystical contemplation is no longer practised by monks alone. In German mysticism, the artisan who withdraws into his room to practise mystical contemplation (e.g. Jakob Boehme) makes his appearance. Religion is no longer exclusively a matter of the community. It becomes privatized, solitary contemplation. The intimate life space of the individual becomes the vehicle of his religious experience; the four walls of his abode are transmuted, so to speak, into a soul-space.

We have already touched upon this heightened dignity of the space of everyday experience in connection with the 'intimate realism' of late medieval art. At this point, we may mention a related cultural symptom. Painting during the period we are discussing definitely severs its earlier close connection with architecture, and easel paintings (of religious subjects) make their appearance in private homes as wel. as public offices, e.g., of gilds.[1] Easel paintings require a 'distance' that is most appropriate to a 'democratized' public; the earlier media of painting —the monumental mural on the one hand, the miniature on the other—called for a distance that was either too great or too small. Monumental paintings as well as miniatures were removed from the everyday environment of the average individual. The former decorated the public buildings in which the exercise of authority in the hierarchial, stratified society was centred; the latter could be seen only by one individual, that is, an aristocratic collector. Easel paintings, however, may be placed where people congregate in their everyday pursuits —in homes as well as in the offices of autonomous corporations.

A final point concerning the manifestations of a 'dedistantiating' trend in late medieval art: the discovery of true perspective in painting falls into the same period. Early medieval painting is two-dimensional. The figures represented are removed from the space of everyday experience. They stand in

[1] Cf. Dehio, *op. cit.*, vol. IV, p. 296; also Bechtel, *op. cit.*, pp. 271, 274 ff.

a mystical, metaphysical space of their own, and their appearance stresses their attributes as divine or holy personages. The background is often a flat expanse of gold. Later, the figures become three-dimensional and their background also acquires depth. In this illusionistic style, the pictorial space is a continuation of the spectator's own space. A direct connection is established between the spectator and the object represented, a connection that does not break up the continuity of ordinary, everyday experience.

8. As we pointed out above, the democratizing tendency of the late Middle Ages (and of the early Renaissance) later gave way to a retrograde movement towards 're-feudalization'. The distance between élite and mass grew immeasurably with the advent of absolutism. It must be noted, however, that retrograde movements of this kind neither revive the hierarchial forms displaced by the earlier democratization nor eliminate the cultural results of the preceding democratizing process completely. The 're-feudalization' of European society during the 16th and 17th centuries by no means restored early medieval feudalism; it rather combined feudal elements with novel forms of stratification and novel techniques of control. In so far as the cultural evolution is concerned, it is a fundamental postulate of the sociology of knowledge that whatever has come into being in the cultural process cannot simply disappear; it will enter into later cultural configurations in changed form. Thus, the authoritarianism of the Church reasserted itself in the Counter-Reformation, and in politics the absolute monarchy became dominant at the same time. Both these authoritarian control systems, however, made use of the achievements of the preceding rationalistic eras. In art and science, the Baroque is a continuation of the Renaissance. What the new age did was to neutralize the effects of the earlier conquests of the *Ratio*, by blunting its cutting edge where it could be a menace to the new absolute authority. This was done, for example, by introducing new 'supra-rational' elements into the rational system of the Renaissance.

Baroque religion is ecstatic, not in the manner of the mystic contemplation practised by isolated monks and artisans, but in the form of an intensification of fervour beyond all measure, in a kind of overheated and sublimated eroticism. Baroque art, on the other hand, does not abandon the earlier illusionistic realism of the Renaissance; on the contrary, it exaggerates it to the point of of extreme naturalism, but for the purpose of conveying a transcendent, metaphysical message.

The supra-rational principle of the Baroque is the heroic and superhuman. The emphasis is upon the incomparable power of the ruling individual. At the same time, Baroque art, and Baroque culture in general, emphasizes rational calculation and classic measure. Classical conventions and models predominate, guiding imagination in pre-existent channels. Baroque art is cool, conventional, and yet fervent and declamatory. It depended on circumstances which aspect of this culture—the rational or supra-rational one—became dominant. The calculating rationalism of its ruling groups could produce a wholly this-wordly, critical state of mind from which some of the impulses responsible for the Enlightenment flew.

Also, Baroque society was by no means wholly permeated by the authoritarian and aristocratic spirit. The middle class, though crushed and overawed by the enormous prestige of the aristocracy, lived its own life, had its own corporate institutions, and cultivated its own intellectual and artistic taste. Besides official, heroic art, there is also the intimate art of the Dutch painters, and some of the writers of the period show considerable acumen in their ironic, disillusioned analysis of society.[1]. . .

9. Our contemporary culture is characterized by a radical negation of 'distance' both in social relationships and in the realm of culture. Our field of experience tends to become homogeneous, without the earlier hierarchical gradations between 'high' and 'low', 'sacred' and 'profane'. In all earlier ages, such divisions were all-pervasive. In the medieval university, branches of learning were divided into 'higher' and 'lower'. In ancient Greece, as Zilsel has pointed out, poetry was considered infinitely more honourable than plastic art, simply because the sculptor and painter had their social origin in the class of craftsmen who were often slaves.[2] In pre-modern times, among topics of knowledge, 'high' was sharply separated from

1 [Translator's Note: At this point, three pages are missing from the manuscript. The context indicates that these must have dealt with the Enlightenment period and the nineteenth century.]

2 Cf. H. Zilsel, *Die Entstehung des Geniebegriffes*, Tübingen, 1926, Part I.

'low', knowledge of divinity and metaphysics belonging into the former category, knowledge of the objects of everyday experience into the latter. In art, too, representations of ideal beauty ranked high above portrayals of everyday objects, and this distinction was reflected in the formal structure of academic paintings. Their very composition revealed a hierarchical structural principle—the things represented were arranged in a more or less regular design enhancing the dominant position of the central figures. In these academic paintings, the haphazard, random arrangement of things as we encounter them in real experience is replaced by order. As against this, impressionism strives for a 'photographic' effect, reproducing the unregulated, spontaneous freshness of momentary combinations of things. Photography, indeed, expresses well the spirit of modern 'de-distantiation'. It marks the greatest closeness to all things without distinction. The snapshot is a form of pictorial representation that is most congenial to the modern mind with its interest in the unretouched and uncensored 'moment'. (It may be added that, in keeping with the general rule that 'distantiation' always reasserts itself, composition and design tend to reappear in modern, post-academic art.)

In the modern, homogenized field of experience, every single thing is an appropriate object of scrutiny; none has a greater dignity than any other; the study of theological ideas is on a par with that of chemistry or physiology. This, however, leads to a characteristic difficulty which is inherent in the process of democratization. If the field of experience is 'homogeneous', if no object is respected 'above' any other, how can man himself, the individual unit of society, claim any particular dignity? The principle of equality thus comes into conflict with that of vital autonomy—a contradiction which is as yet unsolved. If we stress the one, we can hardly avoid slighting the other. The ideal of 'freedom', of the autonomy of vital selfhood, is difficult to reconcile with the ideal of 'equality', the assertion of the equal to value of all social units. We have to do here with a contradiction, an antinomy that reveals the deep inner conflict of our age.

This conflict manifests itself with particular sharpness in those sciences which deal with man—psychology and sociology. Psychology as a natural science works with a completely homogenized field of experience. It is not only that all individuals are treated on the same footing; in addition to this, classes of psychic phenomena which for the experiencing subject have very unequal value and dignity are just data, without any difference of rank, for the scientific psychologist. Sense data or religious striving—for psychology, they are just empirical phenomena subject to ascertainable laws. In this way, forms of experience are 'de-distantiated', just as individuals and objects are. This is inherent in the scientific attitude, but it leads to a discrepancy between the image of man as drawn by science, and the self-image of man as given in immediate experience.

In sociology, similar problems arise in connection with the problem of freedom. Sociology seeks to ascertain regularities of behaviour in a homogenized field. Now if these behavioural regularities alone are observed, disregarding individual choices and their meaningful *rationale*, all human groups will begin to resemble calculable mechanisms. But if we start from the individual and his vital selfhood, we shall discover that there is another side to behaviour, and that human actions considered in themselves result from choices due to autonomous initiative. Each individual is the centre of his own universe, and is free in this sense. It is difficult for behaviour science, with its predominant interest in observable regularities of behaviour, to render justice to this other side of the problem. We cannot undertake here to solve this antinomy; all we can do is to call attention to it.

The homogenization of the field of experience is by no means a matter of the scientific approach only. We can observe it also in everyday experience. Just as science obliterates the differences of rank among different classes of objects and phenomena, the modern attitude towards time tends to disregard the distinction between 'working day' and 'holiday'. The articulation of time in terms of periodically recurrent, 'distantiated', sacred dates has not for modern man the decisive importance it had for earlier generations. 'Holidays' tend to acquire a purely utilitarian, functional character as times for rest and recreation, even when they coincide with religious dates. (In Soviet Russia, an attempt was even made to do away with this coincidence, by substituting staggered rest days on the basis of a five-day week for the Sunday rest—a reform which, by the way, did not take root.)

Analogous trends can be observed in art and philosophy. It is characteristic of modern art that it stresses the 'how', the manner of representation, instead of the 'what', the represented object. A still life of vegetables may be just as 'high' art as a Madonna—it is all a matter of the quality of painting. The world of the objects represented is 'homogenized'; this is one of the principles of 'l'art pour l'art'. But we must enter a *caveat* at this point. The motto of 'l'art pour l'art' itself shows that for the artist the field of experience is by no means wholly homogenized. Art as such has a high dignity of its own; it is 'distantiated'. (The same is true of science as an activity.) What we observe here is not that *all* distantiation is done away with, but that distantiation is limited to the general type of activity that one is engaged in—an activity which, while itself 'distantiated', treats all its objects as being on the same level.

In philosophy, too, we may observe the levelling of the objects of speculation. The modern line of evolution in philosophy leads from theism to deism, pantheism, naturalism. One of the characteristic features of modern philosophy is its rejection of the 'reduplication of Being' ('Seinsverdoppelung'). Pre-modern philosophy tended to distinguish between purely phenomenal Being (the world of tangible and observable things) and true, noumenal Being (the metaphysical Essence). This introduced a hierarchy into the world of things: they could be ordered according to their distance from 'true' Being. Now we cannot say that all metaphysics, all 'reduplication of Being', is of aristocratic origin, just as it is wrong to assert that 'distantiation' arises only in aristocratic cultures. It is, however, correct to say that whatever tendency towards 'reduplication of Being' exists is very sharply threatened by the democratization of culture. The origin of this threat lies in the propensity of the democratized mind to homogenize the field of experience.

In the history of metaphysical thought, the idea of a personal God, God the Father, marks the maximum of 'distantiation'. (This corresponds to the steeply hierarchical, 'distantiated' character of patriarchal cultures.) From this, the trend goes in modern times towards a growing stress upon 'immanence'. The divine principle increasingly loses its transcendent character, until—passing through the phase of Deism with its minimization of the transcendent and personal traits of Divinity—we reach pantheism. In this philosophy, God is wholly immanent in Nature, and every existing thing acquires a particle of the divine essence. From a certain point of view, this represents the culminating point of the democratizing tendency, for it is here that the 'vital selfhood' of all elements receives its fullest recognition.

The modern evolution, however, does not stop here. Relentlessly, it pursues its path towards ever more complete 'de-distantiation'. The metaphysical aura which surrounds the things of the world in pantheism is dispersed in modern naturalism, positivism, and pragmatism. As a result of this radical this-worldiness, the mind of man becomes perfectly congruent with 'reality'—'reality' being understood as the sum of manipulable things. We have to do here with a radically analytical and nominalistic outlook that leaves no room for the 'distantiation' and idealization of anything. The modern type of distantiation mentioned above—that in which group integration mechanisms and institutions were treated as embodying 'higher' principles—tends to be corroded by this radical nominalism. The metaphysical concepts of People, History, and State succumb to its critique. This is inevitable in the long run, for two reasons. For one thing these concepts become party labels and thus must undergo the invidious scrutiny of the adverse party. For another, the thinking of democratized élites tends to become more and more analytical, and they therefore cease to believe in metaphysical 'substances'. The mythical image of institutions is decomposed; they are broken down into a mass of observable, empirical facts. All the rest is treated as mere 'ideology'.

(e) *The Cultural Ideals of Aristocratic and Democratic Groups*

1. In the preceding section, we tried to show how different principles of élite selection (the aristocratic and the democratic) give rise to characteristic differences in the 'culture' of the societies in question in such fields as art, philosophy, and religion, as well as in the current everyday interpretation of life. The underlying mechanism at work here is an 'unconscious' one in the sense that the subjects engaged in creation and interpretation need not have an awareness of the sociological

background and of the 'aristocratic' or 'democratic' origin of their impulses and activities. The uncovering of such more or less unconscious mechanisms of the cultural process does not, however, exhaust the matter. Basic cultural aspirations and norms ('Bildungsideale') are also entertained by various groups on a conscious level, and it is to such cultural ideals[1] of an aristocratic or democratic nature that we now turn.

In our own society, there is sharp conflict and competition between two such cultural ideals, a relatively aristocratic and a more democratic one. The former is the 'humanistic' ideal; the latter, a democratic one that seeks to displace it. It will be useful for understanding if we can demonstrate that the rival ideals are those of two different, and differently constituted, élite groups.

2. The humanistic cultural and educational ideal by no means represents an extreme type of aristocratic thought. It is too universalistic to be tailored to the needs of small and closed privileged castes. Relatively speaking, however, it is still the ideal of an élite group, that of the 'cultivated' bourgeoise, an élite that seeks to distinguish itself from the proletarian or petty bourgeois mass. As we shall see, the humanistic ideal has marked 'aristocratic' traits in this sense.

The humanistic ideal is, first of all, steeped in the values of classical antiquity. It finds in antiquity, on the one hand, those elements which are best suited to developing harmonious, integrated and many-sidedly cultivated personalities, and on the other, a universe of 'pure' ideas that can help modern man to rise above the sordid and profane concerns of everyday life. In both these aspects of the humanistic ideal one may perceive the aristocratic principle of 'distantiation' at work.

In order to become a universally cultivated, harmonious and integrated personality, one needs leisure. This is an ideal of ruling groups. The average man who must work for a living cannot become a harmonious and many-sided personality; specialization is his destiny. He has no time to devote himself

[1] [Translator's Note: The German terms 'Bildung' and 'Bildungsideal' are difficult to render in English. What they designate partakes of both 'culture' and 'education'. 'Bildung' comprises whatever makes a 'cultivated' man. The 'ideals' discussed in the text refer to the image that various societies and groups have of what it takes to be 'cultivated'].

to the acquisition of social graces characteristic of aristocratic cultures (see p. 208 f., above).

The lack of specialization, the many-sidedness of the humanistic ideal might suggest, at first glance, something like the impartial openness of the democratic mind to which all things are equally interesting and absorbing. In reality, however, the humanistic many-sidedness has nothing to do with this, for its objects of interest, though manifold, are severely selected. Not all manifestations of life are worthy of interest and exploration, but only their most sublimated aspects, and, in particular, their reflection in the world of ideas. Things are admitted to consciousness only as embalmed in the flawless creations of classic art or poetry. There is no risky experimentation with real-life impulses. There is a closed horizon beyond which one is forbidden to venture.

The modern form of humanism has a twofold nature. As against the 'courtly' ideal of the aristocrat and cavalier, it is decidedly democratic. It does not stress social graces and elegant speech alone. It strives for 'cultivation' in a higher sense, in the sense of spiritualization. But this ideal is not fully democratic either. It neither wants to nor could be a possession of all men. We find its devotees among sons of upper-middle-class parents as well as among literati; but it is also worth noting that the pioneers of this cultural ideal (Shaftesbury, Humboldt) came from the nobility. The cultivated, intellectualized aristocrat was the first model for the upper middle class.[1]

This humanism creates a 'distance' from everyday life and hence unavoidably, whether intentionally or not, a distance from the common man, the mass, also. To this it adds another aristocratic trait: that of 'self-distantiation'. The humanist aspires to be, above everything else, a 'personality' in his own right. He does not turn to classical antiquity for its own sake, like a specialized historian. He needs the classical background in order to enhance his own personality, to set it off against the uncultivated. There must be a foil, a backdrop against the contemporary world; in order to be a 'personality', one needs that second world in order to feel elevated beyond the contingent circumstances of one's everyday situation.

[1] Cf. W. Weil, 'Die Entstehung des deutschen Bildungsideals', in *Schriften zur Philosophie und Soziologie*, vol. IV, Bonn, 1930.

This is a genuine, universal aspiration that we find in all ages in many varied forms. It finds its mythical expression in most religions. In fact, images of the Beyond and of salvation reflect man's striving to overcome the contingencies of his life. The mystics, and particularly the 'urbanized' mystics of the late Middle Ages, were a typical 'cultivated élite' in this sense; their ecstatic contemplation helped them overcome the limitations of everyday life. They, of course, strove for communion with God—they did not want to become 'personalities'. Yet their solitary ecstacies differed essentially from the collective ecstasies of rural 'folk' groups. In their way they were just as individualistic as the later literati who also cultivated a kind of solitary, ecstatic contemplation. For all humanists, the deepest fulfilment is found in occupation with things of the intellect and of the spirit, in seclusion from this world.

Solitude, then, becomes for the humanist of the secular type, the type which no longer seeks communion with God, something positive rather than the merely negative lack of human company. Its essence is 'communion with oneself' and enrichment through that communion. Through this self-cultivation, the humanist becomes more than himself, more than one or the other of his potentialities, more than the concrete situation in which he finds himself.

We had to stress these positive aspects of the humanistic ideal (today critically menaced if not already doomed) before discussing some of its limitations. If the humanistic ideal is about to be discarded by our culture, it is not because of the inadequacy of its ultimate aspirations but because it cannot provide enrichment of life for broader masses. Because of the conditions of mass existence, the humanistic ideal in its present form cannot be meaningful for the average man. Nevertheless, it is our opinion that this ideal contains elements indispensable for a full and rich life, and cultural ideals of a more universal appeal should make use of these elements in changed form.

We shall now turn to some of the limitations of the humanistic ideal as we see them; they are:

(*a*) Its confusion of its own élite sector with 'the' world itself. The humanist pretends that he is 'universally' interested, while in reality he is interested only in the world of his own educated sector. Within this universe, the humanist has an abnormally acute sense for nuances of meaning. Beyond it, he lacks the most primitive understanding of elementary facts. Men of a radically different background are needed to compensate for the one-sidedness of this so-called 'universal' outlook. The humanist cannot get over this limitation by himself.

(*b*) Its lack of contact with the stark realities of life. 'Cultivation' can become a prime object in life only for people who are never confronted by matters of life or death, safety or disaster, triumph or decline. For groups always faced by such realities, the ideal is too soft. They cannot understand why contemplation and book learning should be the finest things in life and why the vital struggle in itself should be considered ignoble. For these latter groups it may be a good thing to practise contemplation or to play with pure ideas once in a while, but they can have no truck with people who feel so secure that they can only make words about the tragedies of life.

(*c*) Its purely aesthetic relationship to things. Art has a universal function in neutralizing the sense of doom that threatens all human existence. But when art becomes the be-all and end-all of life, as it does in groups addicted to the cult of Art for Art's sake, it shuts out that sense of doom from awareness altogether, instead of merely sublimating and counterbalancing it. This attitude again is possible only for groups far removed from the rough-and-tumble of life, and wholly secure in a rentier's, patrician's, or aristocrat's existence. The reaction against this among groups fully engaged in struggle in the social arena is understandable. The latter want no 'pure' art but art carrying a practical message. This attitude threatens to abase art and to turn it into propaganda; but we should not forget that the opposite extreme, art for art's sake, also drains the life-blood out of living art. The really great art of classical Greece, for example, had an organic function in the life of the *polis*.

(*d*) Its neglect of the personal, biographical, and contingent element in literary or artistic creation. The *person* of the creative artist was completely neglected in favour of the 'work' as such. Works, then, did not appear as the products and manifestations of life; life was conceived as a means to produce works, and the latter alone deserved attention. Interest in the personal, biographical background was denounced as a profanation, as base 'psychological curiosity'.[1]

(*e*) Its antipathy towards the dynamic and unexpected. In its endeavour to produce 'harmonious', 'integrated' personalities, humanism was led to turn its back upon human potentialities whose manifestations could not be fully anticipated. Its classical canon claimed to encompass every human potentiality worthy of notice, and to provide a valid model for every situation. In this, humanism profoundly misunderstood life. One of man's supreme faculties is that of mobilizing entirely new potentialities in meeting new and critical situations. Life, then, cannot be hemmed in by the regulations and restrictions of any pre-existent canon. In defending the orderliness of its world, humanism merely betrayed a desire to maintain a wholly artificial security, based upon entrenched economic privilege.

3. It is not easy to give an idea of the contrary ideal of democratized groups, for this is still in the process of emerging and cannot be reduced to ready-made formulas. All we can do is to enumerate some of the symptoms of these novel cultural aspirations. In doing so, we shall pay particular attention to potentialities inherent in the new outlook that are not yet generally recognized.

As we shall see, the various elements of the new cultural ideal are sharply antithetical to the dominant features of humanism. Here as elsewhere, life works with antitheses; when new groups enter the arena and want to express themselves, they begin by rejecting what they find entrenched. The new is complementary to the old; this is how the historical process seeks to achieve totality.

The following points about the democratic cultural ideal deserve especial mention:

(*a*) In contrast to the humanistic ideal, it stresses the ideal of *vocational specialization*. Humanism is the ideal of an élite that does no specialized work, and considers such work (echoing in this the mentality of classical antiquity) as beneath its dignity. Man can become 'cultivated' only if he does not 'work'

[1] [Translator's Note: This criticism is directed against the school of 'Geistesgeschichte', and in particular against the literary historian Friedrich Gundolf.]

but merely 'occupies himself' with things. The new ideal, however, is work-oriented. Man can become 'cultivated' only through and within a concretely goal-oriented practice. (Political 'cultivation', too, is seen in contemporary groupings to be linked to participation in active political work, rather than to mere familiarity with doctrines.) The emphasis is upon the concrete situation, calling for active intervention, in which the individual happens to find himself. While the humanist, so to speak, hovered above the situation, the new democratized type recognizes the compelling force of the moment. In the 'homogenized' experiential field of this type, any concrete vocational task may provide equal fulfilment.

Pure specialization has traditionally been considered as antithetical to 'cultivation', and we have to admit the truth contained in this traditional view. Mere specialization as such cannot make one 'cultivated', even in a thoroughly democratized world. According to the democratic cultural ideal of which we are speaking, however, specialization as such is not the sole content of personal culture. The democratic type, too, strives to broaden his horizon beyond his specialty; he is fully aware of the fact that one cannot be a cultivated man without this. But he goes about it in a different way than did the humanist, for he starts from his concrete situation and never loses sight of it, whereas the humanist, in order to be cultivated, severed all connection with his own concrete situation.

This can be illustrated by a concrete example. A necessary phase in the acquisition of 'cultivation' in the humanistic sense is the 'grand tour' or educational trip. One has to go to Italy and Greece and see the monuments of classical antiquity. One's profession or occupation is entirely irrelevant in this respect; the prescription is the same for the student, the business man, and the lawyer. And this neutrality towards the professional horizon of the various individuals 'cultivating' themselves is essential, for the practice described unconsciously serves a very definite purpose. This consists in providing a common universe of communication among the different sectors of the cultivated élite as differentiated from the mass. To have made the grand tour was the entrance ticket to this select circle. Communication was achieved in terms of a second world besides the workaday one.

For the democratic type, too, cultivation reaches beyond specialization, but the process of cultivation starts from one's everyday occupation and remains organically linked to it. This is exemplified by the skilled worker who takes an extension course in order to gain more knowledge about his speciality, or who studies economics and management in order to have a clearer idea of where he stands in his social environment. Some workers study in order to become trade union functionaries. These people do not seek to 'cultivate' themselves in a free-floating sense; they want to be better able to control their situation and to broaden their own perspective in the process. There are no limits set to this gradual and organic process; there is a way from the trade union branch into municipal and national politics, or into the international labour movement. In any case, the process of self-cultivation is deliberate and continuous, rather than dictated by 'a priori' concepts or sudden, subjective impulses or mere curiosity.

It is an advantage of this self-cultivation programme that thought becomes congruent with life—one does not acquire knowledge about things that do not matter to one. The man who follows this path will be able to live the things he is talking about, while the man who follows the humanistic course will often repeat things that he knows about only at second-hand and that have no personal meaning for him.

(*b*) Politics, in the pre-democratic world, was no specialized vocation. Political offices were filled by amateurs who did not 'work' at politics but merely 'occupied themselves' with it.[1] In the age of early, pre-democratic parliamentarianism, we see epic rivalries arise between fashionable coteries and old aristocratic houses. In their oratory, the politicians of that period draw upon classical erudition and general philosophical principles; they seek to persuade, to obtain the adhesion of uncommitted individuals, free to decide for themselves. Clearly, the political struggle does not yet reflect a clash of massive economic interests. When these begin to dominate politics, a specialized knowledge of the economic effects of governmental

[1] Cf. Max Weber, 'Politik als Beruf', translated as Ch. IV in H. H. Gerth and C. Wright Mills, *From Max Weber: Essays in Sociology*, London and New York, 1946. For a good characterization of this type of politician, see R. Lennox, *Edmund Burke und sein politisches Arbeitsfeld in den Jahren* 1760–1709, Munich and Berlin, 1923.

and legislative action becomes indispensable. The political amateur, the orator dealing with universal principles and generalities, must then yield to the specialist. The real political decisions are taken in closed committee, on the basis of bargaining among interest groups; the plenary sessions of the parliaments with their set speeches are mere make-believe, staged for the benefit of the rank-and-file.

The committees and caucus rooms are an excellent school for party functionaries rising from the ranks. As they advance into higher policy-making bodies, their perspective becomes broadened. Assuming larger responsibilities, they lose the one-sidedness of their original orientation which was circumscribed in narrow geographical or class terms. In this process, the politicians of the new era typically expose themselves to the charge of being renegades and traitors; their rank-and-file suspects them of having 'sold out' to the 'interests'. But this need not be the case at all. The politician's evolution from a narrow particularist to a responsible statesman may represent the genuinely democratic type of political 'self-cultivation'.

(*c*) In essence, the type of 'cultivation' attained by the specialist consists in his acquiring a deeper and more adequate understanding of his own particular position, by learning to approach it from different sides. In this respect, the specialized man of the modern age is better off than the specialized man of earlier ages. For the latter, it was difficult indeed to transcend the narrow limits of his specialization, or, if he was a politician wedded to very narrow interests, to achieve a more comprehensive perspective. In modern society, however, specialization both can and must go beyond itself, for the interconnectedness and interdependence of fields of specialization and of particular interests becomes more and more evident. This is why today 'specialization' can be a good starting-point for 'cultivation', whereas this was not the case in earlier ages. Today one may become 'cultivated', not in the purely quantitative sense of acquiring more knowledge, but in the deeper sense of becoming able to advance from familiarity with an immediately given concrete situation to the understanding of the structural pattern behind that same situation.

While the humanist achieved 'cultivation' by advancing from everyday reality to a 'higher' reality of the world of Ideas, modern man attains the same goal by advancing from immediate experience to a structural view of reality. The realm of 'structure'[1] is no 'second world' of pure Essences behind the real world. It is immanent in reality, and achieving 'structural' understanding is not a matter of going beyond reality but rather of the intensity with which one experiences reality. In every field of specialization, there are people who have a merely routine interest in their activities, besides others who are so passionately interested that they have a need to penetrate to the underlying mechanism; for example, bankers who are mere technicians of finance, as against others who try to *understand* finance. Or, to return to the field of educational theory and practice: there are routiniers of education who want to know only how to keep discipline in the classroom and how to transmit the required amount of knowledge, as against true educators for whom each child represents a unique challenge. For the true educator, the pupils are not identical targets of 'education', but individualities with their own social backgrounds and their psychologically and biologically determined needs, demands, and potentialities. Such an educator will seek to fulfil his task by achieving insight into the underlying structural pattern of the schoolroom situation.

Adherents of the humanistic educational ideal often deprecate 'vocational' education as lacking in the elements of 'cultivation'. These humanists do not know how truly 'cultivated' practitioners of real stature can be. Above all, they overlook the fact that thought rooted in actual practice is likely to be more genuine than thought developed around mere topics of 'cultivated' conversation. In contrast to purely verbal knowledge, knowing achieved by doing establishes an organic relationship between the knower and the known. If such knowledge transcends one-sidedness by a broadening of the knower's perspective, it will be more truly many-sided and universal than the purely verbal universality of humanistic 'cultivation'. This type of knowledge also has the best chance of escaping the danger of becoming an 'ideological' screen for unavowed and unrealized self-centred and group-centred interests.

[1] [Translator's Note: For the role of the concept of 'structure' in Karl Mannheim's thinking, see the Introduction to *Essays in Sociology and Social Psychology*, London and New York, 1953.]

All this should not be taken, of course, as an advocacy of purely vocational education or of a cult of mere technical expertness. We do not hold that children should be taught only 'what they will need to know in practical life'. Such a view completely misses both the real nature of specialized knowledge and the educational aims and potentialities of an organic connection between 'knowing' and 'doing'. If education transmits a lot of 'practical' knowledge but still fails to enable the pupil to become oriented in his own life environment, it is in no way superior to purely verbal, humanistic education. Specialized vocational education in this sense is a symptom of decadence rather than of progress.

Hence, modern education can approximate to an ideal of 'cultivation' only by giving more than specialized knowledge, narrowly circumscribed. Such knowledge must be supplemented by more general disciplines that have orientation in life and in social reality as their subject matter. Sociology is particularly appropriate to fulfil this task in the modern world. Traditionally, philosophy was entrusted with the task of providing general principles of orientation, and we do not assert that the philosophical approach has become valueless or that philosophy should be banished from the curriculum. The dominant tradition of Western philosophy, however, is still that of idealism, of the 'reduplication of Being', of seeking a second world behind reality; such a philosophy is not able to give modern man the orientation that he needs. The idealistic tradition, on the other hand, is being more and more corroded within modern philosophy itself, as the recent trend towards pragmatism and positivism shows. There is hardly any conflict in principle between these philosophies and the sociological approach.[1]

E THE PROBLEM OF ECSTASY

In so far as 'cultivation' means a broadening of one's existential perspective, the democratic cultural ideal seems to be superior to the humanistic one: as we have seen, it achieves that broadening in a more organic fashion. Cultivated existence,

[1] [Translator's Note: The necessity to transcend the purely pragmatist and positivist approach is the argument of the next concluding section of this paper.]

however, also has another aspect: that of self-distantiation. This is an organic part of the cultural ideal of the humanistic élite, whereas the modern, democratic concept of cultivation seems to offer little in the way of 'self-distantiation' and 'ecstatic' contemplation. Is this a shortcoming of the modern ideal, or was self-distantiation an unjustified aspiration of old élites? Such questions about ultimate values are difficult to answer, and it is still more difficult to give a reasoned argument for and against the possible answers. We shall therefore state our position without entering into its pros and cons; it is that achieving from time to time a certain distance from his own situation and from the world is one of the fundamental traits of man as truly a human being. A man for whom nothing exists beyond his immediate situation is not fully human. But even the 'democratized' way of cultivation discussed above, which consists in gaining an increasingly broader situational perspective, does not suffice. We inherited from our past another need: that of severing from time to time *all* connection with life and with the contingencies of our existence. We shall designate this ideal by the term 'ecstasy'. Supposing that this ideal is a valid one, and that 'ecstasy' is a necessary element of true 'cultivation', the question facing us is this: Is it true that the democratic cultural ideal is antithetical to ecstasy and offers no avenues towards it?

Our answer is that if we consider the potentialities inherent in the democratic approach, it will appear to be eventually conducive to a new type of 'ecstasy' and of true 'cultivation'. It may even be suggested that ecstasy can be a general, universally shared form of experience only in a democratized culture. But this democratization of culture does not attain that stage at one stroke. To begin with, radical democratization means de-distantiation; this has to be overcome before new forms of ecstasy can emerge. Democratized culture must go through a dialectical process before it can realize its full potentialities.

We shall examine this dialectical process under three headings, that is, from the point of view of the new, democratic relationship between (*a*) the 'I' and the object, (*b*) between the 'I' and the 'Thou', and (*c*) between the 'I' and the 'myself', that is, self-distantiation.

(*a*) *The I-object relationship.* As we have seen, full democratization means, to begin with, radical de-distantiation of all objects, non-human as well as human. This makes for a flat, uninspiring, and unhappy world. There is no Beyond; the existing world is not a symbol for the eternal; immediate reality points to nothing beyond itself. At the stage of full democratization, human types who experience reality in this flat and uninspiring perspective do, indeed, abound. They are found among business men and scientists, educators and politicians. Their thinking is fully congruent with their doing, since they seek nothing beyond what they can actually achieve by practical manipulation. In this sense, they describe themselves as 'realists': after all, they have done away with all myths, with all concepts that are not fully operational. But are these people truly realists? We hold that they are not. For 'realism' cannot consist in doing away with all historically given forms of distantiation and then equating the remainder with 'the' world itself. There is more to the world and, in particular, to man as a real being than is open to manipulation. It may be extremely useful for a man who wants to achieve control over things and other men to consider them all for a while as if they consisted in nothing but a bundle of responses. We understand quite well that our modern culture, driven by an overwhelming need to perfect techniques of control, comes to reduce both things and men to their regular patterns of responding to stimuli. In this context, the achievements of the behaviouristic approach must be recognized. But one cannot say that this particular perspective exhausts the full reality of man. Man cannot be reduced to the sum of his responses to stimuli. Some aspects of human reality call for intuitive 'understanding' ('Verstehen'), even if we may be driven for a while to ignore these aspects for technical and methodological reasons.

The danger inherent in the modern ontology, then, is that it tends to succumb to the temptation to take its specific perspective, that of the manipulator, to be that of absolute truth. A true ontology cannot be such a partial, perspective-bound one. We have to show these 'realists' and pragmatists that they do not yet face 'the world' but only a limited segment of it, the segment corresponding to practical manipulative operations. When they equate this segment with the whole, their thinking is not 'realistic' but very 'unreal'.

Such self-deception is possible only for a human type which has suppressed his essential human-ness in his approach towards reality. This ontological error has to be corrected by the recognition of the *partial* nature of the manipulative approach. When this is achieved, the specialist will cease to take himself seriously as an arbiter of ontological truth. Since, however, the tendency towards overcoming partial perspectives is inherent in democratization, we may indeed expect that the ontological error will eventually be corrected, and that the way will be open for new distance-creating experiences.

(*b*) *The I-Thou relationship.* Democratization implies that all purely *social* distance between 'high' and 'low' tends to be levelled. This levelling may produce a colourless monotony. All individuals then will appear as interchangeable; the 'other' will play a purely instrumental role in the individual's life. When social distance is abolished and no other form of distantiation takes its place, there is a void in inter-human relationships: no person as a person can mean anything to another. In this respect, however, we shall also discover, if we look more closely, that democratization involves not only a danger but also, and more importantly, a supreme opportunity. In fact, the levelling of purely social distance may enable the purely 'existential' distance[1] to come into its own. When I am no longer compelled to meet the other in his role as a social superior or inferior, I can establish pure existential contact with him as a human being. And this form of relationship between the 'I' and the 'thou' can become a general pattern only on the basis of democratization. We perceive in this sense, at the stage of the democratization of cultures, the emergence of new forms of distance, just as in earlier ages purely spatial avoidance may have yielded to more sublimated psychic distance and to vertical social distance. At the democratic stage, it becomes possible to 'love' or 'hate' the other as a person, irrespective of any social mask he may wear.

Creating a basis for purely existential human relationships is the greatest potential achievement of democracy. In earlier ages, existential, supra-social, person-to-person relationships did exist. But as a rule, they were embedded in social, vertical relationships. Thus, to mention one example, the priest did

[1] Cf. above, p. 207.

speak to the penitent as a person, and his words at times stirred the soul of the believer in its innermost depth. Yet, at the same time, the priest was also the representative of social authority. In all such relationships, a purely personal appeal could make itself heard only through the impersonal medium of authority and vertical social distance.

The emergence of sublimated erotic 'love' in the knightly culture of the Middle Ages was one of the most important chapters in the history of the I-thou-relationships. The troubadours of Provence created an image of the beloved that reflected a purely 'existential' relationship; in their poetry, love was a way to self-purification and salvation. And yet, one can observe, in this as in other cases, that 'existential' relationships do not have a language of their own. They speak the language of purely 'social' distance. The troubadours represented themselves as the 'servants' of the beloved lady, in a kind of feudal relationship, and we still echo this in the ritual and language of our own sublimated erotic relationships. We even use the feudal metaphor of 'courting'. (In other 'existential' relationships, too, we tend to use the vocabulary of vertical social distance, e.g. when we designate our purely ethical appreciation for another as 'respect', although it has little to do with 'respect' for social authority.) It is, in fact, difficult for us to express our experience of existential 'distance' in non-social terms. In recent times, ritual and language begin to change, and we hear complaints about the matter-of-factness of modern erotic relationships, about the decline of 'romantic' love. In the course of social de-distantiation, the beloved woman no longer is seen as a 'higher' being. People who consider themselves 'advanced' welcome this rejection of romantic 'sham'. According to them, love relationships should be matter-of-fact and natural; they also hold that in a democratic world, man and woman ought to consider themselves as 'comrades' and 'collaborators', even in their erotic relationship with each other. This, however, is a misunderstanding. The true potentialities inherent in democratization are not yet realized when we put *horizontal* social relationships in the place of *vertical* ones in expressing our person-to-person attitudes and feelings. The real opportunity that democratization gives us consists in being able to transcend *all* social categories and experience love as a purely personal and existential matter.

It becomes apparent, then, that the 'sociological' orientation we are advocating by no means implies that we recognize 'sociological' categories as the only ones in terms of which human experience can express itself. On the contrary, one of the reasons why we seek to subject human reality to radical sociological analysis is that we need to know the effects produced by social factors in order to be able to counteract them when they are inimical to man. The positive type of modern thinker, in our view, will become increasingly sociological in his thinking, not in order to deify the social, but in order to neutralize its negative effects concerning ultimate human values.

(*c*) *The I-myself relationship*. The primary business of man is to come to terms with the outside world and with his fellows. Gradually, however, he becomes aware of the need to know himself and to develop an idea of his own being and aspirations. Every culture has, in this sense, its own characteristic conception of man's relationship to himself, in addition to its characteristic I-object and I-thou relationships. In hierarchically organized societies, however, man tends to think of himself in terms of his place in the social hierarchy. He is compelled to experience himself, not as a person, but as the specimen of a social category. The 'personality' ideal, the wish to achieve unique dignity as this person, is specifically modern. This aspiration is closely related to the 'existential' I-thou relationship just discussed, for a man can become a 'person' *for himself* only to the extent that he is a 'person' for others and others are 'persons' for him. In fact, to our view, the 'existential', personal I-thou relationship is fundamental to the development of a personal self-image. We hold it to be an idealistic delusion that man first becomes a person in his own, individual self-assessment and then proceeds to meet others as persons. It is the other way round: man's human and social environment must first develop in such a way that he can become a person for others and be addressed as such on numerous occasions before he can see himself as a person.

It follows that a democratic social order, with its tendency to minimize vertical social distance, provides the most favourable conditions for the development of 'internalized' personality. This is misunderstood by the modern intellectual élite whose members are proud of being able to see themselves in purely existential terms but ignore the fact that they owe this to a social trend they instinctively reject, that of social levelling. It is because the hierarchial, social evaluation of man no longer is all-pervasive and dominant that he can, from time to time, possess himself as he is in his supra-social essence, stripped of conventional and social masks, and unconstricted by his contingent social situation.

It is in this way that democratic social reality opens up new avenues towards the age-old goal of escaping the contingency of the world, of achieving ecstasy. This was, at bottom, the meaning of the aspirations of all *homines religiosi*. Escape from the world and from the contingent situation was first achieved by the use of intoxicants, later by asceticism, and finally through solitary contemplation. In all this, freedom from the tyranny of the contingent world was achieved, but not as yet a purely existential relationship to the self. The experience of salvation was articulated through mythical and religious symbols—symbols which often were the projections of social authority relationships. In this way, man who sought to escape contingent, everyday social reality was led back, in roundabout fashion, to that which he hoped to escape. A more radical liberation from contingency has become possible only in the modern age.

Whatever one may say against the modern cultural type, one cannot deny him one virtue, that of truthfulness. Other cultures may have had more sublime ideals, more challenging utopias, a more colourful reality, a greater wealth of nuances. Our modern age has sacrificed all that, for the sake of possessing truth unadorned and unfalsified. It wants to stand in its own undistorted reality; this is why it has done away with all distantiation. The individual of this culture also wants to be 'himself' as he is, not as he appears clothed in the trappings of his social status. Therein lies the greatness that the modern individual may achieve—the dissatisfaction with a socially determined relation to himself. He must pay for this, however, first of all, by the loss of that sense of security which only well-defined status can give. Orientation in status-bound societies is easy; everybody knows what he can aspire to and what he can expect. As against this, modern life no longer offers sure expectations but only an infinite challenge. In earlier times, only the poor had infinite dreams, since they could not expect finite rewards.[1] In this sense, we have all become poor. *Insecurity as a general destiny, no longer limited to submerged strata, is one of the characteristics of the modern age.* Former élites may deplore this. To be exposed to insecurity is a tragic experience. But it also opens up an avenue towards moral and cultural growth. It is wholly wrong to interpret the collapse of old hierarchies and patterns of order as a symptom of moral and cultural decay. We must see in this, on the contrary, a potentially positive factor in the education of mankind. If society with its fixed hierarchies no longer can give us a safe orientation and a basis for self-evaluation, we must for that very reason meet the challenge of developing a new pattern of orientation based upon a deeper and more genuine human truth.

This is the real task of the democratized age, and this task is yet to be done. The modern mind misunderstands itself if it assumes that by becoming wholly thing-oriented and operational it has fulfilled its potentialities. If we probe deeper, we shall see that this culture will not be able to maintain itself unless it breaks through the screen of purely social self-assessment and achieves communion with the existential self, stripped of all social masks.

[1] According to Max Weber, only oppressed strata developed a missionary consciousness, cf. *Gesammelte Aufsätze zur Religions-soziologie*, 1920–21, vol. I, p. 248.

SUBJECT INDEX

SUBJECT INDEX

SUBJECT INDEX

NAME INDEX

NAME INDEX

NAME INDEX